L.D 3/04

Vest Pocket ARABIC

TITLES IN THIS SERIES

VEST POCKET SPANISH
VEST POCKET FRENCH
VEST POCKET GERMAN
VEST POCKET ITALIAN
VEST POCKET RUSSIAN
VEST POCKET MODERN GREEK
VEST POCKET JAPANESE
VEST POCKET ARABIC
VEST POCKET ENGLISH
(Inglés En El Bolsillo)

VIETNAMESE IN A NUTSHELL

Vest Pocket ARABIC

Formerly published as: ARABIC IN A NUTSHELL

By
DILAVER BERBERI, Ph.D.
St. Mary's College
formerly of the American University in Cairo, U.A.R.
and the Institute of Modern Languages, Washington, D.C.

PUBLISHED BY

INSTITUTE FOR LANGUAGE STUDY
Westport, Connecticut 06880

DISTRIBUTED TO THE BOOK TRADE BY
HENRY HOLT & COMPANY

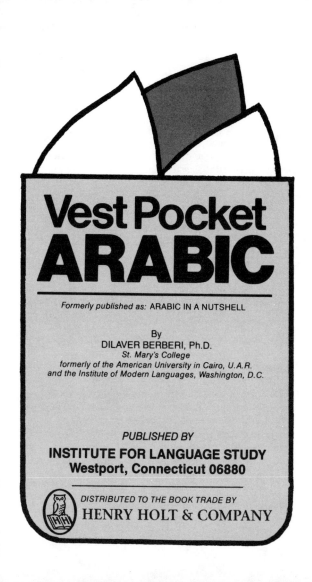

Library of Congress Cataloging-in-Publication Date

Berberi, Dilaver.
Vest Pocket Arabic.

Previously published as: Arabic in a Nutshell.
1. Arabic language – Dialects—English. 2. Arabic language – Conversation and phrase books—English.
3. Arabic language—Grammar. I. Title.
PJ6779.B4 1989 492'.783421 89-15367
ISBN 0-8489-5109-3

Printed in the United States of America
HH Editions 9 8 7 6 5 4 0306-5M

HOW TO USE THIS BOOK

Because Arabic is spoken in 21 countries throughout the Middle East, it is an essential tool for anyone planning to visit or work in this fascinating region. Egypt's considerable economic, political and cultural influence in the Middle East makes the Egyptian colloquial Arabic taught in this text well understood throughout the Arab world. Colloquial Arabic is used in conversation, most letters, advertising, and film and television entertainment, which originates primarily in Egypt. VEST POCKET ARABIC provides a step-by-step approach to the study of Arabic which simplifies and clarifies all aspects of this useful language.

The phonemic transcription used throughout the book provides stress marks and vowels, which are normally omitted from Arabic script. In the transcription the articles, pronouns, and tense markers are separated from the substantives by dashes. Thus the student learns correct pronunciation and gains an understanding of Arabic structure and syntax.

Another advantage of the text is the use of both literal and free translations. Arabic regularly uses affixes (prefixes, suffixes and infixes) and has a completely different word order from English. The literal translation is essential as it illustrates Arabic structure graphically by indicating the position and meaning of each word and affix. The free translation provides the idiomatic English equivalent.

Each unit begins with a natural conversation dealing with a topic a foreigner living in or visiting an Arab country is likely to encounter. Approximately 2000 high-frequency words are introduced. The conversations acquaint the learner with both the practical and cultural aspects of the language while he learns about the Arabs and their customs.

A clear grammar discussion follows each conversation. A unfamiliar terminology is explained and examples are given t illustrate each point. Tables of verbs and pronouns, as well a lists of nouns, adjectives, and prepositions, are included fc easy reference. Thus the student learns gradually, unit by uni all the essential grammatical features of Arabic.

Vest Pocket Arabic has everything required for a basi foundation in colloquial Egyptian Arabic. By applying the fol lowing suggested procedures systematically, the student will b well on his way to mastering Arabic:

1. Study the Spelling and Pronunciation Guide carefully making sure you know how to pronounce both the Arabic script and phonetic symbols correctly.
2. Read the conversations aloud until you feel comfortable saying them. You may read only the phonetic transcription, or try to read the Arabic script checking yourself with the transcription. If a sentence is long, break it down and work on a section at a time, until you are ready to read the whole sentence.
3. Next, look at the free translation while practicing the Arabic sentences, and associate the meaning with what you are saying.
4. Now analyze the sentence structures and learn the meanings of individual words by comparing the Arabic with the literal translations.
5. Next study the grammar discussion carefully. Learn the additional vocabulary and the verb paradigms, as they are essential for a basic foundation in Arabic. Study the examples carefully and refer back to the conversations which incorporate the grammatical principles. Be sure you understand all the grammar before going on to the next unit.

To further aid the student, the dialogues of the text have been flawlessly reproduced on records and tapes. The foreign voices are those of professionals who have been selected for their perfect pronunciation and accent, as well as for their pleasant voice quality.

TABLE OF CONTENTS

ABBREVIATIONS USED IN THIS TEXT

adj	*adjective*	pl	*plural*
c	*consonant*	pr	*bound pronoun*
cn	*collective noun*	pt	*present tense (marker)*
cs	*construct state*	S	*subject*
d	*dual*	sg	*singular*
f	*feminine*	un	*unit noun*
ft	*future tense (marker)*	V	*short vowel*
m	*masculine*	$\bar{V}$	*long vowel*
neg	*negative*	( )	*includes explanation*
P	*predicate*	/	*either or*

ARABIC SPELLING AND PRONUNCIATION

Because the Arabic spelling and some of the Arabic sounds are unfamiliar to most English speaking people, the introduction of a special writing system is necessary. This writing system, commonly called phonetic transcription, represents the Arabic dialect of Egypt as spoken by most native speakers of Cairo. The Arabic script in this book is an adaptation of literary Arabic.

The tables below present the Arabic letters and their respective phonetic symbols; in addition, some examples in both Arabic script and phonetic transcription show the different shapes the letters take in three positions in a word and in isolation.

ARABIC SCRIPT AND PHONETIC TRANSCRIPTION

Arabic symbol	*Phonetic symbol*	*Approximate English correspondence*
	PLAIN CONSONANTS	
ب	[b]	as *b* in boy
ف	[f]	as *f* in fat
ت	[t]	as *t* in take
ث	[s]	as *s* in sin
د	[d]	as *d* in dad
س	[s]	as *s* in sin
ز ، ذ	[z]	as *z* in zeal
ش	[š]	as *sh* in ship
ج	[ž]	as *ge* in beige or *j* in jack

Arabic symbol	*Phonetic symbol*	*Approximate English correspondence*
ك	[k]	as *k* in kate or *c* in cat
ق	[q]	no English correspondence (glottal stop)
	[q̇]	as *q* in queen or *c* in coin
ج	[g]	as *g* in go
ه	[h]	as *h* in hat
ء	[']	no English correspondence (glottal stop)
ر	[r]	as *r* in ring
ل	[l]	as *l* in let
م	[m]	as *m* in mother
ن	[n]	as *n* in night

EMPHATIC CONSONANTS

ط	[ṭ]	as *t* in tall
ض	[ḍ]	as *d* in dark
ص	[ṣ]	as *s* in suck
ظ	[ẓ]	as *z* in zebra

LARYNGAL OR THROAT CONSONANTS

ح	[ḥ]	as *h* in hall
خ	[x]	no English correspondence
ع	[ع]	no English correspondence
غ	[ġ]	no English correspondence

VOWELS, SEMIVOWELS, AND DIPHTHONGS

أَ	[a]	as *a* in Patrick and as *a* in carbon
أُ	[u]	as *u* in put
إِ	[i]	as *i* in stick
ي	[ī]	as *i* in machine
	[ē]	as *ei* in beige
	[y]	as *y* in yes
	[ay]	as *a* in Kate and as *i* in high

Arabic symbol	*Phonetic symbol*	*Approximate English correspondence*
و	[ū]	as *oo* in loot
	[ō]	as *oa* in boat
	[w]	as *wh* in what
	[aw]	as *ow* in cow
ا	[ā]	as *a* in car or bat
اً	[an]	as *en* in pen
ة	[a]	as *a* in mama
	[t]	as *t* in pit
	[it]	as *it* in summit
ى	[a]	as *a* in Zsa Zsa

The examples below show the varying shapes the Arabic letters take in various word positions and in isolation:

In isolation	*Initially*	*Medially*	*Finally*
ب	بلد [bálad]	لبن [lában]	كلب [kalb]
ف	فكر [fikr]	مفرش [máfraš]	تلف [tálaf]
ت	تلج [talg]	نتيجه [natīga]	تحت [taḥt]
ث	ثورة [sáwra]	مثل [másal]	حديث [ḥadīs]
س	سكن [síkin]	فسحة [fúsḥa]	لبس [líbis]
چ	چكتة [žakítta]	اباچور [abažūr]	جراچ [garāž]
ج	جميل [gamīl]	نجار [nagār]	تلج [talg]
ك	كسلان [kaslān]	تكس [taks]	ملك [milk]
ق	قلم [qálam]	نقل [naql]	حقّ [ḥaqq]
ل	لغة [lúġa]	ملح [malḥ]	كل [kul]
م	مشمش [míšmiš]	سمك [sámak]	قلم [qálam]
ن	نفس [nafs]	بنت [bint]	فين [fēn]
ط	طرد [ṭard]	نطق [nuṭq]	شخط [šáxaṭ]
ظ	ظبط [ẓabṭ]	مظبوط [maẓbūṭ]	حظ [ḥaẓẓ]
ض	ضرب [ḍarb]	فضل [fáḍḍal]	حفض [ḥáfaḍ]
ص	صباح [ṣábaḥ]	حصل [ḥáṣal]	بصبص [báṣbaṣ]
ح	حمل [ḥámal]	لحم [laḥm]	نصح [náṣaḥ]
خ	خصر [xíṣir]	سخن [súxun]	مخ [muxx]
ع	علم [ɛálam]	بعد [baɛd]	مع [maɛ]
غ	غدا [ġáda]	شغلة [šúġla]	بلغ [bállaġ]

د	درس	[dars]	مدينة	[madīna]	بلد	[bálad]
ذ ، ز	ذاكر	[zākir]	نزل	[nízil]	حجز	[hágaz]
ر	ريشة	[rīša]	كرسى	[kúrsi]	قمر	[qámar]
ه	هنا	[hína]	فهم	[fáhim]	نبيه	[nabīh]
ء	أدب	[ádab]	مسألة	[mas'ála]	جلاء	[galā']
أ	أصل	[aṣl]	تمن	[táman]	كِدا	[kída]
أ	أخت	[uxt]	تين	[tīn]	درسُوا	[dárasu]
إ	إسم	[ism]	فوق	[fōq]	إنتِ	[ínti]
ى	إيد	[īd]	كاتب	[kātib]	فى	[fī]
و	أودة	[ōda]			أبُو	[abū]
آ	آسف	[āsif]			باشا	[bāša]

KEY TO ARABIC SPELLING

1. Arabic is written from right to left.

2. Classical Arabic words keep their traditional spelling; phonetically, however, they are transcribed according to the colloquial (spoken) sound system. As shown in the table above, the Classical Arabic ذ (as *th* in *th*an) and ظ (also as *th* in *th*an, but emphatic) are pronounced in colloquial as [z] and [ẓ] respectively. Moreover, ث is pronounced as [s].

3. Arabic letters take different shapes according to their occurrence: in isolation, in final, medial, or initial position in a word. Letters written in isolation and in final position have almost the same shape, as is also true for those written initially and medially.

4. Six of the Arabic letters ز , ذ [z], د [d], ر [r], و [w], and ا [ā] or alif, can be joined to a preceding letter but never to a following one.

5. Both [q] (a glottal stop) and [q̇] (a velar consonant) are represented in Arabic script by ق .

6. The glottal stop in this book is represented by two symbols in both the Arabic script and the phonetic transcription: ء ['] or hamza and ق [q]. The latter is a vestige of the Classical Arabic ق [q̇] or q̇af.

7. The original glottal stop or hamza ـٔ ['] is usually written over a letter, but never attached to it.

8. Short vowels are rarely indicated in Arabic script. When they are, it is by a diacritical mark above or below a letter. Such diacritics are not used in this book since the phonetic transcription indicates the pronunciation.

9. When the short vowels ـَ [a] or fatḥa, ـُ [u] or ḍamma, and ـِ [i] or kasra are marked in Arabic script, fatḥa and ḍamma are marked above the letter and kasra below the letter. ـّ CC (shidda, the sign for gemination, or the occurrence of two identical consonants), like fatḥa and ḍamma, is marked above the letter.

10. Short vowels in initial position in Arabic script are usually written with an ا (alif) and a hamza (over [أ] for fatḥa and ḍamma and below [إ] for kasra).

11. Short vowels in final position are usually spelled in Arabic script as long vowels. Frequently, in other positions also, some short vowels of classical Arabic or foreign words are spelled as long vowels in Arabic script, although they are short vowels in pronunciation.

12. The semivowels [y], the diphthong [ay], and the long vowels [ī] and [ē] are all spelled in Arabic script with ي . The semivowel [w], the diphthong [aw], and the long vowels [ū] and [ō] are spelled in Arabic script with و .

13. ة or ta marbuta, which is the sign for the feminine gender of nouns and adjectives, occurs finally in a word.

14. ى , which is written as ي without dots, occurs only finally and not too frequently.

KEY TO ARABIC PRONUNCIATION

There are three types of consonants: plain, emphatic, and throat, all of which are described below.

Plain Consonants

Most of the Arabic plain consonants have approximate counterparts in English; they do not present, therefore, any special problem. However, some remarks on the following consonants and phonetic symbols are necessary:

1. As in many other languages, some of the Arabic consonants are voiced, e.g. [b, d, z, ž, g]; and some are voiceless, e.g. [f, t, s, š, k]. The difference in pronunciation between voiced and voiceless consonants can be heard if the fingers are pressed against the ears: during the pronunciation of a voiced consonant, there is a musical buzz (the vocal cords are vibrating); whereas, during the pronunciation of voiceless consonants, this buzz is not heard (the vocal cords are not vibrating).

2. Arabic has no [p] or [v] consonants; however, [b] is sometimes pronounced as [p] and [f] as [v].

3. [š] is the symbol for *sh* as in *sh*ip, fi*sh*, etc. [ž] is the symbol for *s* as in plea*s*ure, mea*s*ure, etc., or for *ge* in words borrowed from French such as bei*ge* or rou*ge*.

4. [q̇] is a velar consonant as *c* in *c*ow or *k* in *kid* (pronounced like [k] but further back in the mouth) and occurs in a few words of classical Arabic, such as قانون q̇anūn 'law' or قاهرة qāhira 'Cairo'.

5. The glottal stop is a consonant in Arabic. Its presence or absence makes a difference in meaning in some Arabic words. It is heard as a sudden break at the beginning and at the end of a vowel, as in the expression "oh, oh!" This Arabic consonant has no counterpart in any of the English consonants. Hamza, which is one of the two symbols which represent the glottal stop both in Arabic script (أ , إ) and phonetic transcription ['], is not marked phonetically in this book in initial position in a word. In this position, hamza is rarely marked in Arabic script either. For example, the word ألبنت 'il-bint 'the girl', is written in this book as البنت il-bint without the glottal stop in initial position.

6. [q], the other symbol for the glottal stop, is always marked both in phonetic transcription and Arabic script. It is sometimes pronounced by educated speakers as [q̇].

Emphatic Consonants

7. Emphatic consonants are slightly different from their plain counterparts: during their articulation, the muscles of the tongue are tense and the throat cavity is slightly narrowed. This phenomenon is commonly called velarization.

Phonetically, emphatic consonants are written as their plain counterparts with a subscript dot: [ṭ ḍ ṣ ẓ].

8. [r], [l], [y], and especially their doubles [rr], [ll], and [yy] can also be emphatic on their own, usually with the back vowels [a] and [ā].

Throat Consonants

Throat consonants are unlike anything in English. For their pronunciation, an articulatory description is not sufficient. A good aid for their approximate pronunciation is offered by citing examples of similar consonants of other languages when possible:

9. [ḥ] is pronounced as *h* in *h*at with the throat cavity slightly narrowed.

10. [x] is pronounced like an [ḥ] with a strong friction in the throat cavity as in clearing the throat. It is the same sound as the German *ch* in na*ch*t, or the Greek χ before back vowels [a, o, u], as in χαρά.

11. [ɛ] is pronounced as *a* in f*a*ther, but further back in the throat which is slightly narrowed. However, this is a consonant in Arabic and not a vowel.

12. [ġ] is pronounced like a [x] but the air, instead of being ejected, is compressed in the throat cavity as in gargling gently. It is similar to the French Parisian rolled *r* or the Greek γ before back vowels [a, o, u] as in γάτι.

Vowels

There are three short [i, u, a] and five long [ī, ē, ū, ō, ā] vowels. The pronunciation of each vowel varies more or less from its norm according to its position in a word:

13. [i] in final position is pronounced as *i* in mach*i*ne; in other positions as *i* in b*i*t or as *e* in b*e*t.

14. [u] in final position as *oo* in b*oo*t; in other positions as *u* in p*u*t or as *o* in p*o*rtable.

15. [a] in proximity to emphatic and next to throat consonants is pronounced as *a* in c*a*rbon; elsewhere, as *a* in m*a*d*a*m.

16. [ī] as *ee* in m*ee*t, [ē] as *a* in f*a*te, [ū] as *oo* in l*oo*t, and [ō] as *oo* in d*oo*r.

17. The preceding four long vowels and the two short [i] and [u] with emphatic and throat consonants become more centralized and heavier than their norms.

18. [ā] is pronounced as *a* in f*a*ther when near to emphatic and next to throat consonants; elsewhere, pronounced as *a* in m*a*d.

Semivowels and Diphthongs

19. The two semivowels of Arabic, [y] and [w], are pronounced approximately as English *y* in *y*es and *w* in *w*ant.

20. The most frequently used diphthongs are [ay] and [aw]. [ay] is pronounced as *i* in h*i*gh and [aw] as *ou* in d*ou*bt.

21. Three other diphthongs [iy, iw, uy] are seldom used. [iy] is pronounced as *ee* in s*ee*, [iw] as *ew* in n*ew*, and [uy] as *we* in *we*aver.

22. In final position of words used in isolation, ة is pronounced as *a* in m*a*m*a*, followed by a puff of air. In connected speech, it is pronounced as either [t] or [it].

23. ى is pronounced as *a* in c*a*rbon.

CONSONANT AND/OR VOWEL COMBINATIONS

24. **Consonant clusters.** Three consecutive consonants do not occur within a word; they may, however, occur in word boundary (between words). With a few exceptions of two consonants in initial position in a word, clusters of two consonants may occur only medially and finally.

25. **Double consonants and semivowels.** In Arabic, double consonants or semivowels (two consecutive identical consonants or semivowels) are both pronounced, but are written as one. In ambiguous cases, the sign ّ (shidda), which indicates two identical consonants or semivowels, is marked over the double consonant or semivowel. For example, درس daras 'he studied' and درّس darras, 'he taught'; مايو māyu, 'May' and ميّة mayya, 'water'.

26. **Assimilation** (influence of consonants in certain consonant/vowel combinations). Neither this process nor the following ones affect the Arabic spelling.

a. Plain consonants in proximity to emphatic and next to throat consonants are pronounced like them.

b. For the influence of consonants on vowels, see the discussion of the pronunciation of vowels.

27. **The Nonoccurrence of Two Consecutive Short Vowels.** In affixes and/or stem combinations, when two short vowels occur next to each other, usually the vowel of the shorter form drops. For example, [wi] + [izzāy] becomes [w-izzāy]. However, because of the omission of the hamza (a glottal stop) in initial position, two consecutive short vowels may occur in word boundary (between words) in this book, e.g.

ísm-i áḥmad
Name-my Ahmad
My name is Ahmad.

28. **The Helping Vowel.** Between a word ending in two consonants and one beginning with one, a short vowel, usually [i], may be inserted to avoid the difficulty of pronouncing three consecutive consonants, which usually do not occur in Arabic. For example:

[bint] + [gamīla] becomes [bint (i) gamīla].

29. **Elision.** In the combination of words and affixes, the unstressed vowels [i] and [u] in initial or final syllables usually drop, unless three consecutive consonants would result. However, the vowel of [-it], the suffix for the 2nd f. sg. in the complete stem, is not dropped. For example, [šírib] 'he drank' + [u] becomes [šírb-u] 'they drank'; but [šírb-it] 'she drank' + [u] remains [širb-ít-u] 'she drank it'.

30. **The Lengthening of Short Vowels.** Any final vowel of a stem is lengthened before adding a suffix: [máda] + [ha] becomes [madā-ha] 'he signed it'; [málu] + [ha] becomes [malū-ha] 'they filled it'.

31. **The Shortening of Long Vowels.** Long vowels do not occur before two consonants. Whenever suffixation brings about the occurrence of two consonants after a long vowel or shifts the stress, the long vowel is shortened in the following ways: [ī] and [ē] both become [i], [ū] and [ō] both become [u], and [ā] becomes [a]. For example: [kitāb] + [ha] becomes [kitáb-ha] 'her book'; [ašūf] + [kum] becomes [ašúf-kum] 'I will see you'; [yōm] + [ēn] becomes [yum-ēn] 'two days'; [šīl] + [ha] becomes [šíl-ha] 'carry/lift it'.

32. **Stress or Accent.** Words in Arabic have one stress only. Throughout the book, stress is indicated by [´] over the stressed vowel. However, stress is not marked in words with only one vowel or in polysyllabic words which contain a long vowel. In words with more than one vowel, stress can fall on any one of the last three vowels in a word according to the following rules:

a. Usually stress falls on the next to the last vowel: [maktába] 'library'.

b. A long vowel is always stressed. Phonetically, a word in Colloquial Arabic may contain only one long vowel: [ɛayān] 'sick'.

c. A short vowel followed by two consonants in the last syllable is always stressed: [katábt] 'I or you (m. sg.) wrote'.

d. If a word contains three or more short vowels and none of the last three is followed by two consonants, then, stress falls on the third from the last vowel: [kátab-it] 'she wrote'; [ištáġal-u] 'they worked'. However, the following are exceptions: 1) regardless of the structure of a word, the vowel of [it] (2nd f. sg. in the complete stem), when followed by another suffix, attracts the stress: [istámal-it] + [ha] becomes [istamal-ít-ha] 'she used it'; 2) some plural nouns with three short vowels, of which the first two are [i]'s or [u]'s, have the stress on the next to the last: [sibíta] 'baskets'.

33. **Syllable Pattern** (C = consonant, V = short vowel, V̄ = long vowel). There are five types of syllables: CV, CVC, CV, CVC, and CVCC. Thus, in principle, no word in Arabic begins with a vowel. Every syllable has a vowel and, with few exceptions, one and only one consonant before a vowel. However, in this book vowels appear in initial position in words because the hamza, a glottal stop, is not written phonetically when it occurs at the beginning of a word.

Unit I.

أهلاً وسهلاً. إزّيّك ؟

áhlan wi sáhlan. izzáyy-ak?

Greetings. How are you?

CONVERSATION

سعيدة يا محمّد. صباح الخير.

SAM. — saɛīda, ya maḥámmad, ṣabāḥ il-xēr.
Hello, oh Muhammad, morning the-good.
Hello, Muhammad, good morning.

صباح الخير عليكم. أهلاً وسهلاً.

MUHAMMAD. — ṣabāḥ il-xēr ɛalē-kum, áhlan wi sáhlan.
Morning the-good on-you (pl), greetings.
Good morning, good to see you.

إزّيّك يا محمّد؟

ESTHER. — izzáyy-ak, ya maḥámmad?
How-you (m), oh Muhammad?
How are you, Muhammad?

أنا كويّس، الحمد لله.

MUHAMMAD. — ána kwáyyis, il-ḥámd(u) li-llāh.
I fine, the-praise to-God.
I am fine, praise to God.

أهلاً وسهلاً! وحشتونى والله.

MUHAMMAD. — áhlan wi sáhlan! waḥaš-tū-ni w-allāhi.
Greetings! Made lonesome-you (pl)-me by-God.
Good to see you! I missed you very much.

أيوه، فاتوا سنتين من يوم ما سبت أمريكا.

ESTHER. — áywa, fāt-u sana-t-ēn min yōm ma-síb-t amrīka.
Yes, passed-(pl) year- (cs)-(d) from day when-left-you (m) America.
Yes, it has been two years since you left America.

إنت كمان وحشتنا ، يا محمد .

ESTHER. — ínta kamān waḥaš-t-ína, ya maḥámmad.
You (m) also made lonesome-you (m)-us, oh Muhammad.
We have missed you too, Muhammad.

إزّاى صحّتكم ؟ وازّاى أولادكم ؟

MUHAMMAD. — izzāy ṣiḥḥ-ít-kum? w-izzāy awlád-kum?
How health-(cs)-your (pl)? And-how boys-your (pl)?
How is your health? And how are your children?

مشْ بطّالة . بسّ البنت الكبيرة عيّانة شويّة .

SAM. — miš baṭṭāl-a. bass il-bínt ik-kibīr-a ʿayyān-a šwáyya.
Not bad-(f). Only the-girl the-big-(f) sick-(f) little.
Not bad. Only the older daughter is a little sick.

سلامتها ! مالها ؟ عندها إيه ؟

MUHAMMAD. — salam-ít-ha! má-l-ha? ʿand-áha ēh?
Safety-(cs)-her! What-to-her? At-her what?
Speedy recovery! What is wrong with her?

لا ، حاجة بسيطة . شويّة برد بسّ .

ESTHER. — lá', ḥāga basīṭ-a, šwáyy-it bard bass.
No, thing trifling-(f), little-(cs) cold only.
Nothing serious, just a cold.

إزّاى والدك ووالدتك . يا مدام ؟

MUHAMMAD. — izzāy wáld-ik wi wald-ít-ik, ya madām?
How father-your(f) and mother-(cs)-your(f), oh madam?
How are your father and mother, madam?

أمّى وأبوى كويّسين . متشكّرة .

ESTHER. — úmm-i w-abū-ya kwayyis-īn, mutšakkír-a.
Mother-my and-father-my well-(pl), thankful-(f).
My mother and my father are fine, thank you.

1. 1. Cultural notes. Greetings are an important feature of the Arabic language. We give only a few of the large number of greetings used by the Arabs. Note that the forms of greetings vary, depending on whether a man, a woman, or several persons are greeted.

The traditional Moslem greeting of Arab Moslems given by one who comes or goes is:

السّلام عليكم is-salām ɛalē-kum, Good to see you!

and the response is:

وعليكم السّلام wi ɛalē-kum is-salām, Good to see you!

The greeting to one who is leaving is:

مع السّلامة máɛa-s-salāma, Goodbye!

and the response is:

الله يسلّمك allāh yi-sallím-ak, Goodbye!

The form سعيدة saɛīda, which is invariable and a less formal greeting, is usually used for both "hello" and "good-bye" by non-Moslems.

The formal greeting for "how are you, sir?" is formed by the word إزّاى izzāy 'how', plus one of the three words for "you, sir":

إزّاى حضرتك ؟ izzāy ḥaḍrít-ak? How are you, sir?
إزّاى جنابك ؟ izzāy ganāb-ak? How are you, sir?
إزّاى سيادتك ؟ izzāy syádt-ak? How are you, sir?

When addressing a lady or several persons, the ending -ak in the above sentences changes to -ik for a lady and -kum for several persons.

The informal greeting for "how are you?" is:

إزّيّك ؟ izzáyy-ak? (to a man)
إزّيّك ؟ izzáyy-ik? (to a woman)
إزّيّكم ؟ izzayy-úkum? (to several people)

عن العيلة العربيّة

ɛan il-ɛēla il-ɛarab-í-yya

Unit 2. About the Arab Family

CONVERSATION

يا زكى ، قل لى حاجة عن العيلة العربيّة .

JIM. — ya záki, qúl-l-i hāga ɛan il-ɛēla il-ɛarab-í-yya.
Oh Zaki, tell-to-me thing on the-family the-Arab-(adj)-(f).
Zaki, tell me something about the Arab family.

عادة العيلات العربيّة كبيرة قوى .

ZAKI. — ɛādatan il-ɛil-āt il-ɛarab-í-yya kibīr-a qáwi.
Habitually the-family-(pl) the-Arab-(adj)-(f) big-(f) very.
Usually Arab families are very large.

فى عيلتى ، مثلا ، إحنا عشرة أنفار .

ZAKI. — fi ɛíl-t-i, másalan, íḥna ɛášar-t-anfār.
In family-(cs)-my, for example, we ten-(cs)-persons.
For example, there are ten in my family.

الأوّل ، والدى ووالدتى ، وتمانية أولاد .

ZAKI. — il-áwwil, wáld-i wi wald-ít-i, wi táman-t-awlād.
The-first, father-my and mother-(cs)-my, and eight-(cs)-children.
First, father and mother, plus eight children.

لك كام أخّ وكام أخت ، يا زكى ؟

JIM. — li-k kām axx wi kām uxt, ya záki?
At-you(m) how many brother and how many sister, oh Zaki?
How many brothers and sisters do you have, Zaki?

لىّ تلات اخوات صبيان وأربع اخوات بنات .

ZAKI. — l-íyya tálat ixwāt ṣubyān wi árbaɛ ixwāt banāt.
At-me three brothers boys and four brothers girls.
I have three brothers and four sisters.

أنا سمعت انّ الأبّهات العرب شداد مع أولادهم .

JIM. — ána simíع-t inn il-abbahāt il-عárab šudād maع awlád-[hum.
I heard-I that the-fathers the-Arab strong with children-their.
I have heard that the Arab fathers are strict with their children.

أفتكر ده صحيح عن كلّ الأبّهات اللى فى العالم .

ZAKI. — a-ftíkir da ṣaḥīḥ عan kull il-abbahāt ílli f-il-عālam.
I-think that true on all the-fathers who in-the-world.
I think that is true of all fathers around the world.

إنّما صحيح إنّ الأمّهات ألطف فى كلّ حتّة .

ZAKI. — ínnama ṣaḥīḥ inn il-ummahāt álṭaf fi-kúll(i) ḥítta.
But true that the-mothers nicer in-all piece.
Nevertheless, it is true that mothers are nicer everywhere.

لمّا يتجوّز أخوك الكبير حايسيب البيت ، مش كده ؟

JIM. — lámma yi-tgáwwiz axū-k il-kibīr ḥa-y-sīb il-bēt, miš [kída?
When he-get married brother-your(m) the-big (ft)-he-leave the-house, [not so?
When your older brother marries, he will leave the house, [won't he?

لا ، فى العادة الاولاد يقعدوا مع أهلهم .

ZAKI. — la', f-il-عāda il-awlād yi-qعúd-u maع ahl-úhum.
No, in-the-custom the-boys he-stay-(pl) with folks-their.
No, usually the boys stay with their parents.

يا زكى ، لىّ أخّ واحد وأختين .

JIM. — ya záki, l-íyya axx wāḥid w-uxt-ēn.
Oh Zaki, at-me brother one and-sister-(d).
Zaki, I have one brother and two sisters.

كلّهم متجوّزين ، ولهم بيوتهم .

JIM. — kull-úhum mitgawwiz-īn, wi l-úhum biyút-hum.
All-them married-(pl), and to-them houses-their.
All are married, and they have their own homes.

2. 1. Structure of Arabic words. Three notions are fundamental to the structure of Arabic words: *root* (the underlying part of a word), vowel pattern (various combinations of vowels and consonants), and *affixation* (various affixes added to the root). Not all roots can take affixes. Those roots which take affixes are called *stems*.

A. Three consonantal system. Most Arabic words are built from roots, each of which usually consists of three consonants called the radicals, e.g., k t b, d r s, f t h, s l m. There are a few words of two consonants as the verbs شاف šāf 'see'; and جيب gīb 'give' and of four consonants as ترجم tárgim 'translate'.

B. Vowel pattern and affixation. According to various patterns, vowels combine with one root to form other related words. Furthermore, additional vowels and/or consonants may be added to a root at the beginning (prefixes), at the end (suffixes), or inside the root (infixes). The root carries the basic lexical meaning of the word. The various vowel patterns and affixes in combination with the root yield a number of different words with various shades of the original meaning of the root. For example, from the root k t b, which embodies the idea of writing, we obtain the following words:

كتب	kátab	he wrote	كتابة	kitāba	act of writing
اكتب	íktib	write!	مكتب	máktab	office, desk
يكتب	yí-ktib	he writes	مكاتب	makātib	offices, desks
كاتب	kātib	clerk, having written	مكتبة	maktába	library
كتبة	kátaba	clerks	مكتوب	maktūb	written (m)
كتاب	kitāb	book	مكتوبة	maktūba	written (f)
كتب	kútub	books	مكتوبين	maktubīn	written (pl)

2. 2. Cultural notes. The triconsonantal root system is a characteristic feature of all Semitic languages of which Arabic is the most important. Other Semitic languages are Amharic, the modern language of Ethiopia; Hebrew, the language of the state of Israel; Aramaic, the language spoken in Palestine at the time of Christ and spoken today in a few villages in northern Lebanon; and dead languages as Syriac, Akkadian, and Phoenician.

2. 3. Nouns of the family members.

	SINGULAR		PLURAL
أبّ	abb, father	أبّهات	abbahāt
أمّ	umm, mother	أمّهات	ummahāt
والد	wālid, father (parent)	والدين	waldēn, parents
والدة	wáld-a, mother (parent)		
بابا	bāba, father		
ماما	māma, mother		
طفل	ṭifl, child	أطفال	aṭfāl
عيّل	ɛáyyil (m) child	عيال	ɛiyāl
عيّلة	ɛayyíl-a (f)		
صبي	ṣábi (m) youngster	صبيان	ṣubyān
صبيّة	ṣabí-yya (f)		
ولد	wálad, boy/ child	ولاد — أولاد	wilād, awlād
إبن	ibn, son	أبناء	abnā'
بنت	bint, daughter/ girl	بنات	banāt
أخّ	axx, brother	إخوان	ixwān
أخت	uxt, sister	إخوات	ixwāt
ستّ	sitt, wife/ woman/ lady/ grandmother	ستّات	sitt-āt
مراة	mára, woman/ wife	نسوان	niswān
مرات	mirāt, wife		
زوجة	zōg-a, wife	زوجات	zog-āt
جوز	gōz, husband	أزواج	azwāg
زوج	zōg, husband		
خال	xāl, uncle (maternal)	خيلان	xilān
خالة	xāl-a, aunt (maternal)	خالات	xal-āt
عمّ	ɛamm, uncle (paternal)	أعمام	aɛmām
عمّة	ɛámm-a, aunt (paternal)	عمّات	ɛamm-āt
جدّ	gidd, grandfather	جدود	gudūd
جدّة	gadda, grandmother	جدّات	gadd-āt

حفيد	ḥafīd, grand-child	أحفاد	aḥfād
قريب	qarīb, relative (of blood)	قرايب	qarāyib
نسيب	nasīb, relative (in-law)	نسايب	nasāyib

The plurals of the following compounds are formed by using the plurals of the first noun:

ابن خال ibn(i)-xāl, cousin (maternal)
ابن عمّ ibn(i)-ɛámm, cousin (paternal)
بنت أخت bint-úxt, niece
بنت أخّ bint-axū, niece
ابن أخت ibn-úxt, nephew
ابن أخّ ibn-axū, nephew
جوز أخت gōz-uxt, brother-in-law
مرات أخّ mrat-axū, sister-in-law

When the nouns أبّ abb 'father' and أخّ axx 'brother' are first members of a construct state (that is, when they are followed by another noun or bound pronoun), their forms are أبو abū and أخو axū:

أبو حسن abū ḥássan, Hassan's father
أبوك abū-k, your (m) father
أبوىَ abū-ya, my father
أخو المدرّس axu-l-mudárris, the teacher's brother
أخوكِ axū-k-i, your (f) brother
أخوىَ axū-ya, my brother

However, with the first singular bound possessive pronoun, there is also the regular form:

أبي áb-i, my father أخي áx-i, my brother

The word والد wālid, which also means father, takes the bound pronouns in the regular way; however, the unstressed *i* drops (unless three consecutive consonants would result) and the long vowel is shortened:

والدي wáld-i, my father والدها walíd-ha, her father

التعرف بالطلبة

Unit 3. *it-taʿárruf b-iṭ-ṭálaba* Meeting Students

CONVERSATION

يا عادل ، هوّ مين مصطفى ؟

ROBERT. — ya ʿādil, húwwa mīn muṣṭáfa?
Oh Adil, he who Mustafa?
Adil, who is Mustafa?

مصطفى هوّ أبو أحمد .

ADIL. — muṣṭáfa húwwa abū áḥmad.
Mustafa he father Ahmad.
Mustafa is the father of Ahmad.

هوّ ده الرّاجل إللى شفته امبارح فى بيتك ؟

ROBERT. — húwwa da-r-rāgil ílli šúf-t-uh imbāriḥ fi-bēt-ak?
He this/that(m)-the-man whom saw-I-him yesterday in-house-your(m)?
Is he the man I saw yesterday at your home?

أيوه . هوّ مصطفى النّجّار .

ADIL. — áywa. húwwa muṣṭáfa-n-naggār.
Yes. He Mustafa-the-carpenter.
Yes. He is Mustafa Nagar.

وفاطمة بنته كمان ؟

ROBERT. — wi fáṭma bínt-uh kamān?
And Fatma girl-his also?
And is Fatma his daughter?

أيوه ، فاطمة أخت أحمد .

ADIL. — áywa, fáṭma uxt áḥmad.
Yes, Fatma sister Ahmad.
Yes, Fatma is Ahmad's sister.

وغير كده ، هىّ خطيبتى .

Adil. — wi ġēr kída, híyya xatíb-t-i.
And besides so, she fiancee-(cs)-my.
What's more, she is my fiancee.

همّ طلبة فى الجـّامعة ؟

Sandra. — húmma ṭálaba fi-g-gámɛa?
They students in-the-university?
Are they university students?

إحنا التلاتة طلبة فى جامعة القاهرة .

Adil. — íḥna-t-talāta ṭálaba fi-gámɛ-it il-q̇āhira.
We-the-three students in-university-(cs) the-Cairo.
All three of us are students at Cairo University.

إنت تخصّصك ايه ، يا عادل ؟

Robert. — ínta taxáṣṣuṣ-ak ēh, ya ɛādil?
You specialization-your(m) what, oh Adil?
What is your field, Adil?

تخصّصى الهندسة ، لـكن بأحبّ الصّحافة .

Adil. — taxáṣṣuṣ-i-l-handása, lākin b-a-ḥíbb iṣ-ṣiḥāfa.
Specialization-my-the-engineering, but (pt)-I-like the-journalism.
My field is engineering, but I like journalism.

جامعة القاهرة دى موسّسة كبيرة ؟

Robert. — gámɛ-it il-q̇āhira di mu'assása kibīr-a?
University-(cs) the-Cairo this/that(f) institution big-(f)?
Is Cairo University a large institution?

أيوه ، دى أكبر وأهمّ واحدة فى الشرق الأوسط .

Adil. — áywa, di ákbar w-ahámm wáḥd-a f-iš-šárq il-áwsaṭ.
Yes, this/that(f) biggest and-most important one-(f) in-the-East-
[the-Middle.
Yes, it is the largest and most important one in the Middle
[East.

3. 1. Verbless sentences. Many Egyptian Arabic sentences have no verb and are called verbless sentences in contrast to verbal sentences which always contain a verb.

There are two types of verbless sentences in Egyptian Arabic: one which corresponds to English sentences with the verb "to be" in the present tense, and the other which corresponds to English sentences with the verb "to have".

The latter type of verbless sentences will be discussed in a later unit.

In this unit, we discuss the first type of verbless sentences. There is no word in Egyptian Arabic for the English verb forms "am", "is", or "are". Like English sentences, Egyptian Arabic verbless sentences are of the pattern: Subject (S) + Predicate (P), but without the verb. In such sentences:

A. The subject is always definite and may be a noun phrase (a noun with the definite article or with a possessive bound pronoun with or without modifiers) or a free pronoun such as personal pronouns, demonstratives, or interrogative pronouns.

B. The predicate may be:

	P S	S		P
1) a noun:	الراجل مدير	ir-rāgil		mudīr.
		The-man		director.
		The man	is	a director.
2) a noun phrase:	الولد إبنى	il-wálad		íbn-i.
		The-boy		son-my.
		The boy	is	my son.
3) an adjective:	البنات حلوين	il-banāt		ḥilw-īn.
		The-girls		pretty- (pl).
		The girls	are	pretty.
4) a participle	أنا مشغول	ána		mašġūl.
used as an		I		busy.
adjective:		I	am	busy.

An adjective or participle in a predicate position does not take the definite article.

	P S	S		P
5) a free pronoun:	مين هيَّ	mīn		híyya?
		Who		she?
		Who	is	she?
6) an adverb:	البنت هنا	il-bínt		hína.
		the-girl		here.
		The girl	is	here.
7) a prepositional phrase:	الدهب فى الشنطة	id-dáhab		fi-š-šánta.
		The-gold		in-the-purse/bag.
		The gold	is	in the purse.

C. The usual order of subject + predicate may be reversed for emphasis:

8)	فى الشّنطة الدهب	fi-š-šánta-d-dáhab.
		in-the-purse-the-gold.
		In the purse is the gold.

زيارة للجيران

ziyāra li-l-girān

Unit 4. A Visit to the Neighbors

CONVERSATION

يا لطفي ، أنا عايز أزور جيراننا بيت عفافة .
JACK. — ya lúṭfi, ána ɛāyiz a-zūr girán-na bēt ɛafāfa.
Oh Lutfi, I wanting I-visit neighbor-our house Afafa.
Lutfi, I want to visit our neighbors Afafa.

دى فكرة كويّسة ! أنا عايز آجى معاك .
LUTFI. — di fíkra kwayyís-a! ána ɛāyiz āgi maɛā-k.
This idea good-(f). I wanting I come with-you(m).
That is a good idea. I want to come with you.

صاحبى الطيّب والعزيز السيّد عفافة راح لبنان .
LUTFI. — ṣáḥb-i iṭ-ṭáyyib wi-l-ɛazīz is-sáyyid ɛafāfa rāḥ [libnān.
Friend-my the-good and-the-dear the-mister Afafa he went Lebanon.
My good and dear friend Mr. Afafa has gone to Lebanon.

لكن أفتكر مراته الستّ الظّريفة موجودة .
JACK. — lākin a-ftíkir mrāt-uh is-sítt iẓ-ẓarīf-a mawgūd-a.
But I-think wife-his the-lady the-gracious-(f) present-(f).
But I think his wife who is a gracious lady is here.

أيوه . أنا النّهارده شفتها مع بنتها الصّغيّرة .
LUTFI. — áywa. innahárda šuf-t-áha máɛa bint-áha- [ṣ-ṣuġayyár-a.
Yes. Today saw-I-her with daughter-her-the-small-(f).
Yes. Today I saw her with her little daughter.

أنا أعرف ابنهم الكبير من وقت ما زار أمريكا .
JACK. — an-á-ɛraf ibn-úhum il-kibīr min wáqt(i)ma zār [amrīka.
I-I-know son-their the-big from time when he visited America.
I have known their elder son since his visit to America.

أهلا ! إزيّك ، يا ستّ هانم ؟
JACK & LUTFI. — áhlan! izzáyy-ik, ya sítt(i)hānim?
Greetings! How-you(f), oh woman lady?
Greetings! How are you, madam?

سعيدة ! أهلا بيكم . اتفضّلوا ، ادخلوا .
MRS. AFAFA. — saɛīda! áhlan bī-kum. itfaḍḍál-u, idxúl-u.
Hello! Greetings with-you(pl). Welcome-you(pl), enter-you(pl).
Hello! Nice to see you. Welcome, come in.

يا مدام ، بيتك جميل ونضيف قوى .
JACK. — ya madām, bēt-ik gamīl wi-nḍīf qáwi.
Oh Madam, house-your(f) beautiful and-clean very.
Mrs. Afafa, your house is very beautiful and clean.

يا چاك ، دول عندهم جنينة ظريفة حوالين البيت . [il-bēt.
LUTFI. — ya Jack, dōl ɛand-úhum ginēna ẓarīf-a ḥawalēn
Oh Jack, these/those at-them garden nice-(f) around the-house.
Jack, they have a beautiful garden around the house.

يالله نروح الجنّينة ونشرب شاى متلّج .
MRS. AFAFA. — yálla ni-rūḥ ig-ginēna wi ní-šrab šāy mi-
Come on we-go the-garden and we-drink tea iced. [tállig.
Let's go into the garden and have iced tea.

إحنا آسفين للزّيارة القصيّرة دى . لازم نروّح . [ni-ráwwaḥ.
LUTFI. — íḥna asf-īn li-z-ziyāra il-quṣayyár-a di; lāzim
We sorry-(pl) for-the-visit the-short-(f) this/that(f); must we-go
We are sorry for the short visit, we must go home. [*home.*

لا مؤاخذة ، عندنا لسّه ورانا مشوار طويل .
JACK. — la mu'áxza, ɛand-ína líssa warā-na mišwār ṭawīl.
No objection, at-us still behind-us errand long.
Excuse us, we still have many things to do.

مع السّلامة ! لازم تتفضّلوا تانى ضرورى .
MRS. AFAFA. — máɛa-s-salāma! lāzim t-itfaḍḍál-u tāni
With-the-peace! Must you-be welcome-(pl) other certainly. [ḍarūrī.
Good-bye. I hope you will come again.

4. 1. Verbal sentences. Verbal sentences in Arabic consist of:

A. at least a verb stem:

كتب.	اكتب !	كلم !	شاف .	شوف !
kátab.	íktib!	kállim!	šāf.	šūf!
He wrote.	Write!	He spoke/Speak!	He saw.	See!/Look!

B. a verb stem with a bound subject pronoun (a pronoun attached to the verb stem):

كتبت .	اكتبوا !	يكتب .	أعرف .
kátab-it.	iktíb-u!	yí-ktib.	á-ɛraf.
Wrote-she.	*Write-you! (pl)*	*He-write.*	*I-know.*
She wrote.	Write! (pl)	He writes.	I know.

C. a verb cluster (two or three verbs in sequence):

نحب نغنّي .	نحب نتعلّم نغني .
ni-ḥíbb ni-ġánni.	ni-ḥíbb ni-tɛállim ni-ġánni.
We-like we-sing.	*We-like we-learn we-sing.*
We like to sing.	We like to learn to sing.

D. any of the foregoing A, B, and C with modifiers which occur only at the beginning and/or the end of the sentence.

A preceding modifier (at the right of the verb in Arabic script, but at the left of the verb in phonetic transcription and English translation) may be:

1. a (free or unattached) subject pronoun or a subject noun:

هوّ يعرف .	الرّاجل يعرف .
húwwa yí-ɛraf.	ir-rāgil yí-ɛraf.
He he-know.	*The-man he-know.*
He knows.	The man knows.

2. a noun phrase (two or more nouns or a noun with a modifier).

مندوب الشركة مضاها .
mandūb iš-šírka maḍā-ha.
Delegate the-company signed-her.
The delegate of the company signed it.

3. A present tense prefix *bi-*, or a future tense prefix *ḥa-*, with or without a preceding adverb of time:

بكرة حانروح.	دلوقتي بيمشي.
(búkra) ḥa-n-rūḥ.	(dilwáqti) bi-yi-mši.
(Tomorrow) (ft)-we-go.	*(Now) (pt)-he-goes/is going.*
(Tomorrow) we will go.	(Now) he is going.

4. the auxiliary verb كان kān or a modal auxiliary:

كان بيكتب.	ناويين يسفروا.
kān bi-yí-ktib.	nawy-īn yi-sáfr-u.
Was (pt)-he-write.	*Intending-(pl) he-leave-(pl).*
He was writing.	They intend to leave.

A following modifier may be:

5. an object noun or noun phrase:

كتبنا جواب طويل.
Katáb-na gawāb ṭawīl.
Wrote-we letter long.
We wrote a long letter.

6. a bound pronoun (direct or indirect) or any adverb:

ورّها له.	جينا ناخد صورتك كمان.
warra-hā-l-uh.	gē-na n-āxud ṣúrt-ak kamān.
Showed-her-to-him.	*Came-we we-take picture-your (m) also.*
He showed it to him.	We came to take your picture too.

4. 2. Classification of verbs. Verb stem and verb form. In Arabic, a verb form consists of a verb stem with or without affixes (prefix, suffix, or infix). A verb stem is a verb form without any affix. The verb stem, then, is the base form from which all other verb forms are derived by adding affixes. According to the various forms verbs may take and their meaning and the relationship to each other, five criteria classify verbs into various categories. The following classifications facilitate the understanding of the mechanics of the construction of the various verb forms and their uses:

A. Derived versus non-derived (simple) **verb classification.** Basically, there are simple and derived verbs.

This classification is based on the fact that some verbs are formed from other verbs or from other parts of speech through some modification. For example:

Simple verbs	*Derived verbs*
درس dáras, study	درّس dárris, teach
فهم fíhim, understand	فهّم fáhhim, explain
رجع rígiع, return	راجع rāgiع, revise

B. Consonant—Vowel structure classification. This classification includes only simple verbs and is based on the consonant-vowel structure of the various verb stems:

1. Triconsonantal verbs (verb stems with three radical consonants):

كتب kátab, write   شرب šírib, drink   فتح fátaḥ, open

2. Double verbs (verb stems with three radical consonants, of which the last two are identical):

سدّ sadd, block   مرّ marr, pass   حبّ ḥabb, like/love

3. Hollow verbs (verb stems with two radical consonants and a medial long vowel):

شاف šāf, see   قال qāl, say/tell   نام nām, sleep

4. Defective verbs (verb stems with two radical consonants and a final short vowel):

لقى láqa, find   مضى máḍa, sign   مشى míši, walk

5. Four consonant verbs (verb stems with four radical consonants):

لخبط láxbaṭ, confuse   ترجم tárgim, translate   دردش dárdiš, chat

6. Irregular verbs (verb stems which do not follow any of the above patterns):

جه gih, come   كل kal, eat   وقف wíqif, stand

C. Stem classification. Each verb, simple or derived, has three types of stems: imperative, complete, and incomplete. As a rule, each type of stem differs in form and meaning. However, except for stems which begin with a vowel *í* and the irregular verb stems, the imperative and the incomplete stems are the same. The three types of stems will be treated in separate sections in a later unit:

Complete	*Incomplete*	*Imperative*
كتب kátab	يكتب yí-ktib	إكتب íktib, write
قال qāl	يقول yi-qūl	قول qūl, say/tell
شدّ šadd	يشدّ yi-šídd	شدّ šidd, pull
كلّم kállim	يكلّم yi-kállim	كلّم kállim, speak
أنتج ántag	ينتج yí-ntig	إنتج íntig, produce

D. Vowel change classification. This classification is based on the relationship of the complete stem to the incomplete or the imperative stem in terms of vowel change. For a number of verbs, all three stems are the same. For many other verbs, the vowels are different. It is difficult to predict the vowel change; therefore, the student must memorize the change in each verb. On the basis of vowel change, verbs are grouped into the following classes:

	Complete	*Incomplete*
1. Unchanged vowel class:	كسّر kássar	يكسّر yi-kássar, smash
2. Vowel *i* class:	درس dáras	يدرس yí-dris, study
3. Vowel *a* class:	فهم fíhim	يفهم yí-fham, understand
4. Vowel *u* class:	خرج xárag	يخرج yú-xrug, go out

As a rule, all derived forms of the simple verbs have the same complete, incomplete, and imperative stems. Some derived verbs for which the vowel change is optional will be considered as belonging to the unchanged vowel class. The incomplete or imperative stem of simple verbs and some of their derived forms have one or more vowels that are different from the complete stem.

E. Classification according to the ending of the verb forms. This distinction is made to facilitate the understanding of the process of suffixation and is made in terms of the ending of any verb form (a stem with or without suffixes):

1. Verbs ending in one consonant: dáras 'study/learn', kul 'eat!'

2. Verbs ending in two consonants: katáb-t 'I/you wrote', rudd 'answer!'

3. Verbs ending in a vowel: katáb-na 'we wrote', dáras-u 'they studied', máḍa, 'he signed'.

4. Verbs ending in bound pronouns -ik (you, feminine singular) and -h (him/it): šāf-ik 'he saw you' (f), šāf-uh 'he saw him'.

Unit 5.

روح اشتغل ، يا حسّن !

rūḥ ištáġal, ya ḥássan!

Get to Work, Hassan!

CONVERSATION

ايه ده ، يا حسّن ؟ قوم كده وروح اشتغل .

ALI. — ēh da, ya ḥássan? qūm kída wi rūḥ ištáġal.
What this, oh Hassan? Get up so and go work.
What's this, Hassan? Get up and get to work.

إزّاى أشتغل يا ريّس ؟ الورشة مقفولة .

HASSAN. — izzāy a-štáġal, ya ráyyis? il-wárša maqfūl-a.
How I-work, oh chief? The-workshop closed-(f).
How can I work, sir? The workshop is closed.

هوّ انت ما تقدرش تيجى المكتب وتاخد المفتاح ؟

ALI. — húwwa ínta ma-ti-qdár-š t-īgi il-máktab wi t-āxud [il-muftāḥ?
He you (neg)-you-can-(neg) you-come the-office and you-take [the-key?
Can't you come to the office and get the key?

أنا مستنّى فتحى عشان هوّ معاه المفتاح .

HASSAN. — ána mistánni fátḥi ʕašān húwwa maʕā-h il-[muftāḥ.
I waiting Fathi because he with-him the-key.
I am waiting for Fathi because he has the key.

هوّ انت يا راجل ما تعرفش تشتغل من غير فتحى ؟

ALI. — húwwa ínta, ya rāgil, ma-ti-ʕráf-š ti-štáġal min-ġēr [fátḥi?
He you, oh man, (neg)-you-know-(neg) you-work from-other Fathi?
Don't you know, man, how to work without Fathi?

إفرض إنّ فتحى ما جاش النّهارده ؟

ALI. — ífriḍ ínn(i) fátḥi ma-gā-š innahárda?
Suppose that Fathi (neg)-come-(neg) today?
Suppose Fathi doesn't come today?

أنا جيت معاه وهوّ قال لى أستنّاه هنا .
HASSAN. — ána gē-t maɛā-h wi húwwa qál-l-i a-stannā-h
I came-I with-him and he said-to-me I-wait-him here. [hína.
I came with Fathi, and he told me to wait for him here.

راح يشترى شويّة عيش وجبنة يا ريّس .
HASSAN. — rāḥ yi-štíri šwáyy-it ɛēš wi gíbna, ya ráyyis.
Went he-buy little-(cs) bread and cheese, oh chief.
He went to buy a few sandwiches, sir.

بلاش كلام فاضى ! خد المفتاح أهو !
ALI. — balāš kalām fāḍi! xud il-muftāḥ, ahú!
Never mind talk empty! Take the-key, here it is!
Let's stop talking nonsense. Here is the key!

افتح الباب وامسح الأرضيّة قبل كلّ حاجة .
ALI. — íftaḥ il-bāb wi ímsaḥ il-arḍ-í-yya qábl(i) kúll(i) ḥāga.
Open the-door and sweep the-ground-(adj)-(f) before all thing.
Open the door and clean the floor first.

طيّب يا ريّس ، لكن لازم حدّ يساعدنى أدخّل العلبة دى جوّه .
HASSAN. — ṭáyyib, ya ráyyis, lākin lāzim ḥadd yi-saɛíd-ni a-dáxxal il-ɛílba di gúwwa.
Well, oh chief, but must anyone he-help-me I-enter the-box this inside.
Yes, sir, but I need help to carry this box inside.

ياالله بينا ؛ أنا حاساعدك . تعال معاىَ نشيلها . [šíl-ha.
ALI. — yálla bī-na; ána ḥa-sáɛd-ak. taɛāla maɛā-ya ni-
Come on with-us; I (ft)-help-you(m). Come with-me we-carry-her.
Come; I can help you. Come on. Let's lift it.

يا حسّن ، قول لفتحى ييجى يشوفنى لمّا يرجع .
ALI. — ya ḥássan, qūl li-fátḥi y-īgi yi-šúf-ni lámma yí-rgaɛ.
Oh Hassan, tell to-Fathi he-come he-see-me when he-return.
Hassan, tell Fathi to come to see me when he returns.

5. 1. Complete or suffix verb stems. Complete stems convey the meaning of a completed action or condition, which roughly corresponds to the English past tense. The base or citation form of each complete verb stem is the third person masculine singular:

كتب kátab, he wrote/has written
شرب šírib, he drank/has drunk

The entry of each verb, in the vocabulary or any list of verbs, is given in this form. However, the English translation is conventionally given as that of the corresponding English infinitive form without "to":

كتب kátab, write شرب šírib, drink

From this base form, all forms for the other persons, gender, and number are built with the addition of appropriate suffixes (hence, suffix stem), which are the same for all complete stems. The base form, however, with few exceptions, does not remain the same for all persons, gender, and number; its form depends on the type of verb and suffix.

For the negation of the complete verb forms, the split negative form ma...š is used:

ما كتبناش حاجة .
ma katab-nā-š ḥāga.
(Neg) wrote-we-(neg) thing.
We didn't write a thing.

5. 2. The imperative stems. The imperative stems of the verbs in Arabic convey the same meaning as the English imperatives in giving direct orders in the affirmative. The imperative stem has only three forms: second person masculine singular (m), feminine singular (f), and plural (pl) for both masculine and feminine. The base form of the imperative stem is the masculine form. The feminine and the plural forms are obtained by adding to the base stem the suffix *-i* for the feminine and the suffix *-u* for the plural. Except for the defective verbs, which have the same masculine and feminine singular forms, these suffixes are the same for all types of verbs. Moreover, except for the elision of unstressed short vowels and the shortening of long vowels, the stem remains the same for all three forms.

For the negation of the imperative forms, the second person incomplete stem is used with the split negative form ma...š:

كلّم kállim, speak to someone:

كلّم	kállim	speak! (m)
كلّمي	kallím-i	speak! (f)
كلّموا	kallím-u	speak! (pl)
ما تكلّمش	ma-t-kallím-š	don't speak! (m)
ما تكلّميش	ma-t-kallim-ī-š	don't speak! (f)
ما تكلّموش	ma-t-kallim-ū-š	don't speak! (pl)

A common exclamatory imperative is اوعى iwɛa 'watch out!' which, like all imperatives, has three forms:

اوعى	íwɛa! (m)
اوعى	íwɛi! (f)
اوعوا	íwɛu! (pl)

This imperative may be used alone or it may be followed by the interjection ya and a noun or by an incomplete verb form, either affirmative or negative. If this imperative is used alone or followed by a noun, it may be translated into English as either "watch out" or "be careful":

اوعى !	íwɛa!	Watch out!
اوعى يا بنت!	íwɛi, ya bint!	Be careful, girl!

If íwɛa is followed by an incomplete verb form in the affirmative, it conveys the meaning of a negative imperative; however, if it is followed by an incomplete verb form in the negative, íwɛa conveys the meaning of an affirmative imperative of the following verb. If it is followed by a verb form, it may be translated into English as "be sure not to..." or "make sure not to...":

اوعوا تناموا!	اوعوا ما تناموش !
íwɛu t-nām-u!	íwɛu ma-t-nam-ū-š!
Be sure you-sleep-(pl)!	*Be sure (neg)-you-sleep-(pl)-(neg)!*
Be sure you don't sleep!	Be sure you sleep!

5.3. The incomplete or prefix verb stems. Although the complete stems designate past tense, the incomplete stems do not necessarily designate the present tense. The distinction, therefore, is not a matter of time (tense); but rather, it is a matter of completed or not completed action or condition (aspect). In other words, an incomplete verb stem in Arabic may designate: 1) an action or condition being performed or existing in the present (simple, habitual, or continuous present); 2) an action or condition which has started in the past (past progressive); 3) an intended action or condition (future); or 4) a non-temporal state, which may assume the form of (a) an imperative other than the second person; (b) imperatives (orders) in the negative, intentions, wishes; and (c) expressions corresponding to the English infinitives and subjunctives (see below).

The base form of the incomplete stem is the same as the base form of the imperative stem, without the initial vowel (if there is any), preceded by the prefixed subject pronoun.

Formally, the incomplete stems usually occur:

A. After the tense prefixes *bi-* (indicating present tense) and *ḥa-* (indicating future tense):

أحمد بيكتب جواب .
áḥmad bi-yí-ktib gawāb.
Ahmad (pt)-he-write letter.
Ahmad writes/is writing a letter.

أحمد حيكتب جواب .
áḥmad ḥa-yí-ktib gawāb.
Ahmad (ft)-he-write letter.
Ahmad will write a letter.

B. In the second and third positions of a verb cluster or verbal sentence and for a few verbs at the beginning of a verb cluster or verbal sentence:

أحمد يحبّ يسوق العربيّة .
áḥmad yi-ḥíbb yi-sūq il-ƹarabíyya.
Ahmad he-love he-drive the-car.
Ahmad loves to drive the car.

هم طلبوا ييجوا يناموا عندنا .
húmma ṭálab-u y-īg-u yi-nām-u ɛand-ína.
They asked-(pl) he-come-(pl) he-sleep-(pl) at-us.
They asked to come to sleep at our place.

C. After the auxiliary verb كان kān 'was/were' or a modal auxiliary like ناوى nāwi 'intending'.

أحمد كان يكتب جوابات كتير .
áḥmad kān yí-ktib gawab-āt kitīr.
Ahmad was he-write letter-(pl) many.
Ahmad used to write many letters.

إحنا ناويين نزورك بكرة .
íḥna nawy-īn n-zūr-ak búkra.
We intending-(pl) we-visit-you (m) tomorrow.
We intend to visit you tomorrow.

D. In negative imperative constructions:

ما تعملش دوشة ، يا ابنى !
ma-ti-ɛmíl-š dáwša, ya íbn-i!
(Neg)-you (m)-make-(neg) noise, oh son-my!
Don't make noise, son!

E. After participles and most conjunctions in verb clusters and verbal sentences:

أحمد رايح يشترى الدّفتر .
áḥmad rāyiḥ yi-štíri id-dáftar.
Ahmad going he-buy the-copy book.
Ahmad is going to buy the copy book.

قبل ما تسافر أدّينا خبر .
qábl(i)-ma t-sāfir iddī-ni xábar.
Before-when you-leave give-me news.
Before you leave, let me know.

F. As an imperative other than the second person in Arabic (comparable to the English expression "let's..."):

ياالله نروح نعوم .
yálla n-rūḥ ni-ɛūm.
Come on we-go we-swim.
Let's go swimming.

Unit 6.

درس عربي

dars ʕárab-i

An Arabic Lesson

CONVERSATION

يا دافيد ، إنت بتذاكر ايه ؟

Khalid. — ya David, ínta bi-t-zākir ēh?
Oh David, you (pt)-you-study what?
David, what are you studying?

أنا باحاول أتعلّم اللّغة العربيّة .

David. — ána b-a-ḥāwil a-tʕállim il-lúġa il-ʕarab-í-yya.
I (pt)-I-try I-learn the-language the-Arab-(adj)-(f).
I am trying to learn the Arabic language.

إنت بتذاكر عربى فصيح والاّ عامّى .

Khalid. — ínta bi-t-zākir ʕárab-i faṣīḥ wálla ʕámm-i?
You (pt)-you-study Arab-(adj) literary or public-(adj)?
Are you studying literary or colloquial Arabic?

أنا عايز أتعلّم عربى عامّى .

David. — ána ʕāyiz a-tʕállim ʕárab-i ʕámm-i.
I wanting I-learn Arab-(adj) public-(adj).
I want to learn colloquial Arabic.

أوّلاً عشان عايز أتكلّم عربى مع أصحابى العرب هنا .

David. — áwwalan ʕašān ʕāyiz a-tkállim ʕárab-i maʕ-
[aṣḥāb-i-l-ʕárab hína.
Firstly because wanting I-speak Arab-(adj) with-friends-my-the-
[*Arabs here.*
First, because I want to speak Arabic with my Arab friends
[here.

وبعدين عشان ناوى أروح الشّرق الأوسط قريباً . [rīban.
DAVID. — wi baɛdēn ɛašān nāwi a-rūḥ iš-šárq il-áwsaṭ qa-
And then because intending I-go the-East the-Middle nearly.
Then, because I intend to go to the Middle East soon.

يا دافيد ، إنت دلوقتي بتتكلّم عربى كويّس . [kwáyyis.
KHALID. — ya David, ínta dilwáqti bi-ti-tkállim ɛárab-i
Oh David, you now (pt)-you-speak Arab-(adj) well.
David, you already speak Arabic well.

متشكّر ، يا خالد ، ده أنا بقى لى سنتين عمّال أدرس عربى .
DAVID. — mutašákkir, ya xālid. da ána baqā-l-i sana-t-ēn
[ɛammāl á-dris ɛárab-i.
Thankful, oh Khalid. This I has been-to-me year-(cs)-(d) continually I-study Arab-(adj).
Thank you, Khalid. I have been studying Arabic steadily
[for two years.

أنا ابتديت أدرس العربى الفصيح فى انديانا .
DAVID. — ána ibtadī-t á-dris il-ɛárab-i il-faṣīḥ f-Indiana.
I began-I I-study the-Arab-(adj) the-literary in-Indiana.
I started to learn literary Arabic in Indiana.

لكين إنت عارف إنّ ما حدّش بيتكلّم عربى فصيح .
KHALID. — lākin ínta ɛārif ínn(i) m-ḥádd-iš bi-y-itkállim
[ɛárab-i faṣīḥ.
But you knowing that (neg)-anyone-(neg) (pt)-he-speak Arab-(adj)
But literary Arabic is not spoken, you know. [*literary.*

أيوه ، أنا عارف . عشان كده ابتديت أدرس العامّى . [ɛámm-i.
DAVID. — áywa, ána ɛārif; ɛašān kída ibtadī-t á-dris il-
Yes, I knowing; because so began-I I-study the-public-(adj).
Yes, I know; that's why I began to learn the spoken language.

إنت تعرف سرّ دراسة اللغات ؟
DAVID. — ínta tí-ɛraf sirr dirās-it il-luġ-āt?
You you-know secret studies-(cs) the-language-(pl)?
Do you know the secret of learning languages?

أيوه . الواحد لازم يتمرّن عليها ويستعملها دايما .

KHALID. — áywa. il-wāḥid lāzim yi-tmárran ع alē-ha wi [yi-staعmíl-ha dáyman.

Yes. The-one must he-practice on-it and he-use-it always.

Yes. One must practice it and always use it.

6. 1. Verb inflection. Except for the imperative masculine singular verb form and the third person masculine singular of the complete verb form, a verb in Arabic always has a bound subject pronoun. The complete and the incomplete stems are inflected for person, number, and gender. The imperative stems are inflected only for gender and number. The inflection of a stem consists of a verb stem plus affixes which are bound pronouns. The use of a free personal subject pronoun is optional.

A. Person. The imperative stems have only second person. Complete and incomplete stems have three persons each: first, second, and third. Every incomplete stem has a prefixed bound subject pronoun; and except for the third person masculine singular, every complete verb stem has a suffixed bound subject pronoun:

Imperative

اكتب	íktib!	write!	(you m. sg.)
اكتبى	iktíb-i!	write!	(you f. sg.)
اكتبوا	iktíb-u!	write!	(you pl.)

Complete

كتب	kátab	he wrote
كتبت	kátab-it	she wrote
كتبوا	kátab-u	they wrote
كتبت	katáb-t	you (m) wrote
كتبتِ	katáb-t-i	you (f) wrote
كتبتوا	katáb-t-u	you (pl) wrote
كتبت	katáb-t	I wrote
كتبنا	katáb-na	we wrote

Incomplete

يكتب	yí-ktib	he writes
تكتب	tí-ktib	she writes
يكتبوا	yi-ktíb-u	they write
تكتب	tí-ktib	you (m) write
تكتبي	ti-ktíb-i	you (f) write
تكتبوا	ti-ktíb-u	you (pl) write
اكتب	á-ktib	I write
نكتب	ní-ktib	we write

B. Number. As shown above, there are two numbers for each person: singular and plural. Unlike nouns, verbs have no dual number. The plural sign for the second and third person is the suffix *-u*. For the first person, the plural sign is the suffix *-na*; however, the plural signs for both first and third person function also as their respective subject.

C. Gender. Only the third and second person singular have separate forms for masculine and feminine gender. The feminine gender for the third person singular of complete stems is marked by the suffix *-it*; this suffix also functions as the subject of the verb. The suffix *-i* marks the feminine gender for the second person singular of both complete and incomplete stems. The first person and the plural number have no gender.

6. 2. The present tense prefix bi-. This prefix is always attached to an incomplete verb stem to indicate present tense (simple present) and habitual or continuous action (present or past progressive) because Arabic does not make any distinction between "he does" or "he is doing":

أحمد بيلعب كورة .
áḥmad bi-yí-lɛab kōra.
Ahmad (pt)-he-play soccer.
Ahmad (usually) plays/is playing soccer.

أنا شفت أحمد بيسوق عربيّة .
ána šuf-t áḥmad bi-ysūq ɛarabíyya.
I saw-I Ahmad (pt)-he-drive car.
I saw Ahmad driving a car.

Usually, the construction bi + incomplete stem occurs at the beginning of a verbal sentence or verb cluster:

بنخرج نشترى لبن .
bi-nú-xrug ni-štíri lában.
(pt)-we-go out we-buy milk.
We go out/are going out to buy milk.

This construction may be used after kān (habitual past or past progressive) and a few modal auxiliaries:

الرّاجل كان بيلبس برنيطة .
ir-rāgil kān bi-yí-lbis barnēṭa.
The-man was (pt)-he-wear hat.
The man used to wear/was wearing a hat.

لازم بيضحك .
lāzim bi-yí-ḍḥak.
Must (pt)-he-laugh.
He must be kidding.

The *i* of *bi-* is dropped before an incomplete verb stem with the first person singular subject prefix pronoun *a-*; furthermore, *bi-* causes the elision of the unstressed vowel *i* of subject pronouns before some incomplete verb stems:

أنا باشوف كويّس .
ána b-ašūf kwáyyis.
I (pt)-I-see good.
I see/am seeing well.

انت بتشوف بعيد خالص .
ínta bi-t-šūf biɛīd xāliṣ.
You (pt)-you (m)-see far completely.
You see/are seeing very far.

6. 3. The future tense prefix ḥa-. This prefix is always attached to an incomplete verb form to indicate future tense:

حنركب القطر السّاعة عشرة .
ḥa-ní-rkab il-qáṭr is-sāɛa ɛášara.
(ft)-we-mount the-train the-hour ten.
We will take the train at ten o'clock.

حانزل على طول .
ḥ-á-nzil ع ala-ṭūl.
(ft)-I-come down on-length.
I will come down right away.

Like the prefix *bi-*, *ḥa-* loses its *a* and causes the elision of the unstressed vowel *i* of prefix subject pronouns before certain incomplete verb stems.

Unlike all other verb forms, a construction with the prefix *ḥa-* is negated by the word miš.

مش حنروح السّينما النّهارده .
miš ḥa-n-rūḥ is-sínima innahárḍa.
Not (ft)-we-go the-movies today.
We won't go to the movies today.

6. 4. Personal subject pronouns. Personal subject pronouns are of two kinds: free and bound.

A. Free personal pronouns, which stand in a sentence by themselves as subjects of sentences, are:

هوّ húwwa, he	أنتَ ínta, you (m)	أنا ána, I
هىّ híyya, she	أنتِ ínti, you (f)	إحنا íḥna, we
همّ húmma, they	أنتوا íntu, you (pl)	

The use of these pronouns will be explained in a later unit.

B. Bound personal pronouns, which are attached to the verb stems as subjects of sentences, are suffixes or prefixes:

1. With complete verb stems, bound subject pronouns are suffixes. The third person masculine singular is represented by the stem itself (no suffix):

With complete verb stem درس dáras 'study/learn':

درس	dáras	he studied
درست	dáras-it	she studied
درسوا	dáras-u	they studied
درست	darás-t	you (m) studied
درستِ	darás-t-i	you (f) studied

درستوا	darás-t-u	you (pl) studied
درست	darás-t	I studied
درسنا	darás-na	we studied

The bound subject pronouns for the second person masculine singular (m) and the first person singular are the same. Only the context or the free personal pronoun placed before the verb can indicate the person. The suffix *-i* marks the feminine singular (f) and the suffix *-u* marks both the masculine and feminine plural (pl).

2. With incomplete verb stems, bound subject pronouns are prefixes which usually remain the same with any type of verb. In this case all persons are marked by a prefix, but the form of the stem depends on the type of the verb.

With the incomplete verb stem درس dris from درس dáras

يدرس	yí-dris	he studies
تدرس	tí-dris	she studies
يدرسوا	yi-drís-u	they study
تدرس	tí-dris	you (m) study
تدرسى	ti-drís-i	you (f) study
تدرسوا	ti-drís-u	you (pl) study
ادرس	á-dris	I study
ندرس	ní-dris	we study

The bound subject pronoun for the third person feminine and second person masculine are the same. Only the context or the free personal pronoun placed before the verb can indicate the person. The suffix *-i* marks the feminine singular (f) and the suffix *-u* marks both masculine and feminine plural (pl).

3. With imperative verb stems, the stem itself indicates both the second person and the masculine form (no affix). The feminine (singular) form is marked by the suffix *-i* and the plural form (for both masculine and feminine) is marked

by the suffix *-u*. The form of the stem depends on the type of the verb:

With the imperative verb stem إدرس idris from درس dáras

إدرس	ídris	study! (m)
إدرسى	idrís-i	study! (f)
إدرسوا	idrís-u	study! (pl)

تعارف الاصحاب

Unit 7. *taɛāruf il-aṣḥāb*
Introducing Friends

CONVERSATION

يا سام ، آدى أصحابى مصطفى ومنى .

RIFAT. — ya Sam, ādi aṣḥāb-i musṭáfa wi mōna.
Oh Sam, here are friends-my Mustafa and Mona.
Sam, here are my friends Mustafa and Mona.

أهلا وسهلا . فرصة سعيدة . إزيّكم ؟

SAM. — áhlan wi sáhlan. fúrṣa saɛīda. izzayy-úkum?
Greetings. Opportunity happy. How-you(pl)?
Glad to meet you. It's a pleasure. How are you?

دى ساندرا ، مراتى. وهى وصلت النّهارده .

SAM. — di Sandra, mrāt-i; wi híyya wáṣal-it innahárda.
This Sandra, wife-my; and she arrived-she today.
This is Sandra, my wife; she arrived today.

إزيّك ، يا مدام ؟ شرّفتينا والله .

MUSTAFA. — izzáyy-ik, ya madām? šarraf-tī-na w-allāhi.
How-you(f), oh madam? Honored-you(f)-us by-God.
How are you, madam? It is a great pleasure to meet you.

مصطفى طالب فى جامعة الأزهر .

RIFAT. — muṣṭáfa ṭālib fi-gámɛ-it il-ázhar.
Mustafa student in-university-(cs) the-Azhar.
Mustafa is a student at il-Azhar University.

ومنى هىّ خطيبته . هىّ طالبة فى جامعة القاهرة .

RIFAT. — wi mōna híyya xaṭíb-t-uh; híyya ṭāliba fi-gámɛ-it [il-qāhira.
And Mona she fiancee-(cs)-his; she student in-university-(cs) [*the-Cairo.*
Mona is his fiancee; she is a student at Cairo University.

أصحابنا أمريكان . مش كده ؟

MUSTAFA. — aṣḥáb-na amrikān. miš kída?
Friends-our Americans, not so?
Our friends are Americans, aren't they?

أيوه . وعندهم ولد صغيّر وبنت كبيرة .

RIFAT. — áywa. wi ɛand-úhum wálad ṣuġáyyar wi bint [kibīr-a.
Yes. And at-them boy small and girl big-(f).
Yes. And they have a small boy and a grown-up girl.

أنا راجل تاجر فى الزّيوت والأقطان ، ومراتى خيّاطة .

SAM. — ána rāgil tāgir fi-z-zuyūt wi-l-aqṭān, wi mrāt-i [xayyāṭ-a.
I man businessman in-the-oils and-the-cottons, and wife-my seams- [tress-(f).
I am a businessman in oil and cotton, and my wife is a seams- [tress.

أنا شايفة إنّكم فى سكّتكم للجّامعة .

SANDRA. — ána šáyf-a inn-úkum fi-sikk-ít-kum li-g-gámɛa.
I seeing-(f) that-you(pl) in-way-(cs)-your(pl) to-the-university.
I see that you are on your way to the university.

أيوه . هوّ ده الشّارع إللى يوصّلنا هناك .

MONA. — áywa. húwwa da iš-šāriɛ ílli yi-waṣṣál-na hināk.
Yes. He this the-street which it-take-us there.
Yes. This is the street which takes us there.

باردون ، إنتو الاتنين مصريين ؟

SANDRA. — bardōn, íntu il-itnēn maṣr-i-yyīn?
Pardon, you the-two Egyptian-(adj)-(pl)?
Pardon me, are you both Egyptian?

لا ، مصطفى مصرى ، لـكن منى لبنانيّة .

RIFAT. — la', muṣṭáfa máṣr-i, lākin mōna libnan-í-yya.
No, Mustafa Egypt-(adj), but Mona Lebanon-(adj)-(f).
No, Mustafa is Egyptian, but Mona is Lebanese.

7. 1. The noun. Unlike Classical Arabic, nouns in Colloquial Arabic are not declined, i.e., have no case. Nouns are of two kinds: regular nouns which form their plural by adding a suffix to the singular, and irregular or broken plural nouns which form their plural by internal vowel change:

مدرّس mudárris,	teacher	كتاب	kitāb, book
مدرّسين mudarris-īn,	teachers	كتب	kútub, books

7. 2. The definite article. The definite article is ال il, which corresponds to the English article "the"; it is used with nouns and, in some cases, with adjectives and participles. The definite article is placed before the noun, adjective, or participle; it is invariable for gender and number. A noun or adjective used with the definite article is called definite. Proper nouns and nouns with bound pronouns are also considered definite, although they aren't used with the definite article:

الولد	المدرسة	الولدين	الباب المفتوح
il-wálad	il-madrása	il-walad-ēn	il-bāb il-maftūḥ
the-boy	*the-school*	*the-boy-(d)*	*the-door the-open*
		the two boys	the open door

In pronunciation only (not in Arabic spelling), however, the vowel *i* of the definite article drops when it is preceded by a word ending in a vowel:

ورا البيت	مع المدير	والبنت
wara-l-bēt	maʿa-l-mudīr	wi-l-bínt
behind-the-house	*with-the-director*	*and-the-girl*

In addition, the *l* of the definite article before the consonants t, ṭ, d, ḍ, s, ṣ, z, ẓ, š, ž, n, and r is not pronounced; instead the consonant following *l* is doubled in pronunciation, but in Arabic writing, the sign šidda (ّ) may be placed over the letter.

الدّرس	النّور	الشّنطة
id-dárs	in-nūr	iš-šánṭa
the-lesson	*the-light*	*the-purse*

Before the consonants *k* and *g*, the dropping of *l* is optional:

الكلب	الكّلب	الجبل	الجّبل
il-kálb	ik-kálb	il-gábal	ig-gábal
the-dog	*the-dog*	*the-mountain*	*the-mountain*

7. 3. Indefinite nouns. There is no indefinite article in Arabic. Except for nouns with bound pronouns and proper nouns, a noun without the definite article is called indefinite:

الكتاب	كتاب	بيت جديد
il-kitāb	kitāb	bēt gidīd
the-book	*book, a book*	*house new*
		a new house

بيتك الجديد	أحمد الكبير
bēt-ak ig-gidīd	áhmad ik-kibīr
house-your (m) the-new	*Ahmad the-big/great/old*
your new house	the big/great/old Ahmad

However, the numeral واحد wāḥid (m), and واحدة wáḥd-a (f), sometimes functions as an indefinite article:

واحد صاحبك هنا .	جات لى واحدة فرصة كويسة .
wāḥid ṣáḥb-ak hína.	gát-l-i wáḥd-a fúrsa kwayyís-a.
one friend-your (m) here.	*came-to-me one-(f) opportunity good(f)*
A friend of yours is here.	I had a good opportunity.

7. 4. Gender of nouns. Nouns in Egyptian Arabic are either masculine or feminine:

A. Usually, nouns ending in *-a* (in phonetic transcription) or ة (ta marbuta in Arabic writing) and those ending in -āt (ات) are feminine:

كبّاية	شنطة	عربيّات	ستّات
kubbāya	šánṭa	ɛarabiyy-āt	sitt-āt
glass (of water)	*purse, bag*	*car-(pl)*	*lady-(pl)*
		cars	ladies

B. Usually, nouns ending in a consonant and those ending in -yya (يّة) are masculine:

درس	مدرّسين	حرميّة
dars	mudarris-īn	ḥaramí-yya
lesson	*teacher-(pl)*	*thief-(pl)*
	teachers(m)	thieves

There are a few exceptions to the above rules:

C. A few nouns ending in *a* are masculine:

دوا	خواجة	خليفة	عمدة	رجّالة
dáwa	xawāga	xalīfa	ɛúmda	riggāla
medicine	mister, sir	caliph	village chief	men

D. Nouns of natural gender of female human beings which end in a consonant are feminine:

بنت	ستّ	هانم
bint	sitt	hānim
girl/daughter	woman, lady	lady

E. Nouns denoting some parts of the body are feminine:

رجل	بطن	دقن
rigl	baṭn	daqn
foot, leg	belly	beard, chin

F. Most names of cities and countries, and some unspecified nouns which do not end in *a*, are feminine:

مصر	بلد	مركب	شمس
maṣr	bálad	márkib	šams
Egypt/Cairo	town/country	ship	sun

7. 5. Many feminine nouns are formed by adding *-a* (ة) to masculine nouns:

ملك	ملكة	خدّام	خدّامة
málik	malík-a	xaddām	xaddām-a
king	queen	servant (m)	servant (f)

فسحة في الجنينة

fúsḥa fi-g-ginēna

Unit 8. Walking in the Park

CONVERSATION

ياالله ، يا بيل ، نتفسّح فى الجنّينة ؛ الأولاد هناك . [hināk.
IBRAHIM. — yálla, ya Bill, ni-tfássaḥ fi-g-ginēna; il-awlād
Come on, oh Bill, we-take a walk in-the-garden; the-boys there.
Bill, let's take a walk in the park; the children are there.

عندك كام ولد ، يا ابراهيم ؟
BILL. — ع‍ánd-ak kām wálad, ya ibrahīm?
At-you(m) how many boy, oh Ibrahim?
How many children do you have, Ibrahim?

عندى ولدين صغيّرين وبنتين كبار .
IBRAHIM. — ع‍ánd-i walad-ēn ṣuġayyar-īn wi bint-ēn kubār.
At-me boy-(d) small-(pl) and girl-(d) big(pl).
I have two young boys and two grown-up girls.

عندكم جناين كتير هنا فى القاهرة ؟
BILL. — ع‍and-úkum ganāyin kitīr hína fi-l-q̇āhira?
At-you(pl) gardens many here in-the-Cairo?
Do you have many parks here in Cairo?

أيوه ، فيه كتير ، لكن جنينتين بسّ قريّبين لنا .
IBRAHIM. — áywa, fī-h kitīr, lākin ginin-t-ēn bass qurayyab-īn
Yes, in-it many, but garden-(cs)-(d) only near-(pl) to-us. [l-ína.
Yes, there are many, but only two parks are near here.

اليومين دول أنا عايز أزورهم ، يا ابراهيم .
BILL. — il-yum-ēn dōl ána ع‍āyiz a-zúr-hum, ya ibrahīm.
The-day-(d) these I wanting I-visit-them, oh Ibrahim.
Ibrahim, one of these days I would like to visit them.

أيوه ، ضرورى . آدى البنتين بتوعى ، يا بيل .

Ibrahim. — áywa, ḍarūri. ādi il-bint-ēn bitūع-i, ya Bill.
Yes, certainly. Here are the-girl-(d) belonging to-me, oh Bill.
Certainly. Here are my two girls, Bill.

أهلا وسهلا ، يا حلوين يا حلويّات !

Bill. — áhlan wi sáhlan, ya ḥilw-īn, ya ḥalawiyy-āt!
Greetings, oh pretty-(pl), oh candy-(pl)!
Good to see you, lovely girls!

ياالله ناخد البنات ونمشى فى الجنينة .

Bill. — yálla n-āxud il-banāt wi ní-mši fi-g-ginēna.
Come on we-take the-girls and we-go in-the-garden.
Let's take the girls to the park.

الجنينة دى لها بابين وكل باب عليه أسدين .

Ibrahim. — ig-ginēna di l-áha bab-ēn wi kúll(i) bāb عalē-h [asad-ēn.
The-garden this to-her door-(d) and all door on-him lion-(d).
This park has two gates and each gate has two lions.

شوف ، الأولاد جايّين مع صاحبتينهم .

Ibrahim. — šūf, il-awlād gayy-īn maع ṣaḥb-it-ín-hum.
See, the-boys coming-(pl) with friend-(cs)-(d)-their.
Look, my boys are coming, with their two girl friends.

ازيّك ، يا أفندينا ؟ إن شاء الله حضرتك مبسوط هنا .

Shaban. — izzáyy-ak, y-afandī-na? in-ša'allāh ḥaḍrít-ak [mabsūṭ hína.
How-you(m), oh-mister-our? If-willed God sir-your(m) happy here.
How are you, sir? I hope you like it here.

أهلا ، يابنى . أنا أحبّ أسمعك تتكلّم انجليزى .

Bill. — áhlan, ya íbn-i. ána a-ḥíbb a-smáع-ak ti-kkállim [inglīzi.
Hello, oh son-my. I I-love I-hear-you(m) you-speak English.
Hello, son. It's nice to hear you speak English.

8. 1. Number of nouns. Nouns in Arabic have three numbers: singular (sg), dual (d), and plural (pl)

موظّف	muwáẓẓaf,	clerk
موظّفين	muwaẓẓaf-ēn,	two clerks
موظّفين	muwaẓẓaf-īn,	clerks

ولد	wálad,	boy
ولدين	walad-ēn,	two boys
أولاد	awlād,	boys
شنطة	šánṭa,	purse/bag
شنطتين	šanṭ-it-ēn,	two purses
شنط	šúnaṭ,	purses

8. 2. Dual number. Unlike Classical Arabic, only nouns have dual number in spoken Egyptian Arabic. The dual is formed by adding the dual suffix ـين ēn directly to the singular form of nouns ending in a consonant:

راجل	rāgil,	man	إيد	īd,	hand
رجلين	ragl-ēn,	two men	إيدين	id-ēn,	two hands
كتاب	kitāb,	book	بيت	bēt,	house
كتابين	kitab-ēn,	two books	بيتين	bit-ēn,	two houses

Singular nouns ending in *a* (ة in Arabic writing) take the construct state (cs) suffix -(*i*)*t* (ت) before taking the dual suffix -ēn (ـين):

اوضة	ōḍa,	room	شركة	šírka,	company
اوضتين	uḍ-t-ēn,	two rooms	شركتين	širk-it-ēn,	two companies

Note in the examples above that the addition of the dual suffix causes short vowels to drop (unless three consecutive consonants would result) and long vowels to become short.

When a noun in dual form is in construct state with another noun (corresponding to English "the man's two girls" for example) or a bound pronoun (corresponding to English "my two girls", for example), the word بتوع bitūع 'belonging to', is usually inserted between the two:

بنت حسن	but	البنتين بتوع حسن
bint ḥássan		il-bint-ēn bitūع ḥássan
girl Hassan		*the-girl-(d) belonging to Hassan*
Hassan's girl		Hassan's two girls

بيتى	but	البيتين بتوعى
bēt-i		il-bit-ēn bitū ع-i
house-my		*the-house-(d) belonging to-me*
my house		my two houses

Dual nouns denoting parts of the body do not follow this rule; however, when this type of dual noun occurs with bound pronouns, then, the dual suffix ين ēn loses the *n*:

رجلين	رجليكم
rigl-ēn	rigl-ē-kum
foot-(d)	*foot-(d)-your (pl)*
two feet/legs	your feet/legs

Adjectives, pronouns, and verbs agreeing with dual nouns take their plural forms. This means that there is no dual number for adjectives, pronouns, or verbs:

بنتين حلوين	الرّاجلين دول بيشتغلوا تمام
bint-ēn ḥilw-īn	ir-ragl-ēn dōl bi-yi-štáġal-u tamām
girl-(d) pretty-(pl)	*The-man-(d) those (pt)-he-work-(pl) right.*
two pretty girls	Those two men are really working.

8. 3. Plural forms. There are two kinds of plural forms for nouns and adjectives: sound or regular plurals and broken or irregular plurals. The plural form cannot be predicted from the singular form; however, note that the various sound and broken plurals have patterns.

A. Sound or regular plurals. Sound plural forms are indicated by the suffixes -īn, -yīn, -āt, and -yya. When any of these suffixes is added to the singular form, the plural suffix attracts the stress; consequently, any long vowel becomes short.

1. Participles, many adjectives, and some masculine noun forms ending in a consonant form their sound plurals by adding to the singular form the suffix -īn:

Singular		*Plural*
جزّار gazzār, butcher		جزّارين gazzar-īn
كويّس kwáyyis (m), كويّسة kwayyís-a (f),	good	كويّسين kwayyis-īn
مكتوب maktūb, مكتوبة maktūb-a	written	مكتوبين maktub-īn

2. Some masculine singular nouns and adjectives ending in *i* form their plurals by adding the suffix -yīn:

Singular		*Plural*
محامى muḥāmi, lawyer		محاميين muḥami-yīn
غالى ġāli, غالية ġály-a	expensive	غاليين ġali-yīn

Note that the plural form for adjectives is the same for both masculine and feminine.

3. A few other masculine singular nouns which also end in *i* form their plurals by adding the suffix -yya:

Singular	*Plural*
حرامى ḥarāmi, thief	حرامية ḥaramí-yya

4. Many sound plurals of feminine nouns are formed by adding the suffix -āt to the singular form. The same suffix is used to form the plural of feminine singular forms of nouns ending in *a* (ة). In the latter case the *a* (ة) is dropped:

Singular	*Plural*
ستّ sitt, woman/lady	ستّات sitt-āt
طيّارة ṭayyāra, airplane	طيّارات ṭayyar-āt

5. A few masculine singular nouns and nouns of foreign origin which have final long vowels take the plural suffix -āt after shortening the long vowel:

Singular	*Plural*
جواب gawāb, letter	جوابات gawab-āt
دوسيه dusēh, file/dosier	دوسيهات dusih-āt

6. Some other masculine singular nouns with final long vowels form their plurals by adding *a* (ة) to the singular:

Singular	*Plural*
بحّار baḥḥār, seaman	بحّارة baḥḥār-a

B. Broken or irregular plurals. Most plural nouns and many plural adjectives in Arabic are formed by internal vowel change, known as the broken plural. These forms should be memorized by the student since their derivation rules are very complicated:

Singular	*Plural*
سوق sūq, market	أسواق aswāq
دكّان dukkān, shop	دكاكين dakakīn
جار gār, neighbor	جيران girān
عالم ع̣ālim, learned man	علما ع̣úlama
بيت bēt, house	بيوت buyūt
مكتب máktab, office	مكاتب makātib
دكتور duktūr, doctor	دكاترة dakátra
كرسي kúrsi, chair	كراسي karāsi
سبت sábat, basket	سبيتة síbita
دوا dáwa, medicine	أدوية adwíya

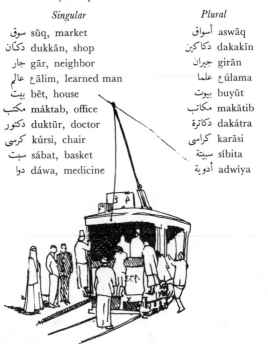

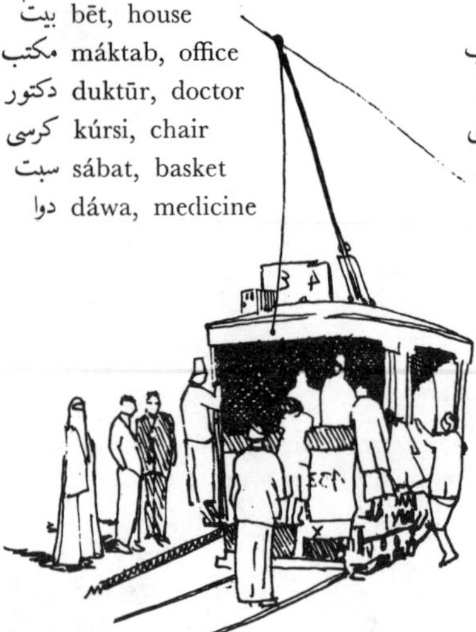

البحث عن شقة

Unit 9. *il-báḥs ɛan šáqqa*
Looking for an Apartment

CONVERSATION

يا صبحي ، أنا بادوّر على شقّة كويّسة .

Bill. — ya ṣúbḥi, ána b-a-dáwwar ɛála šáqqa kwayyís-a.
Oh Sobhi, I (pt)-I-look on apartment good-(f).
Sobhi, I am looking for a nice apartment.

إنت عايز شقّة كبيرة والاّ صغيّرة ؟

Sobhi. — ínta ɛāyiz šáqqa kibīr-a wálla ṣuġayyár-a?
You wanting apartment big-(f) or small-(f)?
Do you want a big apartment or a small one?

وعندك مانع لو تكون في مصر الجديدة ؟

Sobhi. — wi ɛánd-ak māniɛ law ti-kūn fi-máṣr il-gidīd-a?
At-you objection if it-be in-Egypt/Cairo the-new-(f)?
Do you mind if it is in Heliopolis?

لا ، مش مهمّ ، أنا عايز أسكن فى حتّة هادية .

Bill. — la', miš muhímm. ána ɛāyiz á-skun fi-ḥítta hády-a.
No, not important. I wanting I-dwell in-piece quiet-(f).
No, it doesn't matter. I want to live in a quiet place.

كويّس قوى . أنا عارف شقق جميلة فى مصر الجديدة .

Sobhi. — kwáyyis qáwi. ána ɛārif šúqaq gamīl-a fi-máṣr il-gidīd-a.
Good very. I knowing apartments beautiful-(f) in Egypt/Cairo the-new-(f).
Very good. I know some beautiful apartments in Heliopolis.

يا الله ، نروح هناك ونلقى نظرة سريعة .

Bill. — yálla, ni-rūḥ hināk wi ní-lqi náẓra sarīɛ-a.
Come on, we-go there and we-find view quick-(f).
Come on, let's go there and have a quick look.

سعيدة ، يا افندى . عندك شقّة مفروشة للإيجار .

Sobhi. — saɛīda, y-afándi. ɛánd-ak šáqqa mafrūš-a l-il-igār?
Hello, oh-sir. At-you (m) apartment furnished-(f) for-the-rent.
Hello, sir. Do you have a furnished apartment for rent?

أيوه ، يا سيدى . أنا عندى شقّة فاضية كمان .

Landlord. — áywa, ya sīdi. ána ɛánd-i šáqqa fáḍy-a kamān.
Yes, oh-sir. I at-me apartment empty-(f) also.
Yes, sir. I also have an unfurnished apartment.

دى شقّة مريحة ، لكن شبابيكها صغيّرة .

Bill. — di šáqqa murīḥ-a, lākin šababík-ha ṣuġayyár-a.
This apartment comfortable-(f), but windows-her small-(f).
This is a comfortable apartment, but it has small windows.

شوف البلكونة كبيرة إزّاى ، والمنظر جميل .

Mary. — šūf il-balakūna kibīr-a izzāy, w-il-mánẓar gamīl.
See the-balcony big-(f) how, and-the-view beautiful.
Look how big the balcony is, and the view is beautiful.

فيها كمان طرقة طويلة وحمّام صغيّر زيادة .

Mary. — fī-ha kamān ṭúrqa ṭawīl-a wi ḥammām ṣuġáyyar [zyāda.
In-it also corridor long-(f) and bath small more.
It also has a long corridor and a lavatory besides.

الإيجار بتاع الشقّة دى كام ، يا عمّى ؟

Sobhi. — il-igār bitāɛ iš-šíqqa di kām, ya ɛámm-i?
The-rent belonging to the-apartment this how much, oh uncle-my?
How much is the rent for this apartment, sir?

شوف ، يا سيدى ، أنا راجل دغرى : خمسين جنيه فى الشّهر .

Landlord. — šūf, ya sīdi, ána rāgil dúġri: xamsīn ginēh fi-šáhr.
See, oh master, I man straight: fifty Egyptian pound in-month.
Look here, sir, no bargaining: fifty Egyptian pounds per month.

9.1. The adjective. In Arabic, the adjective usually follows the noun it modifies and has three forms: masculine singular (m), feminine singular (f), and plural (pl). The plural form is the same for both masculine and feminine:

الولد الكويّس
il-wálad il-kwáyyis
the-boy the-good
the good boy

البنت الكويّسة
il-bínt il-kwayyís-a
the-girl the-good-(f)
the good girl

الولاد الكويّسين والبنات الكويّسين
il-awlād il-kwayyis-īn wi-l-banāt il-kwayyis-īn
the-boys the-good-(pl) and-the-girls the-good-(pl)
the good boys and the good girls

The masculine singular form is the base form, from which the feminine and the plural forms are derived. The feminine singular adjective is formed by adding to the masculine singular form the suffix *-a* (ة), if the adjective ends in a consonant. If the adjective ends in a vowel, the suffix -ya or -yya (ية) is added.

Adjectives, like nouns, have two kinds of plural forms: sound or regular plurals and broken or irregular plurals. Sound plurals are formed by adding the suffix -īn (ين) to the masculine singular:

MASC. SING.	FEM. SING.	PLURAL	ENGLISH
صغيّر suġáyyar	صغيّرة suġayyár-a	صغيّرين suġayyar-īn	small / young
جاهز gāhiz	جاهزة gáhz-a	جاهزين gahz-īn	ready
كسلان kaslān	كسلانة kaslān-a	كسلانين kaslan-īn	lazy
صبور ṣabūr	صبورة ṣabūr-a	صبورين ṣabur-īn	patient
مبسوط mabsūṭ	مبسوطة mabsūṭ-a	مبسوطين mabsuṭ-īn	content

The broken plurals are formed by an internal vowel change in the singular form.

MASC. SING.	FEM. SING.	PLURAL	ENGLISH
جميل	جميلة	جمال	
gamīl	gamīl-a	gumāl	beautiful
مسكين	مسكينة	مساكين	
maskīn	maskīn-a	masakīn	poor/unfortunate
كريم	كريمة	كرما	
karīm	karīm-a	kúrama	generous

The plural form of مفيد mufīd 'useful' and the feminine and plural forms of قليل qalīl 'few/little' and كتير kitīr 'much/many' are rarely used.

A few adjectives which do not change their forms are also used as adverbs: تمام tamām 'right'; دغرى dúġri 'straight'; طازة ṭāza 'fresh/freshly made'.

هوّ بيشتغل تمام .
húwwa bi-yi-štáġal tamām.
He (pt)-he-work right.
He works well.

هيّ بتمشى دغرى .
híyya bi-t-ímši dúġri.
She (pt)-she-walk straight.
She is a good girl.

Some verbal nouns (like the two examples below), which do not change their forms, are used as both adjectives and abverbs:

غلط ġálaṭ, wrong/mistake
صحّ ṣaḥḥ, right

The adjective has no dual (d) number; an adjective modifying a dual noun is plural in form:

ولدين نبها
walad-ēn núbaha
boy-(d) intelligent (pl)
two intelligent boys

بنتين حلوين
bint-ēn ḥilw-īn
girl-(d) pretty-(pl)
two pretty girls

An adjective may be used as a noun, for example:

انا عايز الطّويل ، مش القصيّر .
ana ɛāyiz iṭ-ṭawīl, miš il-quṣáyyar.
I wanting the-tall, not the-short.
I want the tall one, not the short one.

الكبير مش حا ينفع .
il-kibīr miš ḥa-yí-nfaɛ.
The-big not (ft)-he-be of use.
The big one will not do.

Notice that the form of most adjectives follows a certain pattern (a specific combination of vowels and consonants) and that the change from masculine to feminine or to plural is clear.

The adjectives of color and bodily defect have their own patterns and will be discussed in a separate unit.

9.2. Noun-adjective agreement. In Arabic, the adjective usually agrees with the noun it modifies in definiteness, gender and number:

A. A definite noun must be followed by a definite adjective. A noun and adjective without the definite article are indefinite; however, a noun with a bound pronoun and a proper noun without the definite article are definite:

ولد كبير	الولد الكبير	ابنك الصّغيّر
wálad kibīr	il-wálad ik-kibīr	íbn-ak iṣ-ṣuġáyyar
boy big	*the-boy the-big*	*son-your(m) the-small*
a big boy	the big boy	your small son

مصر القديمة	أحمد الطّويل
maṣr il-qadīm-a	áḥmad iṭ-ṭawīl
Egypt the-old-(f)	*Ahmad the-tall*
the ancient Egypt	the tall Ahmad

B. A masculine noun is followed by a masculine adjective and a feminine noun by a feminine adjective:

راجل طيّب	ستّ طيّبة
rāgil ṭáyyib	sítt ṭayyíb-a
man nice	*lady nice-(f)*
a nice man	a nice lady

C. A singular noun is followed by a singular adjective, and a dual or plural noun is followed by a plural adjective. A plural noun indicating an inanimate object is followed by either a plural adjective or a feminine (singular) adjective, as the speaker chooses:

الشبّاك المفتوح
iš-šubbāk il-maftūḥ
the-window the-open
the open window

البنتين الحلوين
il-bint-ēn il-ḥilw-īn
the-girl-(d) the-pretty-(pl)
the two pretty girls

التلامذة الشاطرين
it-talámza iš-šaṭr-īn
the-students the-clever-(pl)
the clever students

الكتب الجداد
il-kútub il-gudād
the-books the-new (pl)
the new books

الكتب الجديدة
il-kútub il-gidīd-a
the-books the-new-(f)
the new books

D. Exceptions. There are cases in which an adjective following a feminine or plural noun keeps its original form of masculine singular. This occurs when the adjective indicates brand, material, style, specialty or origin of inanimate objects; such an adjective is usually derived from a noun by adding to the latter the suffix *-i* (if it ends in a consonant) and *-wi* or *-ni* (if it ends in a vowel). For other adjectives which do not change their original form see the preceding section.

عربيّات ملاّكى
ɛarabiyy-āt mallāk-i
car-(pl) owner-(adj)
private cars

قهوة فرنساوى
qáhwa fransā-wi
coffee France-(adj)
French coffee

بدل أمريكانى
bídal amrik-āni
suits America-(adj)
American suits

عيش طازه
ɛēš ṭāza
bread fresh
fresh bread

الحكاية تمام .
il-ḥikāya tamām.
The-story right.
The story is correct.

9.3. Intensifiers. Intensifiers do not change and are used to modify adjectives and adverbs:

قوي	qáwi	very	أبداً	ábadan	extremely, at all (more than very)
كتير	kitīr	very	خالص	xāliṣ	extremely, at all (more than very)
جداً	gíddan	very	شويّة	šwáyya	rather (less than very)

All of the above intensifiers may be used with affirmative or negative constructions except أبداً ábadan, which is always used with negative constructions. Note that كتير kitīr and شوية šwâyya are also used as quantifiers and أبداً ábadan as an adverb of manner:

الدّنيا برد كتير النّهارده .
id-dúnya bard kitīr innahárda.
The-world cold very today.
It is very cold today.

هو بيمشي بسرعة خالص .
húwwa b-yí-mši bi súrɛa [xāliṣ.
He (pt)-he-walk fast extremely.
He is walking extremely fast.

الكلام ده مش كويّس أبداً .
ik-kalām da miš kwáyyis ábadan.
The-talk this/that not good very.
That isn't nice talk at all.

محادثة بين أصدقاء

muḥádsa bēn áṣdiqa'

Unit 10. A Friendly Conversation

CONVERSATION

يا حسنى ، إنت تعرف الرّاجل إللى واقف على الباب ؟

SAM. — ya ḥúsni, ínta tí-ع raf ir-rāgil ílli wāqif ع ala-l-bāb?
Oh Hosni, you you-know the-man who standing at-the-door?
Hosni, do you know the man standing at the door?

أيوه ، ده دكتور حسين . هوّ أسْتاذ فى دار العلوم .

HOSNI. — áywa, da duktūr ḥusēn; húwwa ustāz fi-dār il-[ع ulūm.
Yes, that doctor Hussein; he professor in-house the sciences.
Yes, he is Dr. Hussein; he is a professor at Dar il Ulum.

وهوّ مدرّس ابنى فتحى .

HOSNI. — wi húwwa mudárris íbn-i, fáthi.
And he teacher son-my, Fathi.
And he is a teacher of my son, Fathi.

أنا باسأل عشان قابلنا الرّاجل ده قبل كده .

SAM. — ána b-á-s'al ع ašān qabíl-na ir-rāgil da qábl(i) kída.
I (pt)-I-ask because met-we the-man that before so.
I ask because we have met the man before.

طبعاً ، قابلناه الأسبوع إللى فات فى حفلة .

ESTHER. — ṭáb ع an, qabil-nā-h il-usbū ع ílli fāt fi-ḥáfla.
Naturally, met-we-him the-week which passed in-party.
Surely, we met him last week at a party.

الأستاذ حسين له شقّة فى عمارتنا .

HOSNI. — il-ustāz ḥusēn l-uh šáqqa fi-ع imar-ít-na.
The-professor Hussein at-him apartment in-building-(cs)-our.
Professor Hussein has an apartment in our building.

والستّ إللى بتكلّمه ، دى مراته ؟
Esther. — w-is-sítt ílli bi-t-kallím-uh, di mrāt-uh?
And-the-lady who (pt)-she-speak-him, that wife-his?
And the lady who is talking to him, is she his wife?

لا ، أظنّ هىّ كمان مدرّسة .
Hosni. — la', a-ẓúnn híyya kamān mudarríss-a.
No, I-think she also teacher-(f).
No, I think she is a teacher too.

الأستاذ حسين بيتكلّم إنجليزى كويّس قوى .
Sam. — il-istāz ḥusēn bi-yi-tkállim ingilīz-i kwáyyis qáwi.
The-professor Hussein (pt)-he-speak Englishmen-(adj) good very.
Professor Hussein speaks English very well.

طبعاً ، هوّ بيدرّس إنجليزى فى الكلّيّة .
Hosni. — ṭábɛan, húwwa bi-y-dárris ingilīz-i f-ik-kullíyya.
Naturally, he (pt)-he-teach Englishmen-(adj) in-the-college.
Of course, he teaches English at the college.

أنا أعرف بنت مصريّة بتتكلّم أربع لغات .
Esther. — ána á-ɛraf bint maṣr-í-yya bi-ti-tkállim árbaɛ [luġ-āt.
I I-know girl Egypt-(adj)-(f) (pt)-she-speak four language-(pl).
I know an Egyptian girl who speaks four languages.

عندنا فرص كويّسة عشان نتعلّم لغات .
Hosni. — ɛand-ína fúraṣ kwayyís-a ɛašān ni-tɛállim luġ-āt.
At-us chances good-(f) because we-learn language-(pl).
Here we have good opportunities to learn languages.

أصل الشّرق والغرب بيتقابلوا هنا .
Hosni. — aṣl, iš-šárq w-il-ġárb bi-yi-tqábl-u hína.
Origin, the-East and-the-West (pt)-he-meet-(pl) here.
In fact, here the East and the West meet.

10. 1. Noun phrases. A noun phrase may consist of:

A. a single noun, in which case the noun must be definite (either preceded by the definite article or followed by a bound pronoun):

البيت	بيتى
il-bēt.	bēt-i
the-house	*house-my*
the house	my house

B. two or more nouns used attributively:

كبّاية ميّة	الكبّاية الورق
kubbāya máyya	il-kubbāya il-wáraq
glass water	*the-glass the-paper*
a water glass	the paper cup

C. two or more nouns in construct state (corresponding to English possessive constructions):

بيت راجل	بيت الرّاجل	كبّاية ميّة
bēt rāgil	bēt ir-rāgil	kubbāy-it máyya
house man	*house the-man*	*glass-(cs) water*
a man's house	the man's house	a glass of water

D. two or more nouns in subject and predicate position:

الرّاجل مدير .
ir-rāgil mudīr.
The-man director.
The man is a director.

E. a noun preceded and/or followed by a noun modifier. There are various types of noun modifiers such as demonstratives, quantifiers, numerals, adjectives, the word بتاع bitāع 'belonging to', etc. A noun phrase may include several modifiers and may be definite or indefinite:

البيت ده	بيت جديد	البيت الجديد
il-bēt da	bēt gidīd	il-bēt ig-gidīd
the-house this	*house new*	*the-house the-new*
this house	a new house	the new house
البيت بتاعه	العشرين كبّاية	كلّ النّاس
il-bēt bitāع-uh	il-išrīn kubbāya	kull in-nās
the-house belonging to-him	*the-twenty glass*	*all the-people*
his house	the twenty glasses	everyone

10. 2. Attributive nouns. In a noun phrase noun + noun, the second noun may be an attribute of the first and agree with it only in definiteness. Generally, the attribute noun describes the substance of which the first noun is made or the purpose for which it is used:

قميص قطن	القميص القطن	قمصان قطن
qamīṣ quṭn	il-qamīṣ il-qúṭn	qumṣān quṭn
shirt cotton	*the-shirt the-cotton*	*shirts cotton*
a cotton shirt	the cotton shirt	cotton shirts

The student should recognize the differences among this noun phrase, the construct state, and the verbless sentence in which both subject and predicate are nouns. Two nouns in attributive construction are both either definite, with the definite article, or indefinite, without the definite article (see above); whereas in a construct state construction, the first noun never has the definite article and the second noun usually, but not always, has it:

قميص الولد	كبّاية ميّه
qamīs il-wálad	kubbāy-it mayya
shirt the-boy	*glass-(cs) water*
the boy's shirt	a glass of water

In a verbless sentence in which both subject and predicate are nouns, usually the second noun does not have the definite article.

10. 3. Quantifiers. The following words, which are invariable, designate various degrees of quantity and are, therefore, called quantifiers:

معظم múɛẓam, most
بعض baɛḍ, some
كلّ kull, all/every
شويّة šwáyya, a little bit/some
كتير kitīr, much/plenty of/a lot of

The first two quantifiers are used with nouns in the plural

form or with bound pronouns. معظم múɛẓam does not occur before indefinite nouns. If a quantifier is used with a definite noun or bound pronoun, the whole phrase is another construction in construct state:

معظم الرّجّالة مشوا .
múɛẓam ir-riggāla míš-u.
Most the-men walked out-(pl).
Most of the men walked out.

معظمهم مشوا .
muɛẓám-hum míš-u.
Most-them walked out-(pl).
Most of them walked out.

بعض الستّات لسّه هناك .
baɛḍ is-sitt-āt líssa hināk.
Some the-lady-(pl) still there.
Some of the ladies are still there.

بعضهم لسّه هناك .
baɛḍ-úhum líssa hināk.
Some-them still there.
Some of them are still there.

كلّ kull can occur before or after a noun or a numeral; it may also occur with a bound pronoun. If كلّ kull occurs before an indefinite singular noun or a numeral without the definite article, it conveys the meaning of "every". Before a definite noun, a bound pronoun, or a numeral with the definite article, كلّ kull is in construct state and means "all of" or "the whole of". After a noun or pronoun, it must have a bound retrocive * pronoun (in brackets below) which agrees in person, gender, and number with the noun or pronoun to which it refers:

خد كلّ حاجة .
xud kúll(i) ḥāga.
Take all thing.
Take everything.

خد كلّ الدّفاتر .
xud kull id-dafātir.
Take all the-notebooks.
Take all the notebooks.

أنا عارفهم كلّهم .
ána ɛaríf-hum kull-[úhum].
I knowing-them all-[*them*].
I know all of them.

قال لى الحكاية كلّها .
qál-l-i-l-ḥikāya kull-[áha].
Told-to-me-the-story all-[*it*].
He told me the whole story.

Usually, شوية šwáyya occurs before indefinite collective nouns in construct state; and كتير kitīr occurs before and after plural nouns and indefinite collective nouns.

Neither occurs with a bound pronoun.

* For definition see page 101.

أدينى شويّة عيش .
iddī-ni šwáyy-it ع ēš.
Give-me little-(cs) bread.
Give me a little bread.

عندها أولاد كتير .
ع and-áha awlād kitīr.
At-her children a lot of.
She has a lot of children.

إنّهرضة فى لحمة كتير .
innahárḍa fī-h láḥma kitīr.
Today in-it meat much.
There is a lot of meat today.

المنظر من برج القاهرة

il-mánẓar min burg il-qāhira

Unit 11. The View from the Tower of Cairo

CONVERSATION

برج القاهرة ده عمل عظيم ، يا لطفى .

MARION. — burg il-qāhira da ʿámal ʿaẓīm, ya lúṭfi.
Tower the-Cairo this work great, oh Lutfi.
Lutfi, the tower of Cairo is a magnificent work.

ده واحد من أعمال النّظام الجديد .

LUTFI. — da wāḥid min aʿmāl in-niẓām ig-gidīd.
This one from works the-organization the-new.
This is one of the works of the new regime.

يا لطفى ، ايه المبنى الجديد ده تحت ؟

MARION. — ya lúṭfi, ēh il-mábna-l-gidīd da taḥt?
Oh Lutfi, what the-building-the-new-(f) that under?
Lutfi, what is that new building below?

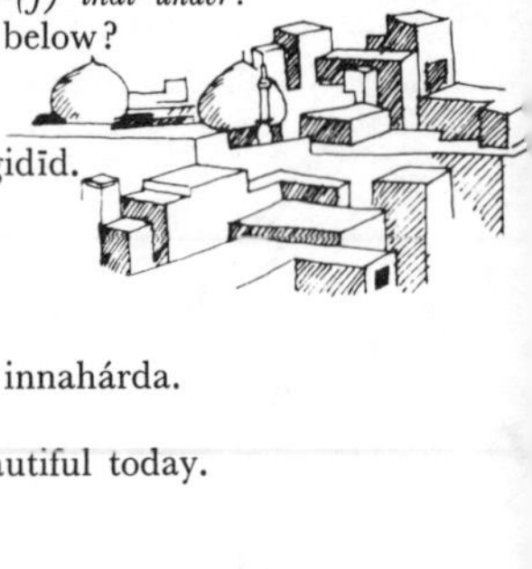

ده نادى الظبّاط الجديد .

LUTFI. — da nādi-ẓ-ẓubbāṭ ig-gidīd.
That club-the-officers the-new.
That is the new officers' club.

لون النّيل جميل قوى النّهارده .

LUCY. — lōn in-nīl gamīl qáwi innahárda.
Color the-Nile beautiful very today.
The color of the Nile is very beautiful today.

ياالله نقعد وناخد فنجان قهوة .

LUTFI. — yálla nú-qʿud wi n-āxud fingān qáhwa.
Come on we-sit and we-take cup coffee.
Let's sit down and have a cup of coffee.

يا لوسى ، معاكى علبة السّجاير إللى اديتهالك ؟

MARION. — ya Lucy, maع̣ā-ki عílb-it is-sagāyir ílli iddi-t-[hā-l-ik?
Oh Lucy, with-you(f) box-(cs) the cigarettes which gave-I-it-to-[you(f)?
Lucy, do you have the pack of cigarettes I gave you?

يا ريّس ، عايزين فنجانين قهوة وقزازة بيرة .

LUTFI. — ya ráyyis, عayz-īn fingal-ēn qáhwa wi qizāz-it bīra.
Oh chief, wanting-(pl) cup-(d) coffee and glass-(cs) beer.
Waiter, we want two cups of coffee and a bottle of beer.

كبّاية ميّة ، من فضلك ، يا جرسون .

LUCY. — kubbāy-it máyya, min-fáḍl-ak, ya garsōn.
Glass-(cs) water, from-bounty-your(m), oh waiter.
Waiter, a glass of water, please.

عايز تاخد صورة الهرم من هنا ؟

LUTFI. — عāyiz t-āxud ṣūra l-il-háram min-hína?
Wanting you(m)-take picture for-the-pyramid from here?
Do you want to take a picture of the pyramids from here?

لا ، أنا حاخد صورة لجبل المقطّم .

LUCY. — la'. ána ḥ-āxud ṣūra li-gábal il-muqáṭṭam.
No. I (ft)-take picture to-mountain the-Mukattam.
No. I am going to take a picture of Mukattam hill.

شوفى قبّة القلعة بتلمع إزّاى !

MARION. — šūf-i qúbb-it il-q̇álعa bi-tí-lmaع izzāy!
See-(f) dome-(cs) the-citadel (pt)-it-shine how!
Look how the dome of the citadel shines!

يا معلّم ، حسابنا كام ، من فضلك ؟

LUTFI. — ya muعállim, ḥisáb-na kām, min-fáḍl-ak?
Oh teacher, bill-our how much, from-kindness-your(m)?
Waiter, how much is our bill, please?

11. 1. Possession — construct state. There are four constructions to indicate possession:

A. *Noun + Noun:* This construction indicates possession and various other similar relationships, such as the English "of", "'s", and many nouns used attributively with other nouns as "taxi driver" and "government employee".

قلم التّلميذ	بيت حسّن	فنجان قهوة
qálam it-tilmīz	bēt ḥássan	fingān qáhwa
pencil the-pupil	*house Hassan*	*cup coffee*
the pupil's pencil	Hassan's house	a cup of coffee

فنجان القهوة	سوّاق تكسى	سوّاق التكسى
fingān il-qáhwa	sawwāq táxi	sawwāq it-táxi
cup the-coffee	*driver taxi*	*driver the-taxi*
the cup of coffee	a taxi driver	the taxi driver

B. *Possessive pronoun:* noun + bound pronoun:

ولده	بلدنا	شغلهم
wálad-uh	balád-na	šuġl-úhum
boy/son-his	*country-our*	*work-their*
his son	our country	their work

C. *The word* بتاع bitāع, *'belonging to/of'*: bitāع + noun/bound pronoun.

بتاع المدرّس	بتاعه	بتاع السّجاير
bitāع il-mudárriss	bitāع-uh	bitāع is-sigāyir
belonging to the-teacher	*belonging to-him*	*belonging to the-cigarettes*
of the teacher	of him/his	cigarette seller

The above constructions are in construct state. The characteristic features of the construct state are:

1. It consists of two juxtaposed elements.

2. The first element, which usually is a noun (possessed), does not have the definite article, although in English translation this noun is definite.

3. The second element, if it is a noun (possessor), may or may not have the definite article.

4. If the first element ends in *a* (usually the sign for feminine gender), the *a* drops in pronunciation only, and the construct state suffix (cs) -t / it, 'of / 's' is added: -t is added after a word ending in a consonant; -it, after a word

ending in two consonants (*i* is inserted to avoid the combination of three consecutive consonants):

شنطة šánṭa, bag / purse
مدرسة madrása, school

مدرسة البنات	شنطة البنت
madrás-t il-banāt	šánt-it il-bínt
school-(cs) the-girls	*bag-(cs) the-girl*
the girl's school	the girl's bag

5. The student should remember the difference in form between an attributive construction of two nouns and a noun used attributively with another noun in construct state: two nouns in attributive construction may be either both definite or indefinite:

سكة حديد	السكة الحديد
síkka ḥadīd	is-síkka-l-ḥadīd
road iron	*the-road-the-iron*
a railroad	the railroad

Whereas, in a construct state construction, the first noun never has the definite article:

باب البيت	كبّاية الميّة
bāb il-bēt	kubbáy-t il-máyya
door the-house	*glass-(cs) the-water*
the door of the house	the glass of water

6. If the first noun (possessed) is modified by an adjective, the latter may follow either the construct state unit or the noun it modifies. If the adjective follows the first noun, the word بتاع bitāʿ 'belonging to', is used between the adjective and the other noun indicating the possessor:

كتاب الطالبة الجّديد
kitāb it-ṭálb-a-g-gidīd
book the-student-(f)-the-new
the student's new book

الكتاب الجديد بتاع الطالبة
ik-kitāb ig-gidīd bitāع it-ṭálb-a
the-book the-new belonging to the-student-(f)
the student's new book

7. Usually, dual nouns do not occur in construct state. In order to indicate possession in the construction dual number noun + noun/bound pronoun, the word بتوع bitūع, 'belonging to', is used:

الولدين بتوع الستّ	الولدين بتوعك
il-walad-ēn bitūع is-sítt	il-walad-ēn bituع-k
the-boy-(d) belonging to the-lady	*the-boy-(d) belonging to-you (m)*
the lady's two boys	your two boys

Exceptions to the above rule. In expressions like *two eyes two hands, two feet,* etc., plus a bound pronoun, the dual form occurs in construct state. The *n* of the dual is dropped before the bound pronoun is added:

رجلين	رجليكم
rigl-ēn	rigl-ē-kum
foot/leg-(d)	*foot/leg-(d)-your (pl)*
two feet/legs	your feet/legs

D. *The retrocive pronoun indicating possession.* This pronoun is a bound possessive pronoun which is attached to a noun indicating the object possessed and refers to an overt noun indicating the possessor. The use of this pronoun offers an alternative construction to indicate possession. Unlike the construct state, the noun indicating the object possessed follows the noun indicating the possession. This pronoun is also used when there are two or more nouns indicating possession. In the following examples, the retrocive pronoun is in brackets:

الستّ اللّى معاك فستنها حلو .
is-sítt ílli maعā-k fustán-[ha] ḥilw.
The-lady who with-you (m) dress-[her] beautiful.
The dress of the lady who is with you is beautiful.

فستان الستّ اللّى معاك حلو .
fustān is-sítt ílli maعā-k ḥilw.
Dress the-lady who with-you (m) beautiful.
The dress of the lady who is with you is beautiful.

قلم البنت ودفترها وكتابها
qálam il-bínt wi daftár-[ha] wi kitáb-[ha]
pencil the-girl and tablet-[her] and book-[her]
the girl's pencil, tablet, and book

في اللوكاندة

Unit 12. *fi-l-lukánda* At the Hotel

CONVERSATION

فين لوكاندتك ، يا ديك ؟ إسمها إيه ؟
HUSSEIN. — fēn lukand-ít-ak, ya Dick? ism-áha ēh?
Where hotel-(cs)-your(m), oh Dick? Name-her what?
Where is your hotel, Dick? What is the name of it?

هيّ فى الجزيرة ، واسمها « البرج » .
DICK. — híyya fi-l-gizīra, w-ism-áha il-búrg.
She in-the-island, and-name-her the-tower.
It is at Gezira, and its name is il Borg.

ياالله نحطّ شنطك فى عربيّتى ونروح .
HUSSEIN. — yálla ni-ḥúṭṭ šúnaṭ-ak fi-ɛarabiyy-ít-i wi ni-rūḥ.
Come on we-put suitcases-your in car-(cs)-my and we-go.
Let's put your suitcases in my car and go.

سعيدة يا أستاذ ، اسمى ديك كلارك .
DICK. — saɛīda, ya ustāz. ísm-i Dick Clark.
Hello, oh professor. Name-my Dick Clark.
Hello, sir. My name is Dick Clark.

أنا حاجز أوضة هنا . هيّ أوضتى جاهزة ؟
DICK. — ána ḥāgiz ōḍa hína. híyya úḍ-t-i gáhz-a?
I reserved room here. She room-(cs)-my ready-(f)?
I have a room reservation. Is my room ready?

أيوه يا أستاذ ، إمبارح وصلنا تلغرافك .
CLERK. — áywa, ya ustāz. imbāriḥ waṣál-na tilliġrāf-ak.
Yes, oh professor. Yesterday reached-us telegram-your(m).
Yes, sir. Yesterday we received your telegram.

آدى مفتاح أوضتك ، يا أستاذ .
CLERK. — ādi muftāḥ úḍ-t-ak, ya ustāz.
Here key room-(cs)-your(m), oh professor.
Here is the key to your room, sir.

الباسبورتات ، من فضلك ؛ جنسيّتكم إيه ؟
CLERK. — il-basabort-āt, min-fáḍl-ak; ginsiyy-ít-kum ēh?
The passport-(pl), from-bounty-your(m); nationality-(cs)-your (pl)
The passports, please; what is your nationality? [*what?*

إحنا أمريكان ، وحنقعد هنا تلاتة ايام بس . [bass.
DICK. — íḥna amrikān, wi ḥa-n-úqʕud hína talát-t-ayyām
We Americans, and (ft)-we-stay here three-(cs)-days only.
We are Americans and will stay here only three days.

يا أستاذ ، الأوضة بتاعتنا بحمّام وميّة سخنة ؟ [súxn-a?
SANDY. — ya ustāz, il ōḍa bitaʕ-ít-na bi-ḥammām wi máyya
Oh professor, the room belonging to-(cs)-us with-bath and water
Does our room have bath and hot water, sir? [*hot-(f)?*

إيوه ، يا هانم . فيه حمّام فالودة نفسها .
CLERK. — áywa, ya hānim. fī-h ḥammām fi-l-ōḍa nafs-áha.
Yes, oh madam. In-it bath in-the-room self her.
Yes, madam. There is a bath in the room.

يا ديك ، بدلتك وفستانى كمان محتاجة لمكوة . [li-mákwa.
SANDY. — ya Dick, badl-ít-ak wi fustān-i kamān miḥtāg-a
Oh Dick, suit-(cs)-your(m) and dress-my also needy-(f) for-ironing.
Dick, your suit and my dress need pressing.

إيوه يا سندى . لكن أنا نفسى حاودّهم لمكوجى . [li-mákwagi.
DICK. — áywa, ya Sandy. lākin ána náfs-i ḥ-a-wadd-íhum
Yes, oh Sandy. But I self-my (ft)-I-take-them to-laundry man.
Yes, Sandy. I will take them to the cleaner myself.

12. 1. Possessive pronouns are suffixes attached to nouns. The mechanics of suffixation is exactly the same as that of the suffix pronouns to prepositions:

A. Nouns ending in one consonant: ولد wâlad 'boy/son'

ولده	wálad-uh	his boy or son	ولدك	wálad-ik	your (f)
ولدها	walád-ha	her	ولدكم	walád-kum	your (pl)
ولدهم	walád-hum	their	ولدى	wálad-i	my
ولدك	wálad-ak	your (m)	ولدنا	walád-na	our

B. Nouns ending in one consonant preceded by a long vowel: كتاب kitāb 'book'

كتابه	kitāb-uh	his book	كتابك	kitāb-ik	your (f)
كتابها	kitáb-ha	her	كتابكم	kitáb-kum	your (pl)
كتابهم	kitáb-hum	their	كتابى	kitāb-i	my
كتابك	kitāb-ak	your (m)	كتابنا	kitáb-na	our

C. Nouns ending in two consonants: درس dars 'lesson'

درسه	dárs-uh	his lesson	درسك	dárs-ik	your (f)
درسها	dars-áha	her	درسكم	dars-úkum	your (pl)
درسهم	dars-úhum	their	درسى	dárs-i	my
درسك	dárs-ak	your (m)	درسنا	dars-ína	our

D. Nouns ending in a short vowel i: كرسى kursi 'chair'

كرسيه	kursī-h	his chair	كرسيك	kursī-ki	your (f)
كرسيها	kursī-ha	her	كرسيكم	kursī-kum	your (pl)
كرسيهم	kursī-hum	their	كرسى	kursí-yya	my
كرسيك	kursī-k	your (m)	كرسينا	kursī-na	our

E. Masculine nouns ending in a short vowel a: مبنى mábna 'building'

مبناه	mabnā-h	his building	مبناك	mabnā-ki	your (f)
مبناها	mabnā-ha	her	مبناكم	mabnā-kum	your (pl)
مبناهم	mabnā-hum	their	مبناى	mabnā-ya	my
مبناك	mabnā-k	your (m)	مبنانا	mabnā-na	our

F. Feminine nouns ending in *a* (ة) take the suffix pronouns after the construct state suffix. This means that ة becomes ت (in Arabic script) and *a* becomes *it* or *t* (in pronunciation).

Therefore, the possessive suffix pronouns added to a feminine noun ending in *a* (ة) are those in A (for *it*) or C (for *t*) above:

Examples: شنطة šánta, purse, bag
مدرسة madrása, school

شنطته	šanṭ-ít-uh	his bag	مدرسته	madrás-t-uh	his school
شنطتها	šanṭ-ít-ha	her	مدرستها	madras-t-áha	her
شنطتهم	šanṭ-ít-hum	their	مدرستهم	madras-t-úhum	their
شنطتك	šanṭ-ít-ak	your (m)	مدرستك	madrás-t-ak	your (m)
شنطتك	šanṭ-ít-ik	your (f)	مدرستك	madrás-t-ik	your (f)
شنطتكم	šanṭ-ít-kum	your (pl)	مدرستكم	madras-t-úkum	your (pl)
شنطتى	šanṭ-ít-i	my	مدرستى	madrás-t-i	my
شنطتنا	šanṭ-ít-na	our	مدرستنا	madras-t-ína	our

madrasa + possessive pronoun on the pattern of šanta + possessive pronoun may also be heard:

مدرسته	مدرستها	مدرستهم
madras-ít-uh	madras-ít-ha	madras-ít-hum, etc.

12. 2. The reciprocal. We have already discussed the use of the word بعض baɛḍ 'some' as a quantifier. When used with verbs and some prepositions, the same word conveys the meaning of reciprocity and means "each other":

A. الأولاد بيحبّوا بعض .
il-awlād bi-y-ḥíbb-u baɛḍ.
The-children (pt)-he-love-(pl) each other.
The children love each other.

B. مع بعض
maɛa-báɛḍ
with-each other
together

زىّ بعض
zayy(i)-báɛḍ
like-each other
the same

جمب بعض
gamb(i)-báɛḍ
near-each other
close together

على بعض
ɛala-báɛḍ
on each other
all together

فوق بعض
fuq-báɛḍ
up-each other
on top of each other

12. 3. The reflexive. The specialized word نفس nafs, 'self' (also pronounced nifs), is used in various ways, conveying different meanings:

A. nafs with possessive suffix pronouns forms the reflexive pronouns:

نفسه	náfs-uh	himself	نفسك	náfs-ik	yourself (f)
نفسها	nafs-áha	herself	نفسكم	nafs-úkum	yourselves
نفسهم	nafs-úhum	themselves	نفسى	náfs-i	myself
نفسك	náfs-ak	yourself (m)	نفسنا	nafs-ína	ourselves

B. nafs with bound pronouns forms a modal auxiliary corresponding to the English verb "to long" or "to want":

نفسى أروح مصر .
nífs-i a-rūḥ maṣr.
Self-my I-go Egypt.
I want to go to Egypt.

C. Used as a unit noun, نفس nafs may mean "appetite":

ما عنديش نفس خالص .
ma-ɛand-ī-š nafs xāliṣ.
(Neg)-at-me-(neg) self completely.
I do not have any appetite at all.

D. In construct state with a noun, nafs has the meaning of "same":

لاقيت فى الأوضة نفس النّاس .
laqē-t fi-l-ōḍa nafs in-nās.
Found-I in-the-room self the-people.
I found the same people in the room.

E. The reflexive pronouns preceded by some of the prepositions convey a variety of meanings:

بنفسه	لنفسه
bi-náfs-uh	li-náfs-uh
by-himself	*to-himself*
alone/he himself	for his own sake/himself

لزوم الادب

luzūm il-ádab

Unit 13. Showing Good Manners

CONVERSATION

يا ولد ، اقعد ساكت على كرسيك .

FATHER. — ya wálad, úqɛud sākit ɛála kursī-k.
Oh boy, sit silent on chair-your(m).
Son, sit still on your chair.

أيوه ، يا بابا ، بسّ القطّة تحت الكرسي بتعاكسني .

BOY. — áywa, ya bāba, bass il-qúṭṭa taḥt ik-kúrsi bi-t-ɛakís-ni.
Yes, oh papa, only the-cat under the-chair (pt)-she-bother-me.
Yes, father, but the cat under the chair is bothering me.

تعالى يا بنتى ، أقعدى بين أبوكِ وأخوكِ .

MOTHER. — taɛāl-i ya bínt-i, úqɛud-i bēn abū-ki w-axū-ki.
Come here-(f) oh girl-my, sit-(f) between father-your(f) and-brother-your(f).
Come, daughter, sit between your father and your brother.

يا ولاد ، لازم دايما تحافظوا على ميعاد الأكل .

FATHER. — ya wilād, lāzim dáyman ti-ḥáfẓ-u ɛála miɛād il-ákl.
Oh children, must always you-observe-(pl) on appointment the-meals.
Children, you must always be on time for meals.

أنا لسّه واصلة من المدرسة ، يا بابا .

GIRL. — ána líssa wásl-a min il-madrása, ya bāba.
I yet arrived-(f) from the-school, oh papa.
I just arrived from school, father.

يا أحمد ، هات شويّة لحمة من التّلاجة ،

MOTHER. — ya áḥmad, hāt šwáyy-it láḥma min-it-tallāga,
Oh Ahmad, bring little-(cs) meat from-the-refrigerator,
Ahmad, get some meat from the refrigerator,

وحطّها هناك ورا الباب .

Mother. — wi ḥuṭṭ-áha hināk wára-l-bāb.
and put-it there behind-the-door.
and put it there behind the door.

ده عشان مين ، يا ماما ، عشان القطط ؟

Girl. — da ɛašān mīn, ya māma, ɛašān il-qúṭaṭ?
This for whom, oh mama, for the-cats?
For whom is this, mother, for the cats?

أيوه . بعد شويّه ، الكلب كمان حياكل .

Mother. — áywa. baɛd šwáyya, ik-kálb kamān ḥa-y-ākul.
Yes. After little, the-dog also (ft)-he-eat.
Yes. After a while, the dog too will eat.

فيه شويّة عضم فى العلبة على الرّف .

Father. — fī-h šwáyy-it ɛaḍm f-il-ɛílba ɛála ir-ráff.
In-it little-(cs) bones in-the-box on the-shelf.
There are some bones in the box on the shelf.

عند الجزّار ما لاقيتش إلاّ الحبّة دول .

Father. — ɛand il-gazzār ma-laqí-t-š ílla il-ḥábba dōl.
At the-butcher (neg)-found-(neg) except the-piece those.
Those few pieces were all I found at the butcher's.

ما فيش حاجة تانية لنا غير ده ، يا ماما ؟

Boy. — ma-fī-š ḥāga tány-a lí-na ġēr da, ya māma?
(Neg)-in-(neg) thing other-(f) for-us except this, oh mama?
Don't we have anything besides this, mother?

خلّيك مؤدّب ، يا أحمد ! كل اللّى قدّامك .

Mother. — xallī-k mu'áddab, ya áḥmad! kul ílli quddām-ak.
Leave-you(m) polite, oh Ahmad! Eat what before-you(m).
Be polite, Ahmad! Eat what is offered to you.

13. 1. Prepositional phrases consist of a preposition followed by a noun, noun phrase, a bound pronoun, or the word بعض baɛḍ 'some/each other'. Usually, a prepositional phrase occurs as a predicate in verbless sentences corresponding to English sentences with the verb "to be" in the present tense, which is lacking in Arabic. Prepositional phrases may be used as adverbial phrases in verbal sentences. Certain prepositional phrases are used to convey the meaning of the corresponding English verb "to have". Some prepositional phrases are also used as subordinating conjunctions:

الولد عند الجزمجى .
il-wálad ʿand il-gazmági.
The-boy at the-shoemaker.
The boy is at the shoemaker's.

بنتى مع بنت المدرّس .
bínt-i máʿa bint il-mudárris.
Girl-my with girl the-teacher.
My daughter is with the teacher's daughter.

13. 2. Form and meaning of prepositions. Prepositions are characteristic of the language to which they belong, that is, their meanings depend on their usage. It is, therefore, impossible to give a consistent translation of the prepositions of one language into another. The following are prepositions in Egyptian Arabic:

مع	máʿa	with	غير	ġēr	except
على	ʿála	on	بين	bēn	between
وايّا	wáyya	with	قصاد	quṣād	opposite
ب	bi	for/with	جنب	gamb	beside/near
فى	fi	in/among	عند	ʿand	at/with
ل	li	to/for	ضدّ	ḍidd	against
من	min	from	بعد	baʿd	after
عن	ʿan	from/for	قبل	qabl	before

فوق	fōq	up
تحت	taḥt	under
قدّام	quddām	in front of
ورا	wára	behind
جوّه	gúwwa	inside
برّه	bárra	outside

Except for bárra 'outside' and gúwwa 'inside', which are usually not used with bound pronouns, the prepositions in the last column may be used independently or with a bound pronoun or followed by a noun or noun phrase. The prepositions in the first two columns are always used with a bound pronoun or followed by a noun or noun phrase.

The prepositions min 'from' and ʿála 'on' also have the forms mi and ʿa (in pronunciation), which are usually used before the definite article of a noun, and minn and ʿann.

Prepositions are negated by placing the word مش miš 'not' before them.

شراء تذكارات من الاسواق

Unit 14. *šíra tizkar-āt min il-aswāq*

Buying Souvenirs at the Bazaars

CONVERSATION

جبتِ من اين الصّينيّة الحلوة دى ، يا حبيبتى ؟

Richard. — gíbt-t-i min-ēn iṣ-ṣaníyya-l-ḥílw-a di, ya ḥabíb-t-i?
Brought-you-(f) from-where the-tray-the-beautiful-(f) this, oh dear-(cs)-my?
Where did you get this beautiful tray, my dear?

أنا اشتريتها من الموسكى ، أنا كنت هناك مع أمينة .

Nancy. — ána ištarí-t-ha min il-múski. ána kún-t(i) hinā̄k maع-amīna.
I bought-I-it from the-Mouski. I was-I there with-Amina.
I bought it at Mouski. I was there with Amina.

همّ باعوهالك بكام ؟

Richard. — húmma baع-u-hā-l-ik bi-kām?
They sold-(pl)-it-to-you by-how much?
For how much did they sell it to you?

الصّينيّة وحاملها ؟ اشتريتهم بتلاتة جنيه .

Nancy. — iṣ-ṣaníyya wi ḥamíl-ha? ištarí-t-hum bi-talāta ginēh.
The-tray and stand-her? Bought-I-them for-three pound.
The tray and the stand? I bought them for three pounds.

أنا شفتك فى دكّان بتفاصلى على سجّادة فارسي .

Rashid. — ána šúf-t-ik fi-dukkān bi-ti-fáṣl-i عála siggāda fáris-i.
I saw-I-you(f) in-shop (pt)-you-bargain-(f) on rug Persia-(adj).
I saw you at a shop bargaining for a Persian carpet.

أنا كنت عايز أشتريها ، لـكن الرّاجل طلب تسعين جنيه .

Nancy. — ána kún-t(i) عāyiz a-štirī-ha, lākin ir-rāgil ṭálab tisعīn ginēh.
I was-I wanting I-buy-it, but the-man asked ninety pound.
I wanted to buy it, but the man asked ninety pounds.

شفتِ سرج الجمل اللّى كان وراكِ فى الدّكّان ؟
Nancy. — šúf-t-i sárg ig-gámal ílli kān warā-k-i fi-d-dukkān?
Saw-you-(f) saddle the-camel which was behind-you-(f) in-the-shop?
Did you see the camel saddle behind you in the shop?

أيوه ، حبّيته قوى ، لَكن حاحطّه فين ؟
Amina. — áywa. ḥabbē-t-uh qáwi, lākin ḥa-ḥúṭṭ-uh fēn?
Yes. Loved-I-it very, but (ft)-put-it where?
Yes. I loved it, but where would I put it?

صحيح ، إحنا جبنا حاجات كتير كان من الصّعب نشيلهم .
Nancy. — ṣaḥīḥ, íḥna gíb-na ḥag-āt kitīr kān min iṣ-ṣáɛb [ni-šíl-hum.
True, we brought-we thing-(pl) much was from the-difficult we- [carry-them.
Indeed, we got so many things it was hard to carry them.

العربيّة كانت مليانة؛ إحنا مليناها بالشّياش .
Amina. — il-ɛarabíyya kān-it malyān-a; íḥna mali-nā-ha [bi-š-šiyāš.
The-car was-she full-(f); we filled-we-it with-the-narghiles.
The car was full; we filled it with water pipes.

الرّجّالة ساعدونا نحطّهم فى شنطة العربيّة .
Amina. — ir-riggāla saɛd-ū-na ni-ḥutt-úhum fi šánṭ-it il- [ɛarabíyya.
The-men helped-they-us we-put-them in bag-(cs) the-car.
The men helped us to put them in the car trunk.

أنا دخلت الدّكّان بعد منكم ولاقيت ريتشارد قبالى .
Rashid. — ána daxál-t id-dukkān báɛd(i) mín-kum wi laqē-t [Richard qubál-t-i.
I entered-I the-shop after from-you(pl) and found-I Richard in front-(cs)-me.
I entered the shop after you and there, in front of me, was [Richard.

قال لى إنّه كان بيدوّر عليكم وأهو لاقاكم .
Rashid. — qál-l-i ínn-uh kān bi-y-dáwwar ɛalē-kum w-ahú [laqā-kum.
Told-to-me that-he was (pt)-he-was looking on-you(pl) and here [found-you(pl).
He told me he was looking for you, and he found you there.

14. 1. Object pronouns with verbs are suffixes. The individual form of each suffix depends on the ending of the verb form to which it is attached. The following is a table of the object pronouns attached to verbs, arranged in groups according to the endings of the verb forms. ($\bar{V}$ = long vowel)

Pronouns attached to verbs ending in:

one consonant	*two consonants*	*a short vowel*	*English correspondence*
C -uh	CC -uh	$V \rightarrow \bar{V}$ -h	him, it
C -ha	CC -áha	$V \rightarrow \bar{V}$ -ha	her, it
C -hum	CC -úhum	$V \rightarrow \bar{V}$ -hum	them
C -ak	CC -ak	$V \rightarrow \bar{V}$ -k	you (m)
C -ik	CC -ik	$V \rightarrow \bar{V}$ -ki	you (f)
C -kum	CC -úkum	$V \rightarrow \bar{V}$ -kum	you (pl)
C -ni	CC -íni	$V \rightarrow \bar{V}$ -ni	me
C -na	CC -ína	$V \rightarrow \bar{V}$ -na	us

A. Except for the first person singular, the suffixation mechanics of the above pronouns is the same as those with both prepositions and nouns.

B. The final *h* (3rd person masculine singular pronoun) is not pronounced; it is written in phonetic transcription in order to be consistent with Arabic script, in which only the Arabic symbol for *h* is written and the short vowel *u* is omitted: زاره zār-uh 'he visited-him/it'.

This unpronounced *h* makes it possible to recognize this suffix pronoun.

C. When the suffix pronouns in the third column are added to a verb form, preposition, or noun ending in a short vowel (V), this vowel is lengthened ($\bar{V}$) before taking a suffix. All these suffixes begin with a consonant.

D. A suffix which begins with a consonant (the first column) shortens the preceding long vowel of the verb, preposition, or noun stem (see šāf below).

E. Since each noun is either feminine or masculine in Arabic there is no separate word for "it". Every object is referred to as "him" for masculine nouns and "her" for feminine nouns.

Verb + object pronoun		Verb: ضرب ḍárab 'beat'
ضربه	ḍaráb-uh	he beat him/it
ضربها	ḍaráb-ha	he beat her/it
ضربهم	ḍaráb-hum	he beat them
ضربتك	ḍarab-ít-ak	she beat you (m)
ضربتِك	ḍarab-ít-ik	she beat you (f)
ضربتكم	ḍarab-ít-kum	she beat you (pl)
ضربتنى	ḍarab-ít-ni	she beat me
ضربتنا	ḍarab-ít-na	she beat us
ضربته	ḍaráb-t-uh	I or you (m) beat him/it
ضربتها	ḍarab-t-áha	I or you (m) beat her/it
ضربتهم	ḍarab-t-úhum	I or you (m) beat them
ضربتك	ḍaráb-t-ak	I beat you (m)
ضربتِك	ḍaráb-t-ik	I beat you (f)
ضربتكم	ḍarab-t-úkum	I beat you (pl)
ضربتنى	ḍarab-t-íni	you (m) beat me
ضربتنا	ḍarab-t-ína	you (m) beat us
ضربوه	ḍarab-ū-h	they beat him/it
ضربوكِ	ḍarab-ū-ki	they beat you (f)
ضربتيها	ḍarab-tī-ha	you (f) beat her/it
ضربتيه	ḍarab-tī-h	you (f) beat him/it
ضربتونى	ḍarab-tū-ni	you (pl) beat me
ضربتونا	ḍarab-tū-na	you (pl) beat us
ضربناك	ḍarab-nā-k	we beat you (m)
ضربناهم	ḍarab-nā-hum	we beat them

Verb + object pronoun		Verb: شاف šāf'see /look'
شافه	šāf-uh	he saw him/it
شافها	šáf-ha	he saw her/it
شافهم	šáf-hum	he saw them
شافك	šāf-ak	he saw you (m)
شافك	šāf-ik	he saw you (f)
شافكم	šáf-kum	he saw you (pl)
شافني	šáf-ni	he saw me
شافنا	šáf-na	he saw us

14. 2. Object pronouns with prepositions. Except for the first person singular suffix pronoun, the mechanics of suffixation of the bound pronouns to prepositions and nouns is almost the same as that of verbs:

A. Prepositions ending in one consonant, like من min 'from' and عن ʕan 'on', double the last consonant before taking a suffix pronoun beginning with a vowel. These prepositions which have another form ending in two consonants and those in B and C below have the first person singular suffix pronoun *-i*. The final *h* of the third person singular pronoun suffix is not pronounced:

منّه	mínn-uh	منّه	mínn-uh	from him/it
منّها	minn-áha	منها	mín-ha	from her/it
منّهم	minn-úhum	منهم	mín-hum	from them
منّك	mínn-ak	منّك	mínn-ak	from you (m)
منّك	mínn-ik	منّك	mínn-ik	from you (f)
منّكم	minn-úkum	منكم	mín-kum	from you (pl)
منّي	mínn-i	منّي	mínn-i	from me
منّنا	minn-ína	منّا	mín-na	from us

B. Prepositions ending in one consonant preceded by a long vowel, like غير ġēr 'except' and بين bēn 'between', shorten the long vowel before taking a suffix pronoun beginning with a consonant.

غيره	ġēr-uh	except him/it	غيرِك	ġēr-ik	except you (f)
غيرها	ġír-ha	except her/it	غيركم	ġír-kum	except you(pl)
غيرهم	ġír-hum	except them	غيرى	ġēr-i	except me
غيرك	ġēr-ak	except you (m)	غيرنا	ġír-na	except us

C. Prepositions ending in two consonants add the pronoun suffixes as follows:

جانبه	gámb-uh	near him/it
جانبها	gamb-áha	near her/it
جانبهم	gamb-úhum	near them
جانبك	gámb-ak	near you (m)
جانبِك	gámb-ik	near you (f)
جانبكم	gamb-úkum	near you (pl)
جانبى	gámb-i	near me
جانبنا	gamb-ína	near us

D. Prepositions ending in the vowel *i*, like ب bi 'with' ف fi 'in' and ل li 'to/for', lengthen this vowel before taking a suffix pronoun (except the first person singular). With these prepositions the first person singular suffix pronoun is -yya:

فيه	fī-h	in him/it	فيكِ	fī-ki	in you (f)
فيها	fī-ha	in her/it	فيكم	fī-kum	in you (pl)
فيهم	fī-hum	in them	فىّ	fí-yya	in me
فيك	fī-k	in you (m)	فينا	fī-na	in us

E. Prepositions ending in *-a* lengthen this vowel before taking a suffix pronoun. The first person singular pronoun is -ya: ورا wára 'behind'.

وراه	warā-h	behind him/it
وراها	warā-ha	behind her/it
وراهم	warā-hum	behind them
وراك	warā-k	behind you (m)
وراكِ	warā-ki	behind you (f)

وراكم	warā-kum	behind you (pl)
وراى	warā-ya	behind me
ورانا	warā-na	behind us

F. The preposition على ʿála plus pronoun suffixes has a characteristic pattern: the first person singular pronoun is -yya, and the final vowel *a* is lengthened to *ē* before adding a suffix other than the first person singular:

عليه	ʿalē-h	on him, it	عليك	ʿalē-ki	on you (f)
عليها	ʿalē-ha	on her, it	عليكم	ʿalē-kum	on you (pl)
عليهم	ʿalē-hum	on them	على	ʿalá-yya	on me
عليك	ʿalē-k	on you (m)	علينا	ʿalē-na	on us

14. 3. The retrocive pronoun. This pronoun is a specialized use of the possessive and object suffix pronouns. It is, therefore, found attached to nouns, verbs, or prepositions. The following examples show the characteristic usage of the object and possessive suffixed pronouns as retrocive pronouns which are included in brackets:

A. The retrocive pronoun accompanies the relative pronoun اللى ílli, 'who/whom/which/that', in sentences as an object pronoun of verbs or prepositions:

البنت اللّى شفتها إمبارح حبيبتى .
il-bínt ílli šuf-t-[áha] imbāriḥ ḥabíb-t-i.
The-girl whom saw-you (m)-[her] yesterday friend-(cs)-my.
The girl you saw yesterday is my girl friend.

البنت اللّى شفتنى معاها حبيبتى .
il-bínt ílli šuf-t-íni maʿā-[ha] ḥabíb-t-i.
The-girl whom saw-you (m)-me with-[her] friend-(cs)-my.
The girl you saw me with is my girl friend.

B. When the object of a verb or preposition is placed before the verb or preposition for emphasis, a retrocive pronoun is used instead of the noun object:

السِتّ دى شفتها إمبارح .
is-sítt di šuf-t-[áha] imbáriḥ.
The-lady that saw-I-[her] yesterday.
I saw that lady yesterday.

C. As we have seen in unit 11, the use of the retrocive pronoun constitutes an alternative device to express possession:

الراجل ده بنته مراتى .
ir-rāgil da bínt-[uh] mrāt-i.
The-man that girl-[his] wife-my.
The daughter of that man is my wife.

مساعدة صديق

Unit 15. *musāɛd-it ṣadīq* Helping A Friend

CONVERSATION

جرى إيه؟ فيه إيه، يا على؟

SAM. — gára ēh? fī-h ēh, ya ɛáli?
Run what? In-it what, oh Ali?
What's up? What's the matter, Ali?

الحقنى، يا سام، امسكه؛ ده سرق محفظتى.

ALI. — ilḥáq-ni, ya Sam; imsík-uh; da sáraq maḥfáẓ-t-i.
Help-me, oh Sam! grab-him! that stole wallet-(cs)-my.
Help me, Sam! Grab him! He has stolen my wallet.

ما تخافش، يا على؛ أنا ماسكه كويّس.

SAM. — ma-t-xáf-š, ya ɛáli; ána másk-uh kwáyyis.
(Neg)-you-be afraid-(neg), oh Ali; I holding-him good.
Don't worry, Ali; I have a good hold on him.

يا شاويش، يا شاويش! اظبط الرّاجل ده من فضلك.

ALI. — ya šawīš, ya šawīš! úẓbut ir-rāgil da min-fáḍl-ak.
Oh sergeant, oh sergeant! Catch the-man this from-bounty-your(m).
Officer, officer! Take this man, please.

ياالله بنا يا سيدى نروح قسم البوليس.

OFFICER. — yálla bī-na, ya sīdi; n-rūḥ qism il-bulīs.
Come on with-us, oh fellow; we-go section the-police.
Come on, fellow; let's go to the police station.

أنا عارفه كويّس؛ ده نشّال معروف.

OFFICER. — ána ɛárf-uh kwáyyis; da naššāl maɛrūf.
I knowing-him well; this pickpocket known.
I know him well; he is a notorious pickpocket.

إيه اللّى حصل ؟ اشرح لى من فضلك .

CAPTAIN. — ēh ílli ḥáṣal? išráḥ-l-i, min-fáḍl-ak.
What which happened? Explain-to-me, from-kindness-your(m).
Would you please explain to me what happened?

أنا وصاحبى سام كنّا راكبين الأتوبيس ، يا حضرة الظّابط .

ALI. — ána wi ṣáḥb-i Sam kún-na rakb-īn il-utubīs, ya
[ḥáḍrit iẓ-ẓābiṭ.
I and friend-my Sam were-we riding-(pl) the-bus, oh mister the-
My friend Sam and I were riding on the bus, sir. *[officer.*

وانا كنت واقف وواحد وشوشنى .

ALI. — w-ána kun-t wāqif wi wāḥid wašwíš-ni:
And-I was-I standing and one whispered-me:
I was standing, and somebody whispered to me:

خلّى بالك ، خلّى بالك ، يا أستاذ ، وأنا ادّوّرت .

ALI. — xálli bāl-ak, xálli bāl-ak, ya ustāz! w-ána iddawwár-t.
Let care-your(m), let care-your(m), oh professor! And-I turned
[around-I.
"Watch out, watch out, sir!" And I turned around.

على مسك إيد الرّاجل ، لٰكن ده فلت ،

SAM. — ع‎áli mísik īd ir-rāgil, lākin da fálat,
Ali grabbed hand the-man, but that escaped,
Ali grabbed the hand of the man, but he got loose,

وحاول ينطّ من الأتوبيس .

SAM. — wi ḥāwil yi-núṭṭ min il-utubīs.
and tried he-jump from the-bus.
and he tried to jump off the bus.

لٰكن على زعّق : حرامى ، يا سام ! وانا مسكته .

SAM. — lākin ع‎áli záععaq: ḥarāmi, ya Sam! w-ána misík-t-uh.
But Ali shouted: thief, oh Sam! And-I grabbed-I-him.
But Ali shouted: "the thief, Sam!" And I grabbed him.

15. 1. Triconsonantal verbs. These simple verbs have three different radical consonants. In terms of vowel change (complete *vs.* incomplete or imperative stems) classification discussed in unit 4, these verbs belong to different vowel classes (vowel *i*, *a*, or *u* class). The complete stem of these verbs may be of the vowel pattern *a-a* or *i-i*:

Complete	*Incomplete*
كتب kátab, he wrote	يكتب yí-ktib, he writes
ضرب ḍárab, he beat	يضرب yí-ḍrab, he beats
خرج xárag, he went out	يخرج yí-xrug, he goes out
نزل nízil, he descended	ينزل yí-nzil, he descends
شرب šírib, he drank	يشرب yí-šrab, he drinks
سكت síkit, he was quiet	يسكت yí-skut, he is quiet

Imperative

اكتب íktib, write!	انزل ínzil, come down!
اضرب íḍrab, beat!	اشرب íšrab, drink!
اخرج úxrug, get out!	اسكت úskut, be quiet!

Inflection in verbs of this type is regular, in the sense that, except for the subject, gender, and number affixes, each type of stem (complete, incomplete, or imperative) of verbs of this kind keeps its respective form unchanged throughout the inflection process (see in unit 6 the inflection of the verbs كتب kátab 'write' and شرب šírib 'drink').

For verbs belonging to the vowel class *u*, the vowel *i* of the prefix pronouns may be replaced optionally by *u*: سكت síkit 'be quiet/stop talking' as a verb:

Complete

3 msg.	سكت	síkit,	stopped talking
3 fmsg.	سكتت	síkt-it	stopped talking
3 pl.	سكتوا	síkt-u	stopped talking
2 msg.	سكتّ	sikít-t	stopped talking
2 fmsg.	سكتّ	sikít-t-i	stopped talking
2 pl.	سكتّوا	sikít-t-u	stopped talking
1 sg.	سكتّ	sikít-t	stopped talking
1 pl.	سكتنا	sikít-na	stopped talking

Incomplete

3 msg.	يسكت	yí/yú-skut	stops talking
3 fmsg.	تسكت	tí/tú-skut	stops talking
3 pl.	يسكتوا	yi/yu-skút-u	stop talking
2 msg.	تسكت	tí/tú-skut	stop talking
2 fmsg.	تسكتى	ti/tu-skút-i	stop talking
2 pl.	تسكتوا	ti/tu-skút-u	stop talking
1 sg.	أسكت	á-skut	stop talking
1 pl.	نسكت	ní/nú-skut	stop talking

Imperative

2 msg.	اسكت	úskut	stop talking!
2 fmsg.	اسكتى	uskút-i	stop talking!
2 pl.	اسكتوا	uskút-u	stop talking!

Usually triconsonantal verbs have two participles (which will be treated in later units) of the following pattern:

Verb	*Active participle*	*Passive participle*
قفل qáfal, close	قافل qāfil	مقفول maqfūl
كتب kátab, write	كاتب kātib	مكتوب maktūb
فهم fíhim, understand	فاهم fāhim	مفهوم mafhūm

15. 2. Quadriliteral verbs. These verbs have four radical consonants and are few in number. They belong to the unchanged vowel class (same vowels in complete and incomplete stems); this means that, except for the prefix pronouns, all three types of stems are the same:

The inflection of this type of verb is regular: ترجم tárgim 'translate'.

Complete

3 msg.	ترجم	tárgim	translated
3 fmsg.	ترجمت	targím-it	translated
3 pl.	ترجموا	targím-u	translated

2 msg.	ترجمت	targím-t	translated
2 fmsg.	ترجمتِ	targím-t-i	translated
2 pl.	ترجمتوا	targím-t-u	translated
1 sg.	ترجمت	targím-t	translated
1 pl.	ترجمنا	targím-na	translated

Incomplete

3 msg.	yi-tárgim	يترجم	translates
3 fmsg.	ti-tárgim	تترجم	translates
3 pl.	yi-targím-u	يترجموا	translate
2 msg.	ti-tárgim	تترجم	translate
2 fmsg.	ti-targím-i	تترجمي	translate
2 pl.	ti-targím-u	تترجموا	translate
1 sg.	a-tárgim	أترجم	translate
1 pl.	ni-tárgim	نترجم	translate

Imperative

2 msg.	ترجم	tárgim	translate!
2 fmsg.	ترجمي	targím-i	translate!
2 pl.	ترجموا	targím-u	translate!

These verbs have only one participle (active or passive).

Verb	*Participle*
ترجم tárgim	مترجم mitárgim

15. 3. Irregular verbs. The following verbs are irregular:

Complete	*Incomplete*	*Imperative*	
جه gih	ييجى y-īgi	تعالى taɛāla	come
كل kal	ياكل y-ākul	كل kul	eat
خد xad	ياخد y-āxud	خد xud	take
وقف wíqif	يقف yú-qaf	اقف úqaf	stop/ stand
وقع wíqiɛ	يقع yú-qaɛ	اوقع úqaɛ	fall

The inflection of these verbs is irregular and should be learned with the verb. However, kal and xad follow the same inflectional pattern, as is also true of wíqif and wíqiع.

جه gih 'come':

		Complete			*Incomplete*	
3 msg.	جه	gih	came	ييجى	y-īgí	comes
3 fmsg.	جت	gat	came	تيجى	t-īgi	comes
3 pl.	جم	gum	came	ييجوا	y-īgu	come
2 msg.	جيت	gē-t	came	تيجى	t-īgi	come
2 fmsg.	جيت	gē-t-i	came	تيجى	t-īgi	come
2 pl.	جيتوا	gē-t-u	came	تيجوا	t-īgu	come
1 sg.	جيت	gē-t	came	آجى	āgi	come
1 pl.	جينا	gē-na	came	نيجى	n-īgi	come

		Imperative			*Participle*
msg.	تعالى	taعāla	come!	جاى	gayy
fmsg.	تعالى	taعāli	come!	جاية	gáyy-a
pl.	تعالوا	taعālu	come!	جايين	gayy-īn

gih before suffixes (pronouns or negative) and gum before the negative suffix take the forms gā and gū, respectively:

جالى جواب امبارح .	لا ، همّ ماجوش النّهارده .
gā-l-i gawāb imbāriḥ.	la', húmma ma-gū-š innahárda.
Came-to-me letter yesterday.	*No, they (neg)-came-(neg) today.*
Yesterday I received a letter.	No, they did not come today.

كل kal 'eat':

		Complete			*Incomplete*	
3 msg.	كل	kal	ate	ياكل	y-ākul	eats
3 fmsg.	كلت	kál-it	ate	تاكل	t-ākul	eats
3 pl.	كلوا	kál-u	ate	ياكلوا	y-áklu	eat

2 msg.	كلت	kal-t	ate	تاكل	t-ākul	eat
2 fmsg.	كلتِ	kál-t-i	ate	تاكلي	t-ákli	eat
2 pl.	كلتوا	kál-t-u	ate	تاكلوا	t-áklu	eat
1 sg.	كلت	kal-t	ate	آكل	ākul	eat
1 pl.	كلنا	kál-na	ate	ناكل	n-ākul	eat

	Imperative			*Participle*			
msg.	كل	kul	eat!	واكل	wākil	واخد	wāxid
fmsg.	كلي	kúl-i	eat!	واكلة	wákl-a	واخدة	wáxd-a
pl.	كلوا	kúl-u	eat!	واكلين	wakl-īn	واخدين	waxd-īn

وقف wíqif 'stop/stand up':

	Complete			*Incomplete*		
3 msg.	وقف	wíqif	stopped	يقف	yú-qaf	stops
3 fmsg.	وقفت	wíqf-it	stopped	تقف	tú-qaf	stops
3 pl.	وقفوا	wíqf-u	stopped	يقفوا	yu-qáf-u	stop
2 msg.	وقفت	wiqíf-t	stopped	تقف	tú-qaf	stop
2 fmsg.	وقفتِ	wiqíf-t-i	stopped	تقفي	tu-qáf-i	stop
2 pl.	وقفتوا	wiqíf-t-u	stopped	تقفوا	tu-qáf-u	stop
1 sg.	وقفت	wiqíf-t	stopped	أقف	á-qaf	stop
1 pl.	وقفنا	wiqíf-na	stopped	نقف	nú-qaf	stop

	Imperative			*Participle*			
msg.	اقف	úqaf	stop!	واقف	wāqif	واقع	wāqiع
fmsg.	اقفي	uqáf-i	stop!	واقفة	wáqf-a	واقعة	wáqع-a
pl.	اقفوا	uqáf-u	stop!	واقفين	waqf-īn	واقعين	waqع-īn

الحج لمكة والقدس

Unit 16. *il-ḥígg(i) li mákka w-il-qúds* Pilgrimage to Mecca and Jerusalem

CONVERSATION

يا أحمد ، بلغني إنّ العرب مسلمين .

ROBERT. — ya áḥmad, baláġ-ni inn il-ɛárab muslim-īn.
Oh Ahmad, reached-me that the-Arabs Moslem-(pl).
Ahmad, I have heard that the Arabs are Moslems.

ممكن تدّيني شويّة معلومات عن الموضوع ده ؟

ROBERT. — múmkin ti-ddī-ni šwáyy-it maɛlum-āt ɛan il-mawḍūɛ da?
Possible you-give-me little-(cs) information-(pl) on the-subject this?
Could you tell me something about this?

طبعاً ، يا روبرت . أنا نفسي عربي .

AHMAD. — ṭábɛan, ya Robert. ána náfs-i ɛárab-i.
Of course, oh Robert. I self-my Arab-(adj).
Of course, Robert. I am an Arab myself.

أيوه ، أكتر العرب مسلمين .

AHMAD. — áywa, áktar il-ɛárab muslim-īn.
Yes, most the-Arabs Moslems-(pl).
The majority of the Arabs are Moslems, yes.

لـكن فيه كمان عرب مسيحيّين وعرب يهود .

AHMAD. — lākin fī-h kamān ɛárab misiḥ-i-yyīn wi ɛaráb yahūd.
But in-it also Arabs Christ-(adj)-(pl) and Arabs Jews.
But there are also Arabs who are Christians and Jews.

بعض النّاس بتفتكر إنّ ما فيش مسلمين غير العرب .

ROBERT. — baɛḍ in-nās bi-ti-ftíkir inn ma-fī-š muslim-īn ġēr il-ɛárab.
Some the-people (pt)-she-think that (neg)-in-(neg) Moslem-(pl) except the-Arabs.
Some people think that only Arabs are Moslems.

لا ، يا روبرت . الإسلام دين عالمى .
AHMAD. — la', ya Robert. il-islām dīn ع ālam-i.
No, oh Robert. The-Islam religion universe-(adj).
No, Robert. Islam is a universal religion.

يا أحمد ، أنا باتلخبط بين مكّة والمدينة .
ROBERT. — ya áḥmad, ána b-a-tláxbaṭ bēn mákka w-il-
[madīna.
Oh Ahmad, I (pt)-I-confuse between Mecca and-the-Medina.
Ahmad, I am confused about Mecca and Medina.

خلّينى أشرح لك . همّ الاتنين مدن الإسلام المقدسة .
AHMAD. — xallī-ni a-šráḥ-l-ak. húmma il-itnēn múdun il-
[islām il-muqaddás-a.
Let-me I-explain-to-you(m). They the-two cities the-Islam the-
[holy-(f).
Let me explain it to you. Both are holy cities of Islam.

النّبى محمّد اتولد فى مكّة ،
AHMAD. — in-nábi muḥámmad itwálad fi mákka,
The-prophet Muhammad was born in Mecca,
The Prophet Muhammad was born in Mecca,

واندفن فى المدينة .
AHMAD. — w-indáfan fi-l-madīna.
and-was buried in-the-Medina.
and was buried at Medina.

المسلمين بيحجّوا لمكّة ، مش كده ؟
ROBERT. — il-muslim-īn bi-y-ḥígg-u li mákka, miš kída?
The-Moslem-(pl) (pt)-he-go to pilgrimage-(pl) to Mecca, not so?
Moslems go on pilgrimages to Mecca, don't they?

أيوه ، زىّ ما المسيحيّين بيروحوا القدس .
AHMAD. — áywa, záyy(i)-ma il-masiḥ-i-yyīn bi-y-rūḥ-u
[il-qúds.
Yes, how-when the-Christ-(adj)-(pl) (pt)-he-go-(pl) the-Jerusalem.
Yes, just as Christians go to Jerusalem.

16. 1. Double verbs. These verbs have three consonants, of which the second and the third are the same. The complete stem of each verb has two vowel patterns: *a* (for third person) and *a-ē* (for second and first person). These verbs belong to vowel classes (complete *vs.* incomplete stem) *i* and *u*.

The inflection of these verbs is not completely regular. Except for the pronoun prefixes, the incomplete and the imperative stems of these verbs are the same.

حبّ ḥabb 'love/like':

	Complete			*Incomplete*		
3 msg.	حبّ	ḥabb	loved	يحبّ	yi-ḥíbb	loves
3 fmsg.	حبّت	ḥább-it	loved	تحبّ	ti-ḥíbb	loves
3 pl.	حبّوا	ḥább-u	loved	يحبّوا	yi-ḥíbb-u	love
2 msg.	حبّيت	ḥabbē-t	loved	تحبّ	ti-ḥíbb	love
2 fmsg.	حبّيت	ḥabbē-t-i	loved	تحبّى	ti-ḥíbb-i	love
2 pl.	حبّيتوا	ḥabbē-t-u	loved	تحبوا	ti-ḥíbb-u	love
1 sg.	حبّيت	ḥabbē-t	loved	أحبّ	a-ḥíbb	love
1 pl.	حبّينا	ḥabbē-na	loved	نحبّ	ni-ḥíbb	love

Imperative

2 msg.	حبّ	ḥibb	love!
2 fmsg.	حبّى	ḥíbb-i	love!
2 pl.	حبّوا	ḥíbb-u	love!

Verbs like this are: عدّ ɛadd 'count'; سدّ sadd 'block'; etc.

ردّ radd 'answer':

	Complete			*Incomplete*		
3 msg.	ردّ	radd	answered	يردّ	yi-rúdd	answers
3 fmsg.	ردّت	rádd-it	answered	تردّ	ti-rúdd	answers
3 pl.	ردّوا	rádd-u	answered	يردّوا	yi-rúdd-u	answer
2 msg.	ردّيت	raddē-t	answered	تردّ	ti-rúdd	answer
2 fmsg.	ردّيت	raddē-t-i	answered	تردّى	ti-rúdd-i	answer
2 pl.	ردّيتوا	raddē-t-u	answered	تردّوا	ti-rúdd-u	answer
1 sg.	ردّيت	raddē-t	answered	أردّ	a-rúdd	answer
1 pl.	ردّينا	raddē-na	answered	نردّ	ni-rúdd	answer

Imperative

2 msg.	ردّ	rudd	answer!
2 fmsg.	ردّى	rúdd-i	answer!
2 pl.	ردّوا	rúdd-u	answer!

Verbs like radd are: بصّ baṣṣ 'look'; حطّ ḥaṭṭ 'put'; etc.

Usually, double verbs have two participles, of the following pattern:

Verb		*Active participle*		*Passive participle*	
ḥabb	حبّ	ḥābib	حابب	maḥbūb	محبوب
radd	ردّ	rādid	رادد	mardūd	مردود
sadd	سدّ	sādid	سادد	masdūd	مسدود

16. 2. Hollow verbs. These verbs have two consonants and a medial long vowel *ā*, which originally was a *w* or *y*. The complete stem of each verb has two vowel patterns: *ā* (for third person) and either *i* or *u* (for second and first persons). Except for the last two verbs below, usually these verbs belong to two vowel classes (complete *vs.* incomplete stem): *i* and *u*. The following are some examples:

Complete		*Incomplete*	*Imperative*
3rd person	2nd and 1st person		
كان kān	كنت kun-t	يكون yi-kūn	كون kūn, be
شاف šāf	شفت šuf-t	يشوف yi-šūf	شوف šūf, see
شال šāl	شلت šil-t	يشيل yi-šīl	شيل šīl, carry
نام nām	نمت nim-t	ينام yi-nām	نام nām, sleep
خاف xāf	خفت xuf-t	يخاف yi-xāf	خاف xāf, be afraid

The inflection of these verbs is not completely regular. Except for the pronoun prefixes, the incomplete and the imperative stems are alike:

qāl 'say/tell':

	Complete			*Incomplete*		
3 msg.	قال	qāl	said/told	يقول	yi-qūl	says/tells
3 fmsg.	قالت	qāl-it	said/told	تقول	ti-qūl	says/tells
3 pl.	قالوا	qāl-u	said/told	يقولوا	yi-qūl-u	say/tell
2 msg.	قلت	qul-t	said/told	تقول	ti-qūl	say/tell
2 fmsg.	قلتِ	qúl-t-i	said/told	تقولى	ti-qūl-i	say/tell
2 pl.	قلتوا	qúl-t-u	said/told	تقولوا	ti-qūl-u	say/tell
1 sg.	قلت	qul-t	said/told	اقول	a-qūl	say/tell
1 pl.	قلنا	qúl-na	said/told	نقول	ni-qūl	say/tell

Imperative

2 msg.	قول	qūl	say/tell!
2 fmsg.	قولى	qūl-i	say/tell!
2 pl.	قولوا	qūl-u	say/tell!

gāb 'bring':

	Complete			*Incomplete*		
3 msg.	جاب	gāb	brought	يجيب	yi-gīb	brings
3 fmsg.	جابت	gāb-it	brought	تجيب	ti-gīb	brings
3 pl.	جابوا	gāb-u	brought	يجيبوا	yi-gīb-u	bring
2 msg.	جبت	gib-t	brought	تجيب	ti-gīb	bring
2 fmsg.	جبتِ	gíb-t-i	brought	تجيبى	ti-gīb-i	bring
2 pl.	جبتو	gíb-t-u	brought	تجيبوا	ti-gīb-u	bring
1 sg.	جبت	gib-t	brought	أجيب	a-gīb	bring
1 pl.	جبنا	gíb-na	brought	نجيب	ni-gīb	bring

Imperative

2 msg.	جيب	gīb	bring!
2 fmsg.	جيبى	gīb-i	bring!
2 pl.	جيبوا	gīb-u	bring!

These verbs have only one participle (active):

Verb		*Active participle*	
šāf	شاف	šāyif	شايف

16. 3. Defective verbs. These verbs have two consonants and a final vowel. The complete stem of these verbs may be of the vowel pattern *a-a* or *i-i*. Furthermore, the complete stem of each verb has two vowel patterns: *a-a* or *i-i* (for third person) and *a-ē* or *i-ē* (for second and first person). These verbs belong to two vowel classes (complete *vs.* incomplete stem), *i* and *a*. The following are some examples:

Complete 3rd person	2nd and 1st person	*Incomplete*	*Imperative*
رمى ráma	رميت ramē-t	يرمى yí-rmi	إرمى írmi, throw
مشى míši	مشيت mišē-t	يمشى yí-mši	إمشى ímši, go
ملا mála	مليت mal-ēt	يملا yí-mla	إملا ímla, fill
نسى nísi	نسيت nisē-t	ينسى yí-nsa	إنسى ínsa, forget

The inflection of these verbs patterns like that of the double verbs.

مضى maḍa 'sign':

	Complete			*Incomplete*		
3 msg.	مضى	máḍa	signed	يمضى	yí-mḍi	signs
3 fmsg.	مضت	máḍ-it	signed	تمضى	tí-mḍi	signs
3 pl.	مضوا	máḍ-u	signed	يمضوا	yí-mḍ-u	sign
2 msg.	مضيت	maḍē-t	signed	تمضى	tí-mḍi	sign
2 fmsg.	مضيتى	maḍē-t-i	signed	تمضى	tí-mḍi	sign
2 pl.	مضيتوا	maḍē-t-u	signed	تمضوا	tí-mḍ-u	sign
1 sg.	مضيت	maḍē-t	signed	أمضى	á-mḍi	sign
1 pl.	مضينا	maḍē-na	signed	نمضى	ní-mḍi	sign

Imperative

2 msg. 2 fmsg.	إمضى	ímḍi!	sign!
2 pl.	إمضوا	ímḍ-u!	sign!

قرأ qara 'read/study':

	Complete			*Incomplete*	
3 msg.	قرأ	qára,	read/studied	يقرأ	yí-qra, reads/studies
3 fmsg.	قرت	qár-it	read/studied	تقرأ	tí-qra reads/studies
3 pl.	قروا	qár-u	read/studied	يقروا	yí-qr-u, read/study
2 msg.	قريت	qarē-t	read/studied	تقرأ	tí-qra read/study
2 fmsg.	قريتى	qarē-t-i	read/studied	تقرى	tí-qr-i read/study
2 pl.	قريتوا	qarē-t-u	read/studied	تقروا	tí-qr-u read/study
1 sg.	قريت	qarē-t	read/studied	أقرأ	á-qra read/study
1 pl.	قرينا	qarē-na	read/studied	نقرأ	ní-qra read/study

Imperative

2 msg.	إقرأ	íqra	read!/study!
2 fmsg.	إقرى	íqr-i	read!/study!
2 pl.	إقروا	íqr-u	read!/study!

Usually these verbs have two participles of the following pattern:

Verb		*Active participle*		*Passive participle*	
مضى	máḍa	ماضى	māḍi	ممضى	mámḍi
قرأ	qára	قارى	qāri	مقرى	máqri
نسى	nísi	ناسى	nāsi	منسى	mánsi

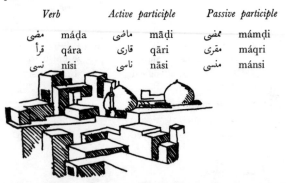

عزومة على عشا عربى

ẓuzūma ẓála ẓáša ẓárab-i

Unit 17. Invitation to an Arab Dinner

سمعت انّ جت لك عزومة الأسبوع اللّى فات .

MOUNIR. — simíẓ-t inn(i) gát-l-ak ẓuzūma il-usbūẓ ílli fāt.
Heard-I that came-to-you(m) invitation the-week which passed.
I heard you received an invitation last week.

أيوه ، احنا اتعزمنا على عشا عربى .

JACK. — áywa, íḥna itẓazám-na ẓála ẓáša ẓárab-i.
Yes, we were invited-we on dinner Arab-(adj).
Yes, we were invited to an Arab dinner.

كانت حفلة ناجحة وانبسطنا من كلّ حاجة فيها .

JACK. — kān-it ḥáfla nágḥ-a, w-imbasáṭ-na min kúll(i) ḥāga [fī-ha.
Was-she party successful(f), and-enjoyed-we from all thing in-it.
It was a successful party; we enjoyed everything.

كلّنا قعدنا على شلت على الأرض .

SANDRA. — kull-ína qaẓád-na ẓála šílat ẓa-l-árḍ.
All-we sat-we on mattresses on-the-ground.
We all sat on pillows on the floor.

مظبوط . ما كانش فيه كراسى .

JACK. — maẓbūṭ. ma-kán-š fī-h karāsi.
Correct. (Neg)-was-(Neg) in-it chairs.
True. There were no chairs.

بنت عربيّة غنّت غنوة عربيّة ، لـكن بالإنجليزى .

SANDRA. — bint ẓarab-í-yya ġánn-it ġínwa ẓarab-í-yya lākin [b-il-ingilīz-i;
Girl Arab-(adj)-(f) sang-she song Arab-(adj)-(f) but in-the-[Englishmen-(adj) ;
An Arab girl sang an Arabic song, but in English;

غنوة ألّفتها هىّ بنفسها .
SANDRA. — ġínwa allif-ít-ha híyya bi-nafs-áha.
song composed-she-it she by-self-her.
a song she herself had composed.

أنا شربت شربات تمر هندى لذيذة لأوّل مرّة . [márra.
SANDRA. — ána šiṙíb-t šarb-āt tamr(i)-hínd-i lazīz-a li áwwil
I drank-I drink-(pl) dates-India-(adj) delicious-(f) for first time.
I drank for the first time a delicious drink, tamarind.

وأكلنا أكل بلدى زىّ الكباب والفول .
JACK. — wikál-na akl bálad-i zayy il-kabāb w-il-fūl.
And-ate-we meal country-(adj) like the-kebab and-the-beans.
And we ate local dishes like kebab and beans.

عملت إيه بعد العشا ؟
MOUNIR. — ʿamál-t ēh baʿd il-ʿáša?
Did-you(m) what after the-dinner?
What did you do after dinner?

دردشنا وسمعنا نكت عربى .
SANDRA. — dardíš-na wi simíʿ-na núkat ʿárab-i.
Chatted-we and heard-we jokes Arab-(adj).
We chatted and listened to Arab jokes.

عمرى ماضحكت فى حياتى زىّ اللّيله دى .
JACK. — ʿúmr-i ma-ḍiḥík-t fi ḥayāt-i zayy il-lēla di.
Age-my (neg)-laughed-I in life-my like the-night that.
I never laughed in my life as I did that night.

وبعدين السّاعة اتناشر النّاس ابتدت تمشى .
JACK. — wi baʿdēn is-sāʿa itnāšar in-nās ibtádi-t tí-mši.
And then the-hour twelve the-people began-she she-go.
Then, at twelve o'clock people started to leave.

17. 1. Derived verbs and form classes. Usually, a derived verb in Arabic is one which is formed from another verb (simple or derived) by some modification which may be internal (infixation) or external (prefixation):

كسر kásar, break → كسّر kássar, smash/break into pieces
رجع rigiʿ, return → راجع rāgiʿ, revise

سرق sáraq, steal → اتسرق itsáraq, be stolen
عمل ع ámal, make, do → استعمل istáعmil, use

Some verbs are derived from other parts of speech like nouns, adjectives, or adverbs:

نضيف niḍīf, clean → نضّف náḍḍaf, clean (verb), make clean
اسم ism, name (noun) → سمّى sámma, name (verb)
آخر āxir, last → أخّر áxxar, get late, delay

Since the various derived verbs have certain characteristics and well defined patterns, they are grouped into form classes.

In Arabic there are at least ten form classes, including simple verbs. Simple triconsonantal verbs yield most of the derived forms; therefore, in this section, only derived verbs obtained from triconsonantal verbs will be discussed. The derivatives of other simple verbs will be described briefly in unit 24.

17. 2. Form class I. This class includes all simple triconsonantal verbs like كتب kátab 'write' and شرب šírib 'drink'. This type of verb has been discussed in unit 15.

Form class II. Derived verbs of this class are the most common and are usually formed from the verbs of class 1 by internal modification. Their stem consists of three different consonants with the second radical doubled (infixation) and the vowel pattern is *a-a* or *a-i*:

كسّر kássar, smash لبّس lábbis, dress someone

Verbs of this form class are transitive, causative, or intensive in meaning and are related in meaning to verbs of form class I. Many intransitive verbs of form class I are made transitive by this derivation process:

جهز gíhiz, be ready جهّز gáhhiz, prepare
درس dáras, study درّس dárris, teach
خبط xábaṭ, knock خبّط xábbaṭ, knock several times

The inflection of these verbs is regular because all three stems (complete, incomplete, and imperative) of the verbs of this class are the same; therefore, these verbs belong to the unchanged vowel class: كلّم kállim 'speak to (someone)'.

	Complete			*Incomplete*		
3 msg.	كلّم	kállim	spoke	يكلّم	yi-kállim	speaks
3 fmsg.	كلّمت	kallím-it	spoke	تكلّم	ti-kállim	speaks
3 pl.	كلّموا	kallím-u	spoke	يكلّموا	yi-kallím-u	speak
2 msg.	كلّمت	kallím-t	spoke	تكلّم	ti-kállim	speak
2 fmsg.	كلّمت	kallím-t-i	spoke	تكلّمى	ti-kallím-i	speak
2 pl.	كلّمتوا	kallím-t-u	spoke	تكلّموا	ti-kallím-u	speak
1 sg.	كلّمت	kallím-t	spoke	أكلّم	a-kállim	speak
1 pl.	كلّمنا	kallím-na	spoke	نكلّم	ni-kállim	speak

Imperative

2 msg.	كلّم	kállim,	speak!
2 fmsg.	كلّمى	kallím-i	speak!
2 pl.	كلّموا	kallím-u	speak!

Like all derived verbs, these verbs have only one participle each, which is formed by prefixing *mi-* to the verb stem. Like most derived verbs, these verbs have verbal nouns, regularly formed on the pattern taCCīC (where C stands for a consonant):

Verb

علّم	ɛállim,	teach
نضّف	náḍḍaf,	clean

Participle		*Verbal noun*	
معلّم	miɛállim, teacher	تعليم	taɛlīm, teaching
منضّف	mináḍḍaf, cleaned	تنضيف	tanḍīf, cleaning

17. 3. Form class III. Derived verbs of this class are less common and are formed from simple verbs by internal modification. The stem consists of three different consonants and the vowel pattern is *ā-i*.

The stems of this class resemble the active participle of the triconsonantal verbs.

Usually, the verbs of this class are transitive: كاتب kātib 'correspond with/write to'.

These verbs belong to the unchanged vowel class because all three stems have the same form. The inflection of these verbs is regular because the stems keep the same form during the inflection process:

قابل qābil 'meet'.

	Complete		*Incomplete*	
3 msg.	قابل qābil	met	يقابل yi-qābil	meets
3 fmsg.	قابلت qábl-it	met	تقابل ti-qābil	meets
3 pl.	قابلوا qábl-u	met	يقابلوا yi-qábl-u	meet
2 msg.	قابلت qabíl-t	met	تقابل ti-qābil	meet
2 fmsg.	قابلتِ qabíl-t-i	met	تقابلى ti-qábl-i	meet
2 pl.	قابلتوا qabíl-t-u	met	تقابلوا ti-qábl-u	meet
1 sg.	قابلت qabíl-t	met	أقابل a-qābil	meet
1 pl.	قابلنا qabíl-na	met	نقابل ni-qābil	meet

Imperative

2 msg.	قابل	qābil	meet!
2 fmsg.	قابلى	qábl-i	meet!
2 pl.	قابلوا	qábl-u	meet!

These verbs also have one participle, which is formed by prefixing mi- or mu- to the verb stem. The verbal noun, except for a few cases (the verbal noun of سافر sāfir is سفر sáfar), is regularly formed by prefixing mi- or mu- (with some vowel change and suffix -a) to the stem on the pattern mi/mu CaCCa .

Verb

ذاكر zākir, study/learn
ساعد sāɛid, help

Participle	*Verbal noun*
مذاكر mi-zākir, having studied	مذكرة muzákra, study
مساعد mi-sāεid, helper/assistant	مساعدة musáεda, help

17. 4. Form class IVa. There are a few verbs in which the base stem begins with *a* on the pattern of form class IV of classical Arabic. These verbs have been borrowed from classical Arabic and are grouped separately to distinguish them from verbs of form class IVb with the prefix *it-*:

أنتج	ántag,	produce
أعلن	áεlan,	announce

The inflection of these verbs is regular in the sense that each stem (complete, incomplete, and imperative) does not change during the inflection process. They have only one participle which is usually formed by adding the prefix *mu-* to the base stem of the imperative: أفاد afād 'be useful'.

	Complete		*Incomplete*	
3 msg.	أفاد afād	was useful	يفيد yi-fīd	is useful
3 fmsg.	أفادت afād-it	was useful	تفيد ti-fīd	is useful
3 pl.	أفادوا afād-u	were useful	يفيدوا yi-fīd-u	are useful
2 msg.	أفدت afát-t	were useful	تفيد ti-fīd	are useful
2 fmsg.	أفدت afát-t-i	were useful	تفيدى ti-fīd-i	are useful
2 pl.	أفدتوا afát-t-u	were useful	تفيدوا ti-fīd-u	are useful
1 sg.	أفدت afát-t	was useful	أفيد a-fīd	am useful
1 pl.	أفدنا afád-na	were useful	نفيد ni-fīd	are useful

	Imperative		*Participle*	
msg.	فيد fīd	be useful!	مفيد mufīd	useful
fmsg.	فيدى fīd-i	be useful!	مفيدة mufīd-a	useful
pl.	فيدوا fīd-u	be useful!	مفيدين mufid-īn	useful

17. 5. Form class IVb. Derived verbs of this form class are obtained from simple verbs by adding the prefix *it-* to the complete base (the third person masculine singular).

There is no corresponding form to this class in classical Arabic. Except for a few verbs, the class IV of classical Arabic does not exist in colloquial Arabic. Usually, the vowel pattern is *a-a* for complete stems and *i-i* for incomplete and imperative stems; therefore, these verbs belong to the vowel class *i*. Usually, these derived verbs are passive or intransitive.

	Simple verb			*Derived verb*	
سرق	sáraq,	steal	اتسرق	itsáraq,	be stolen
وافق	wáfaq,	agree	اتّفق	ittáfaq,	be in accord
وصل	wáṣal,	arrive	اتّصل	ittáṣal,	be in contact

In the last two simple verbs, the initial radical *w* is completely assimilated to the *t* of the prefix *it-*. This is a special case of assimilation (one element becoming like an adjacent element). Other assimilations can be noticed in verbs like اتغلب idġálab 'be defeated' and اسّلخ issálax 'be skinned' where *t* of the prefix *it-* has become *d* and *s*.

The inflection of these derived verbs is regular because the form of each of the three stems (complete, incomplete, and imperative) does not change during the inflection process. Like all derived verbs, these verbs have only one participle, which is formed by adding the prefix *mi-* to the base complete stem (the third person masculine singular):

		Complete			*Incomplete*	
3 msg.	اتولد	itwálad	was born	يتولد	yi-twílid	is born
3 fmsg.	اتولدت	itwálad-it	was born	تتولد	ti-twílid	is born
3 pl.	اتولدوا	itwálad-u	were born	يتولدوا	yi-twílid-u	are born
2 msg.	اتولدت	it-walát-t	were born	تتولد	ti-twílid	are born
2 fmsg.	اتولدت	itwalát-t-i	were born	تتولدى	ti-twílid-i	are born
2 pl.	اتولدتوا	itwalát-t-u	were born	تتولدوا	ti-twílid-u	are born
1 sg.	اتولدت	itwalát-t	was born	اتولد	a-twílid	am born
1 pl.	اتولدنا	ítwaládna	were born	نتولد	ni-twílid	are born

	Imperative	*Participle* (is not used)
2 msg.	اتولد itwílid!	متولد mitwílid, born
2 fmsg.	اتولدى itwílid-i!	
2 pl.	اتولدوا itwílid-u!	

Usually, Arab speakers use the passive participle of the simple verbs instead of the passive form of derived verbs and their participles: ولد wílid 'bear/give birth' مولود mawlūd 'born'.

هوّ مولود سنة ١٩٢١ .
húwwa mawlūd sána-t ١٩٢١.
He born year-(cs) 1921.
He was born in 1921.

17. 6. Form classes V and VI. Verbs of these classes are formed by adding the prefix *it-* to the base stem (complete) of the derived verbs of form class II and III, respectively. All three stems (complete, incomplete, and imperative) of these verbs are the same; therefore, these verbs belong to the unchanged vowel class and their inflection is regular (except for the affixed bound personal pronouns the stems do not change their form). Like all the other derived verbs, they have only one participle. The verbal nouns of these verbs cannot be formed by simple rules. Usually, the meaning of these verbs is either passive or intransitive, while other verbs of form class VI have a reflexive or reciprocal meaning:

Form class II	*Form class III*
كلّم kállim, speak to	راهن rāhin, bet
حرّك ḥárrak, move	حاول ḥāwil, try

Form class V	*Form class VI*
اتكلّم itkállim, speak	اتراهن itrāhin, bet with someone
اتحرّك itḥárrak, be moving	اتحاول itḥāwil, be attempted

	Complete			*Incomplete*		
3 msg.	اتكلّم	itkállim	spoke	يتكلّم	yi-tkállim	speaks
3 fmsg.	اتكلّمت	itkallím-it	spoke	تتكلّم	ti-tkállim	speaks
3 pl.	اتكلّموا	itkallím-u	spoke	يتكلّموا	yi-tkallím-u	speak
2 msg.	اتكلّمت	itkallím-t	spoke	تتكلّم	ti-tkállim	speak
2 fmsg.	اتكلّمت	itkallím-t-i	spoke	تتكلّمى	ti-tkallím-i	speak
2 pl.	اتكلّمتوا	itkallím-t-u	spoke	تتكلّموا	ti-tkallím-u	speak
1 sg.	اتكلّمت	itkallím-t	spoke	اتكلّم	a-tkállim	speak
1 pl.	اتكلّمنا	itkallím-na	spoke	نتكلّم	ni-tkállim	speak

	Imperative			*Participle*		
msg.	اتكلّم	itkállim	speak!	متكلّم	mitkállim	spoken
fmsg.	اتكلّمى	itkallím-i	speak!	متكلّمة	mitkallím-a	spoken
pl.	اتكلّموا	itkallím-u	speak!	متكلّمين	mitkallim-īn	spoken

الاتصال بالاصحاب

il-ittiṣāl bi-l-aṣḥāb

Unit 18. Keeping in Touch with Friends

يا كامل ، تعرف البوسطة فين ؟

JACK. — ya kāmil, tí-ɛraf il-búsṭa fēn?
Oh Kamil, you-know the-post office where?
Kamil, do you know where the post office is?

أيوه . لو تستنّى شويّه حاجى معاك .

KAMIL. — áywa. law t-istánna šwáyya ḥ-āgi maɛā-k.
Yes. If you-wait little (ft)-I come with-you(m).
Yes. If you wait a little, I will come with you.

أنا مستنّى مكالمة تليفونيّة .

KAMIL. — ána mistánni mukálma tilifun-í-yya.
I waiting talk telephone-(adj)-(f).
I am waiting for a telephone call.

تعالَ ، يا كامل ، ردّ ؛ التّليفون بيضرب .

JACK. — taɛāla, ya kāmil, rudd; it-tilifōn bi-y-íḍrab.
Come, oh Kamil, answer; the-telephone (pt)-he-beat.
Come, Kamil, answer; the telephone is ringing.

بختك ، يا چاك . آلو ، أيوه ، أنا اللّى باتكلّم .

KAMIL. — báxt-ak, ya Jack. alō, áywa, ána ílli b-a-tkállim.
Luck-your (m), oh Jack. Hello, yes, I who (pt)-I-speak.
You are lucky, Jack. Hello, yes, speaking.

ياالله ، يا چاك ؛ أنا خلّصت ؛ ياالله نمشى .

KAMIL. — yálla, ya Jack; ána xalláṣ-t; yálla ní-mši.
Come on, oh Jack; I finished-I; come on we-go.
Come on, Jack; I'm finished; let's go.

عايز أشترى ورق بوسطة وظروف جوابات .

JACK. — ʕāyiz a-štíri wáraq búsṭa wi ẓurūf gawab-āt.
Wanting I-buy paper post office and envelopes letter-(pl).
I want to buy some stamps and envelopes.

ممكن تشترى ظروف جوابات من المكتبة .

KAMIL. — múmkin ti-štíri ẓurūf gawab-āt min il-maktába.
Possible you-buy envelopes letter-(pl) from the-stationery.
You can buy envelopes at the stationery shops.

بيبيعوا جوابات البريد الجوى فى البوسطة ؟

JACK. — bi-y-bīʕ-u gawab-āt il-barīd ig-gáww-i fi-l-búsṭa?
(pt)-he-sell-(pl) letter-(pl) the-mail the-air-(adj) in-the-post office?
Do they sell air letters at the post office?

أيوه ، ولازم تلاقى كروت بوسطة هناك كمان .

KAMIL. — áywa, wi lāzim t-lāqi kurūt busṭāl hināk kamān.
Yes, and must you-find cards postal there also.
Yes, and you should find post cards there too.

يا كامل ، فيه حتّه قريّبة نبعت منها تلغراف ؟

JACK. — ya kāmil, fī-h ḥítta qurayyíb-a ní-bʕat mín-ha [tiliġrāf?
Oh Kamil, in-it piece near-(f) we-send from-it telegraph?
Kamil, where is a place nearby to send a cable?

وكمان أنا عايز أطلب ترنك .

JACK. — wi kamān ána ʕāyiz á-ṭlub tránk.
And also I wanting I-ask operator.
I also want to make a long distance call.

عادة اللّوكاندات فيها كل الخدمات دى .

KAMIL. — ʕādatan il-lukand-āt fī-ha kull il-xadam-āt di.
Usually the-hotel-(pl) in-it all the-service-(pl) this.
Usually most hotels provide both services.

18. 1. Derived verbs (cont.). **Form class VII.** Verbs of this class are derived from certain simple verbs by adding to the base stem the prefix *in-* (sometimes *im-*). Although most of these derived verbs are passive, a few are intransitive. The vowel pattern is *a-a* (complete stem) and *i-i* (incomplete and imperative stem). These verbs, belong, therefore, to vowel class *i*:

Complete	*Incomplete*	*Imperative*	
انضرب inḍárab	ينضرب yi-nḍírib	انضرب inḍírib	be beaten
اندهش indáhaš	يندهش yi-ndíhiš	اندهش indíhiš	be surprised
انفجر imfágar	ينفجر yi-mfígir	انفجر imfígir	explode
انبسط imbásaṭ	ينبسط yi-mbísiṭ	انبسط imbísiṭ	be pleased

The inflection of the verbs of this class is regular, that is, the stems do not change. Usually, the participle is formed by adding to the imperative stem the prefix *mu*- or *mi*-. The verbal nouns from verbs of this class are regularly formed on the pattern inCiCāC:

verb	*participle*	*verbal noun*
اندهش indáhaš	مندهش mundíhiš	اندهاش indihāš
انفجر imfágar	منفجر mimfígir	انفجار imfigār

Notice that *n* of *in* before *f* or *b* becomes *m* by assimilation (imbásaṭ, imfágar).

18. 2. Form class VIII. Verbs of this class are formed by prefixing *i* before and infixing *t* after the first consonant of the base form (complete) of simple verbs. Usually, the meaning of these verbs is unpredictable from the meaning of the simple verbs; therefore, their meanings should be learned with the verbs. The vowel pattern is the same as that for verbs of form class VII:

complete	*incomplete*	*imperative*	
افتكر iftákar	يفتكر yi-ftíkir	افتكر iftíkir	think
امتحن imtáḥan	يمتحن yi-mtíḥin	امتحن imtíḥin	examine
احترم iḥtáram	يحترم yi-ḥtírim	احترم iḥtírim	respect

The inflection of these verbs is regular. Usually, the participle is formed by adding to the incomplete stem the prefix *mi*-; and the verbal noun, when it exists, is regularly formed on the pattern iCCiCāC.

verb	*participle*	*verbal noun*
امتحن imtáḥan	ممتحن mimtíḥin	امتحان imtiḥān
احترم iḥtáram	محترم miḥtírim	احترام iḥtirām

18. 3. Form class IX. There are only a few verbs in this class. Most of them are closely related to the adjectives of color. These verbs have the pattern iCCaCC, of which the last two consonants are the same:

إحمرّ	iḥmárr	become or turn red/blush
إصفرّ	iṣfárr	become or turn yellow
إبيضّ	ibyáḍḍ	become or turn white
إسودّ	iswádd	become or turn black
إسمرّ	ismárr	become or turn brown
إحلوّ	iḥláww	become or turn sweet
إخضرّ	ixḍárr	become or turn green
ازرقّ	izráqq	become or turn blue

The inflection of the complete stems is like that of the double verbs.

Except for the prefix subject pronouns, the incomplete stem is the same as the complete. The participle is formed by prefixing *mi*- to the base stem and changing the vowel stem *a* to *i:*

Complete	*Incomplete*
احمرّ íḥmarr, blushed/turned red	يحمرّ yí-ḥmarr
Imperative	*Participle*
احمرّ íḥmarr	محمرّ míḥmirr

18. 4. Form class X. Verbs belonging to this class are few and are characterized by the prefix *ista*-. The meanings of these verbs are unpredictable from the source verbs and must, therefore, be learned with the verbs. The three stems (complete, incomplete, and imperative) of each verb are the same; they belong, therefore, to the unchanged vowel class.

استعمل	istáʿmil,	use
استأذن	istá'zin,	ask permission
استغرب	istáġrab,	wonder
استفهم	istáfhim,	inquire, question
استحمل	istáḥmil,	support, endure, suffer
استعجل	istáʿgil,	hurry
استقبل	istáqbil,	welcome
استحسن	istáḥsin,	choose, prefer
استخرج	istáxrag,	extract
استبدل	istábdil,	exchange
استعمر	istáʿmar,	colonize

The inflection of these verbs is regular because the stems do not change: the suffixes or prefixes, for the formation of the various complete and incomplete forms, are added directly to the verb stem without its being changed. The participle is formed by prefixing *m-* to the base stem, and the verbal noun (if it is used) is formed according to the pattern istiCCāC:

Imperative	*participle*	*verbal noun*
استعمل istáʿmil	مستعمل mistáʿmil	استعمال istiʿmāl

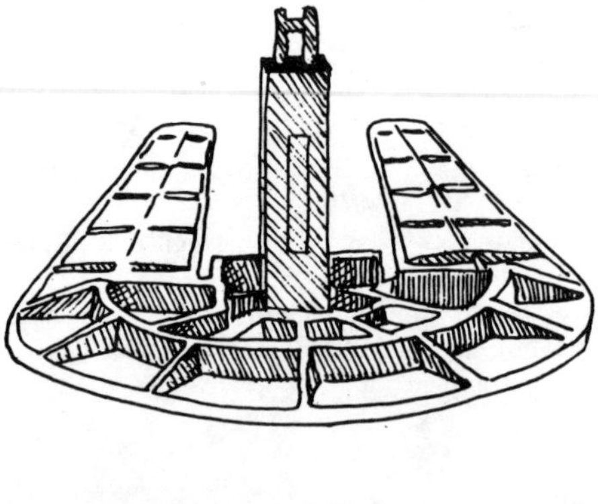

زيارة للارياف

ziyāra li-l-aryāf

Unit 19. A Visit to the Country

يا چون ، عمّى عزمنا نزور عزبته .
ALI. — ya John, ع ámm-i ع azám-na ni-zūr ع izb-ít-uh.
Oh John, uncle-my invited-us we-visit farm-(cs)-his.
John, my uncle has invited us to visit his farm.

دى حاجة لطيفة ، يا على . أنا أحبّ أروح . هىّ فين ؟
JOHN. — di ḥāga laṭīf-a, ya ع áli. ána a-ḥíbb a-rūḥ. híyya fēn?
That thing nice-(f), oh Ali. I I-love I-go. She where?
That's nice, Ali. I would love to go. Where is it?

أنا لازم لى ورقة عشان أرسم خريطة .
ALI. — ána lazím-l-i wáraq-a ع ašān á-rsim xarīṭa.
I must-to-me paper-(one) because I-draw map.
I need a piece of paper to draw a map.

أهى ! عمّى له عزبة كبيرة .
ALI. — ahí! ع ámm-i l-uh ع ízba kibīr-a.
Here! Uncle-my to-him farm big-(f).
Here it is! My uncle has a big farm.

الرّحلة دى جميلة جدّا . يا سلام على المنظر !
BARBARA. — ir-ríḥla di gamīl-a gíddan; ya salām ع ala-l-mánẓar!
The-trip this beautiful-(f) very; oh peace on-the-view!
This trip is very beautiful; and the view, tremendous!

شوفوا الغيطان مزروعة بطّيخ وبطاطس وقوطة .
JOHN. — šūf-u il-ġitān mazrūع-a baṭṭīx wi baṭāṭis wi qūṭa.
See-you(pl) the-fields planted-(f) watermelons and potatoes and tomatoes.
Look at the fields with watermelons, potatoes and tomatoes.

يا عمّى ، ممكن أقطف تفّاحة وبرتقانة ؟

ALI. — ya ɛámm-i, múmkin á-qṭaf tuffāḥ-a wi burtuqān-a?
Oh uncle-my, possible I-pickup apple-(one) and orange-(one)?
Uncle, may I take an apple and an orange?

طبعاً ، اتفضّل ، يا ابنى . عندنا خوخ كمان .

AZIZ. — ṭábɛan, itfáḍḍal, ya íbn-i; ɛand-ína xōx kamān.
Of course, welcome, oh son-my; at-us peaches also.
Of course, help yourself, son; we have peaches too.

دوقى الخوخة دى ، يا باربارا ، شوفى لذيذة إزّاى .

ALI. — dūq-i-l-xōx-a di, ya Barbara, šūf-i lazīz-a izzāy.
Taste-(f)-the-peach-(one) this, oh Barbara, see-(f)tasty-(f) how.
Barbara, taste how sweet this peach is.

شوف البطاطساية دى والقوطاية دى . كبار ازّاى !

BARBARA. — šūf il-baṭaṭsā-ya di wi-l-quṭā-ya di. kubār izzāy!
Look the-potato-(one) this and the-tomato-(one) this. Big(pl) how!
Look at this potato and this tomato. How big!

ياالله ، نقطّع بطّيخة . دى زىّ السكّر .

AZIZ. — yálla, n-qáṭṭaɛ baṭṭīx-a; di zayy is-súkkar.
Come on, we-cut melon-(one); this like the-sugar.
Let's cut a melon; they are very sweet.

فين الموز ، يا عمّى ؟ عايز آكل موزة .

ALI. — fēn il-mōz, ya ɛámm-i? ɛāyiz ākul mōz-a.
Where the-bananas, oh uncle-my? Wanting I eat banana-(one).
Where are the bananas, uncle? I want to eat a banana.

إحنا انبسطنا هنا . متشكّرين جدّاً ، يا عمّ عزيز .

BARBARA. — íḥna imbasáṭ-na hína. mitašakkir-īn gíddan, ya [ɛámm(i) ɛazīz.
We enjoyed-we here. Thankful-(pl) very, oh uncle Aziz.
We enjoyed it here. Thank you very much, Uncle Aziz.

19. 1. Collective nouns. Collective nouns are singular in form but plural in meaning, e.g.:

سمك sámak, fish	بقر báqar, cattle	موز mōz, bananas
برتقان burtuqān, oranges	دبّان dibbān, flies	شجر šágar, trees

ضرب ḍarb, beating ورق wáraq, paper غنم ġánam, sheep
جزر gázar, carrots مشمش míšmiš, apricots فجل figl, radishes

Collective nouns are inflected for definiteness only.

In some cases, collective nouns are treated as plural nouns used with quantifiers, e.g. شوية šwáyya 'some/little' and كتير kitīr 'a lot/much':

شويّة سمك šwáyya sámak, some fish
سمك كتير sámak kitīr, a lot of fish

In other cases, collective nouns are treated as singular nouns as, for example, when used before adjectives:

ده سمك كويّس da sámak kwáyyis. This is good fish.

Most collective nouns are masculine. A few collective nouns end in *a* and are feminine:

كمّترة kummítra, pears قوطة qūṭa, tomatoes

19. 2. Unit nouns. Unit nouns indicate only one unit of a kind and are formed by adding the *-a* (ة), which is the sign for feminine nouns and adjectives, to collective nouns:

لمون lamūn, lemon لمونة lamūn-a, one lemon
جاموس gamūs, water buffaloes جاموسة gamūs-a, one water buffalo

If a collective noun ends in *a* (ة) then the unit noun is formed by lengthening the final *a* and adding -ya:

كمّتراية kummitrā-ya, one pear قوطاية quṭā-ya, one tomato

Unit nouns are treated as feminine nouns because they end in *a* and like feminine nouns, they have three forms: singular, dual, and plural:

Collective	*Unit*	*Dual*	*Plural*	*English*
برتقان burtuqān	برتقانة burtuqān-a	برتقانتين burtuqan-t-ēn	برتقانات burtuqan-āt,	orange
قوطة qūṭa	قوطاية quṭā-ya	قوطايتين quṭay-t-ēn	قوطايات quṭa-yāt,	tomato

The plural form of unit nouns occurs only with numbers three through ten: خمس خوخات xámas xuxāt 'five peaches'. After numbers above ten, the singular form is used:

أربعين بيضة arbiɛīn bēḍa, forty eggs

Some verbal nouns of the simple verb stems (ضرب ḍarb 'beating' from the verb ضرب ḍárab 'beat') derive their unit nouns in the same way, i.e., by adding the suffix *-a*: ضربة ḍárb-a 'a beating'.

There are some collective nouns from which unit nouns cannot be derived by adding the suffix *-a*. In such cases, the unit noun is formed by the collective noun preceded by a noun indicating a unit corresponding to the English expressions "a piece, a grain, a bite", etc. There are few such specialized nouns indicating a unit; usually they are feminine with sound (regular) or broken (irregular) plurals:

Singular		*Plural*	
حتّة ḥítta,	a piece	حتت ḥíttat,	pieces
حبّة ḥábba,	a grain/seed	حبّات ḥabb-āt,	grains/seeds

These nouns are in construct state with collective nouns, e.g.:

لقمة عيش
lúkm-it ɛēš
piece/bite-(cs) bread
a piece of bread

Unit 20. العرب والتّقدّم

il-ɛárab w-it-taqáddum

The Arabs and Progress

ايه رأيك من سفريّاتك ، يا سام ؟

ALI. — ēh rá'y-ak min safariyy-ít-ak, ya Sam?
What opinion-your(m) from traveling-(cs)-your(m), oh Sam?
What is your impression from your traveling, Sam?

قصدك بخصوص زيارتى للبلاد العربيّة ؟

SAM. — qáṣd-ak bi xuṣūṣ ziyár-t-i li-l-bilād il-ɛarab-í-yya?
Intention-your(m) with regard visit-(cs)-my to-the-countries the-[Arabs-(adj)-(f)?
You mean my visit to the Arab countries?

أيوه ، يا سام . أرجو إنّ السّياحة كانت مفيدة .

ALI. — áywa, ya Sam. a-rgū inn is-siyāḥa kān-it mufīd-a.
Yes, oh Sam. I-hope that the-tour was-she useful-(f).
Yes, Sam. I hope the tour has been successful.

طبعاً ، يا على . ده انا استفدت كتير منها .

SAM. — ṭábɛan, ya ɛáli. d-ána istafát-t kitīr mín-ha.
Naturally, oh Ali. This-I took advantage-I much from-it.
Surely, Ali. I benefited a lot from it.

بصراحة فكرتى عن العرب اتغيّرت خالص .

SAM. — bi-ṣarāḥa fikr-ít-i ɛan il-ɛárab itġayyár-it xāliṣ.
With-frankness thinking-(cs)-my on the-Arabs changed-she com-[pletely.
Frankly, it has completely changed my opinion about the [Arabs.

أظنّ إنّك لاقيت استقبال طيّب جدّاً هنا .

ALI. — a-ẓúnn ínn-ak laqē-t istiqbāl ṭáyyib gíddan hína.
I-think that-you(m) found-you(m) reception good very here.
It seems you have had a good reception here.

بلا شكّ ، لازم تفتخر بكرم بلادكم .
SAM. — bi-lā šakk, lāzim ti-ftíxir bi-káram balád-kum.
With-no doubt, must you-be proud with-generosity country-your(pl).
Certainly, you should be proud of your hospitality.

واعتبار العرب للزّاير حاجة عظيمة .
SAM. — w-iɛtibār il-ɛárab li-z-zāyir ḥāga ɛaẓīm-a.
And-consideration the-Arabs for-the-visitor thing great-(f).
And the respect Arabs have for a visitor is great.

لَكن المدهش هنا هوّ التّقدّم الهايل .
SAM. — lākin il-múdhiš hína húwwa it-taqáddum il-hāyil.
But the-outstanding here he the-progress the-tremendous.
But the outstanding thing here is the tremendous progress.

ما تنساش إنّ من وقت التّحرّر من الاستعمار ،
ALI. — ma-ti-nsā-š ínn(i) min waqt it-taḥárrur min il-istiɛmār,
(Neg)-you-forget-(neg) that from time the-liberation from the-[colonialism,
Don't forget that since we won our freedom from colonialism,

الإصلاح فى البلاد العربيّة كان ظاهر ومهمّ جدّاً . [giddan.
ALI. — il-iṣlāḥ fi-l-bilād il-ɛarab-i-yya kān ẓāhir wi muhímm
the-reform in-the-countries the-Arabs-(adj)-(f) was clear and [important very.
the development of the Arab world has been great.

وخصوصاً فى التّعليم ، فهوّ حقّ للجميع دلوقت . [dilwáqti.
SAM. — wi xuṣūṣan fī-t-taɛlīm, fa-húwwa ḥaqq li-l-gámiɛ
And especially in-the-education, and-he right for-the-whole now.
Especially with education, which is now everyone's right.

فعلاً ، يا سام ، كل ده تغيير مهمّ لنا .
ALI. — fíɛlan, ya Sam, kúll(i) da taġyīr muhímm l-ína.
Indeed, oh Sam, all this changing important for-us.
Indeed, Sam, it is an important change for us.

20. 1. Verbal nouns. Usually, each Arabic verb has a noun derived from it. This noun indicates the action of the verb and is called a verbal noun.

In English, nouns derived from verbs can be easily predicted. For example, from the verbs "educate" and "examine" the nouns "education", "educating" and "examination", "examining" are derived. In Arabic, no set rules for the formation of verbal nouns from simple verbs can be supplied. However, there are five types of derived verbs (with few exceptions) which form verbal nouns regularly. These derived verbs belong to verb forms II, III, VII, VIII, and X.

Below are some examples of verbal nouns of simple and derived verbs. Each type of derived verb has its own characteristic pattern for the formation of verbal nouns. The verbal nouns of simple verbs must be memorized.

Simple verb	*Verbal noun*
درس dáras, study	درس dars, lesson
خرج xárag, go out	خروج xurūg, going out/exit

Verbal nouns from derived verbs:

Verb Form II

سجّل sággil, record — تسجيل tasgīl, recording

ربّى rábba, rear/train — تربية tarbíya, educating/good manners

Verb Form III

قابل qābil, meet — مقابلة muqábla, meeting

ذاكر zākir, study — مذاكرة muzákra, studying

Verb Form VII

انفجر imfágar, explode — انفجار imfigār, explosion

امتحن imtáḥan, examine — امتحان imtiḥān, examination

Verb Form VIII

اكتشف iktášaf, discover — اكتشاف iktišāf, discovery

Verb Form X

استقبل istáqbil, receive — استقبال istiqbāl, reception

The verbal noun of سافر sāfir 'travel' is سفر sáfar 'travel/traveling'; and that of غنّى gánna 'sing' is غناء ġinā 'singing'.

In indicating the number of actions performed, verbal nouns of certain simple verbs can be treated like collective nouns, i.e., they can form unit nouns by taking the suffix *-a* (ة):

ضرب ḍarb, beating　　ضربتين ḍarb-it-ēn, two beatings
ضربة ḍárb-a, one beating　　ضربات ḍarb-āt, beatings

The verbal noun may function as a verb complement for emphasis or to indicate the number of actions performed.

ضربه ضرب مظبوط .
ḍárab-uh ḍárb(i) maẓbūṭ.
Beat-him beating good.
He beat him soundly.

شغلتك إيه ؟

Unit 21. *šuġl-ít-ak ēh?* What Is Your Job?

قول لى ، يا على ، مهنتك إيه ؟

JIM. — qúl-l-i, ya ع‎áli, mihn-ít-ak ēh?
Tell-to-me, oh Ali, occupation-(cs)-your(m) what?
Tell me, Ali, what is your profession?

أنا مفتّش فى الجمرك ، يا چيم .

ALI. — ána mufáttiš fi-l-gúmruk, ya Jim.
I inspector in-the-custom house, oh Jim.
I am an inspector at the custom house, Jim.

وانت يا أحمد ، حضرتك مهندس ، مش كده ؟

JIM. — w-ínta, ya áḥmad, ḥaḍrít-ak muhándis, miš kída?
And-you(m), oh Ahmad, sir-your(m) engineer, not so?
And you are an engineer, aren't you, Ahmad?

أيوه ، يا جيم ، كل واحد منّا متخصّص فى مهنة .

AHMAD. — áywa, ya Jim, kúll(i) wāḥid mín-na mitxáṣṣaṣ fi [míhna.
Yes, oh Jim, all one from-us specialized in trade.
Yes, Jim, each one of us has a different profession.

أنا عارف إن واحد من اخواتك حكيم .

JIM. — ána ع‎ārif ínn(i) wāḥid min ixwāt-ak ḥakīm,
I knowing that one from brothers-your(m) physician,
I know that one of your brothers is a physician,

وأخ تانى هوّ ظابط فى الجيش . مش كده ؟

JIM. — wi axx tāní húwwa ẓābiṭ fi-g-gēš, miš kída?
and brother other he officer in-the-army, not so?
and another is an officer in the army, isn't he?

وهم اخواتك بيعملوا ايه ؟

JIM. — wi húmma ixwāt-ak; b-yi-ʿamíl-u ēh?
And they sisters-your(m); (pt)-he-do-(pl) what?
What about your sisters, Ali; what do they do?

واحدة منهم متجوّزة لتاجر فى بيروت .

ALI. — wáḥd-a mín-hum mitgawwíz-a li-tāgir fi-biyrūt.
One-(f) from-them married-(f) to-merchant in-Beirut.
One is married to a merchant in Beirut.

بصراحة جوزها بقّال وعنده محلّ كبير .

AHMAD. — bi-ṣarāḥa gúz-ha baqqāl wi ʿánd-uh maḥáll kibīr.
In-frankness husband-her grocer and at-him place big.
Actually her husband is a grocer and has a big store.

أمّا التانية ، فجوزها ترزى فى القاهرة .

AHMAD. — ámma-t-tány-a, fa gúz-ha tárzi fi-l-qāhira.
As for-the-other-(f), and husband-her tailor in-the-Cairo.
As for the other sister, her husband is a tailor in Cairo.

وهىّ بتزاول فنّ التّجميل فى صلون للستّات .

AHMAD. — wi híyya bi-tzāwil fann it-tagmīl fi ṣalōn li-s-sitt-āt.
And she (pt)-practice art the-beauty in shop for-the-woman-(pl).
And she is a beautician in a shop there.

كمان لنا أخّ فلاّح فى قرية وله عزبة كبيرة .

AHMAD. — kamān lī-na axx fallāḥ fi qárya wi l-uh ʿízba kibīr-a.
Also to-us brother farmer in village and to-him farm big-(f).
Then, we have a brother who is a farmer in the village and has a big farm.

ولسّه أخّ آخر كهربائى فى البلديّة .

ALI. — wi líssa axx āxar kahrabā'i fi-l-balad-í-yya.
And still brother other electrician at-the-country-(adj)-(f).
Still another brother is an electrician for the municipality.

21. 1. Abstract nouns are formed from other nouns or adjectives by adding the suffix يّة -íyya:

مديريّة mudiríyya (mudīr 'manager'), province
حرّيّة ḥurríyya (ḥurr 'free'), freedom

There are some adjectives (feminine) derived from nouns which have the same forms as the abstract nouns:

اشتراك	ištirāk,	participation
اشتراكى	ištirāk-i,	socialist (m)
اشتراكيّة	ištirak-í-yya,	socialist (f) or socialism

However, the adjective حرّ ḥurr 'free (m)' has the feminine form حرّة ḥúrr-a 'free (f)'.

21. 2. Nouns of place. Some nouns can be derived from verbs which indicate the place of the action or the instrument or actor performing the action. Usually, nouns of place are formed by the verb stem with prefix ma-. كتب kátab 'write', مكتب máktab (makātib) 'office/desk'.

21. 3. Nouns of instrument or **actor** are usually formed by the stem of the verb and the prefix mu- or mi- and occasionally ma-: فتح fátaḥ 'open' مفتاح muftāḥ (mafātīḥ) 'key'.

21. 4. Nouns of profession have a characteristic pattern, as those listed below:

بقّال (بقالين)	baqqāl (baqqalīn),	grocer
فلاح (فلاحين)	fallāḥ (fallahīn),	farmer
بسطجى (بسطجيية)	bustági (bustagíyya),	mailman
تاجر (تجار)	tāgir (tuggār),	merchant
حكيم (حكما)	ḥakīm (ḥukáma),	physician

اعياد واجازات

aعyād w-agaz-āt

Unit 22. Holidays and Vacations

يا سام ، يوم الحدّ اللّى جاىّ يوم شمّ النّسيم .

ALI. — ya Sam, yōm il-ḥádd, ílli gayy yōm šamm in-nasīm.
Oh Sam, day the-Sunday, which coming day smell the-breeze.
Sam, this Sunday is Shamm il Nesim.

ده يوم عيد ، والنّاس هنا بتخرج فسحة .

ALI. — da yōm عīd, w-in-nās hiná bi-tí-xrug fúsḥa.
This day feast, and-the-people here (pt)-she-go out stroll.
It is a holiday, and people here go on picnics.

هوّ ده عيد مصرى ، والاّ ايه ، يا على ؟

SAM. — húwwa da عīd máṣr-i, wálla ēh, ya عáli?
He this feast Egypt-(adj), or what, oh Ali?
Is it an Egyptian holiday, or what, Ali?

أيوه ، يا سام ، ده يوم عيد أهلى مصرى .

ALI. — áywa, ya Sam, da yōm عīd áhl-i máṣr-i.
Yes, oh Sam, that day feast people-(adj) Egypt-(adj).
Yes, Sam, it is a popular Egyptian holiday.

افتكر يا على ، عندكم أجازات زيادة عن اللّزوم .

SAM. — a-ftíkir, ya عáli, عand-úkum agaz-āt ziyāda عan [il-lizūm.
I-think, oh Ali, at-you(pl) holiday-(pl) more on the-necessary.
I think you have too many holidays, Ali.

طبعاً ، أكتر من اللّى عندكم يا سام .

ALI. — ṭábعan áktar min ílli عand-úkum, ya Sam,
Naturally more from which at-your(pl), oh Sam,
Certainly more than you have, Sam.

أنهم الأعياد المسيحيّة اللّى بتراعوها هنا ؟
SAM. — ánhum il-aɛyād il-misiḥ-í-yya ílli bi-t-raɛ-ū-ha hína?
Which the-holidays the-Christ-(adj)-(f) which (pt)-you-observe-(pl)-her here?
Which of the Christian holidays do you observe here?

عيد الميلاد ورأس السّنة المسيحيّة وعيد القيامة .
FOUAD. — ɛīd il-milād wi rās ís-sána-l-misiḥ-í-yya wi ɛīd [il-qiyāma.
Feast the-birth and head the-year-the-Christ-(adj)-(f) and feast [the-resurrection.
Christmas, the New Year, and Easter.

قول لى ايه هىّ أطول أجازة للمسلمين ؟
SAM. — qúl-l-i ēh híyya áṭwal agāza l-il-muslim-īn?
Tell-to-me what she longest holiday for-the-Moslem-(pl)?
Tell me, which is the longest Moslem holiday?

اكبر عيد هوّ العيد الكبير أو عيد الأضحى .
ALI. — ákbar ɛīd húwwa-l-ɛīd il-kibīr aw ɛīd il-áḍḥa.
Bigger feast he-the-feast the-big or feast the-immolation.
The biggest one is the Great Holiday or the Holiday of [Sacrifice.

وعندنا العيد الصغيّر أو عيد الفطر .
FOUAD. — wi ɛand-ína il-ɛīd iṣ-ṣuġáyyar aw ɛīd il-fiṭr.
And at-us the-feast the-small or feast the-fastbreaking.
And we have the Small Holiday or the Fastbreaking Holiday.

لكن أهمّ عيد فى العالم الإسلامى هوّ مولد النّبى.
FOUAD. — lākin ahámm ɛīd fi-l-ɛālam il-islām-i húwwa [mūlid in-nábi.
But most important feast in-the-world the-Islam-(adj) he birthday [the-Prophet.
But the most important holiday in the Moslem world is the [Prophet's Birthday.

وعلى فكرة هوّ أقصر الأعياد .
ALI. — wi ɛála fíkra, húwwa áqṣar il-aɛyād.
And on thought, he shortest the-feasts.
Which, by the way, is the shortest of the holidays.

22. 1. Derivation of adjectives. Most adjectives are derived from verbs, nouns, and prepositions or adverbs.

Participles used as adjectives are formed regularly, while other adjectives derived from verbs do not follow any set rules of derivation. A great number of adjectives derived from nouns and prepositions are formed regularly by suffixation. Adjectives derived from nouns are formed by adding *i* to the singular form of a noun ending in a consonant:

مصرى máṣr-i, Egyptian (maṣr, Egypt/Cairo)
غربى ġárb-i, western (ġarb, west)

Nouns ending in *a* form their adjectives either by dropping *a* and adding *i* or by lengthening (or not) *a* and adding *wi* or *ni*:

زراعة ← زراعى zirāεa → zirāε-i, agricultural
سنة ← سنوى sána → sána-wi, yearly
شتا ← شتوى šíta → šít-wi, pertaining to winter

Adjectives derived from some prepositions (or adverbs) and some nouns are formed by adding āni after the last stem consonant:

اسكندرية ← اسكندرانى iskandaríyya → iskandar-ānī, Alexandrian
أمريكا ← أمريكانى amrīka → amrik-āni, American
آجر ← آجرا· āxir → axr-āni, last
جوّه ← جوّانى gúwwa → guww-āni, internal

Most of the feminine and plural forms of derived adjectives are regularly formed by adding the suffixes -yya for the feminine and -yyīn for the plural:

مصرى máṣr-i, Egyptian (m)
مصريّة maṣr-í-yya, Egyptian (f)
مصريّين maṣr-i-yyīn, Egyptian (pl)

Some of the feminine forms are also used as abstract nouns.

بلد bálad, country
بلديّة balad-í-yya, rural (f)
بلديّة balad-íyya, municipality

22. 2. Comparative and superlative forms of adjectives. For comparing the quality of two persons or objects and for expressing the superlative condition of an adjective qualifying a noun, Arabic has a special form of adjective for both which depends on the structure of the adjective:

A. The comparative/superlative pattern of a three consonant adjective is aCCaC, where C is any consonant or *w*, but not *y*, as in the examples below:

صغيّر ṣuġáyyar	اصغر áṣġar,	small, -er, -est
طويل ṭawīl	أطول áṭwal,	long, -er, -est
سهل sahl	أسهل áshal,	easy, easier, easiest

The comparative form of كويّس kwáyyis 'good' is أحسن áḥsan 'better/best'.

B. If the last two consonants of an adjective are the same, the comparative/superlative form is aCaCC:

مهم muhímm	أهم ahámm,	important, more, most
صحيح ṣaḥīḥ	آصح aṣáḥḥ,	true, -er, -est

C. If the adjective ends in *w* or *i*, the comparative/superlative form is aCCa:

حلو ḥilw	أحلى áḥla,	sweet, -er, -est
غنى ġáni	أغنى áġna,	rich, -er, -est

D. If the adjective has more than three consonants, the comparative is formed by the masculine form of the adjective plus either the word أكتر áktar 'more' or أحسن áḥsan 'better':

معروف maɛrūf,	known
معروف أحسن maɛrūf áḥsan,	better known
مشغول mašġūl,	busy
مشغول أكتر mašġūl áktar,	busier

E. The comparative/superlative form does not change for gender or number.

F. The comparative form is always followed by the preposition من min 'from', which introduces the person or object being compared:

الولد أكبر من البنت .
il-wálad ákbar min il-bínt.
The-boy older/bigger from the-girl.
The boy is older/bigger than the girl.

G. Comparison wihout comparative form. Occasionally, the simple adjective followed by the prepositio عن ʕan 'from' is used to express the comparative form:

حسّن كبير عن أخوك .
ḥássan kibīr ʕan axū-k.
Hassan big from brother-your (m).
Hassan is bigger than your brother.

H. To express the superlative degree, the comparative form is used in the following ways:

1. Comparative + indefinite noun or واحد wāḥid, واحدة wáḥda, one:

أحلى بنت áḥla bint, the prettiest girl
أحلى واحدة áḥla wáḥda, the prettiest one

2. Preposition من min + comparative + definite plural noun:

من أحلى البنات min áḥla il-banāt, the prettiest of the girls

3. The definite article + comparative:

الأحلى il-áḥla, the prettiest

4. The superlative form of adjectives with more than three consonants is formed like the comparative, but with a different word order: áktar + indefinite noun + adjective:

النّهارده أنا أكتر راجل مشغول .
innahárda ána áktar rāgil mašġūl.
Today I more man busy.
Today I am the busiest man.

I. For "less than" or "least" constructions, the word أقل aqáll (the comparative form of قليل qalīl 'few/little') is placed after the adjectives:

مهمّ أقلّ muhímm aqáll, less important
متعلّم أقلّ mitʕállim aqáll, less educated

Unit 23. قناة السويس

qanāt is-suwēs

The Suez Canal

يا على ، يوم السّبت ، إحنا رحنا فسحة لقناة السّويس .

Sam. — ya ɛáli, yōm is-sábt, iḥna rúḥ-na fúsḥa li-qanāt [is-suwēs.

Oh Ali, day the-Saturday, we went-we stroll to-Canal the-Suez.

Ali, Saturday we went on an excursion to the Suez Canal.

رحتو فين ، يا سام؟ الإسماعيليّة والسّويس ؟

Ali. — rúḥ-t-u fēn, ya Sam? il-ismaɛlíyya w-is-suwēs?

Went-you-(pl) where, oh Sam? The-Ismailia and-the-Suez?

Where did you go, Sam? To Ismailia and Suez?

ده إحنا رحنا لغاية آخر القناة ، يا على .

Sandy. — da íḥna rúḥ-na liġāyit āxir il-qanāt, ya ɛáli.

That we went-we up to last the-Canal, oh Ali.

We went the length of the canal, Ali.

يعنى من البحر الأبيض للبحر الأحمر .

Ali. — yáɛni min il-báḥr il-ábyaḍ li-l-báḥr il-áḥmar?

That is from the-sea the-white to-the-sea the-red?

You mean from the Mediterranean to the Red Sea?

أيوه ، يا على ، ووقفنا شويّة وزرنا حتت مهمّة بسّ .

Sam. — áywa, ya ɛáli, wi wiqíf-na šwáyya wi zúr-na ḥítat [muhímma bass.

Yes, oh Ali, and stopped-we little and visited-we pieces important [only.

Yes, Ali, and we stopped only at a few places of interest.

حبّيتو إزّاى اختلاف الألوان .

Ali. — ḥabbē-t-u izzāy ixtilāf il-alwān?

Liked-you-(pl) how difference the-colors?

Did you enjoy the contrast of colors?

أيوه . كل أصناف الأزهار إللى لونها أصفر وبمبى .
SAM. — áywa. kull aṣnāf il-azhār ílli lún-ha áṣfar wi bámbi.
Yes. All kinds the-flowers that color-her yellow and pink.
Yes. All kinds of yellow and pink flowers.

أراهنك إنّك رحت تتمشّى فى الصّحرا .
ALI. — a-ráhn-ak ínn-ak ruḥ-t ti-tmáššа fi-ṣ-ṣáḥara?
I-bet-you(m) that-you(m) went-you(m) you-take a walk in-the- *[desert.*
I bet you went for a walk in the desert.

آه طبعاً ، وزرنا عيلة بدويّة عظيمة وطيّبة .
SAM. — āh ṭábɛan, wi zúr-na ɛēla badawì-yya ɛaẓīm-a wi [ṭayyíb-a.
Ah naturally, and visited-we family bedouin-(f) great-(f) and *[good-(f).*
Of course, and we visited a wonderful and kind bedouin [family.

الحاجة العجيبة إنّ بنتهم الصّغيّرة كانت شقرا ؛
SANDY. — il-ḥāga il-ɛagīb-a ínn(i) bint-úhum iṣ-ṣuġayyár-a [kān-it šáqr-a;
The-thing the-strange-(f) that girl-their the-small-(f) was-she *[blonde-(f);*
Strange! The couple's young daughter was blond;

وكانوا ساكنين فى خيمة كبيرة لونها إسود مقلّم رصاصى .
SANDY. — wi kān-u sakn-īn fi xēma kibīr-a lún-ha íswid [muqállam ruṣāṣ-i.
and was-(pl) living-(pl) in tent big-(f) color-her black striped *[lead-(adj).*
and they were living in a big black tent with gray stripes.

أظن أنا أعرف البدوى ده . هوّ مش أقرع خالص ؟
ALI. — a-ẓúnn ána á-ɛraf il-bádawi da. húwwa miš áqraɛ [xāliṣ?
I-think I I-know the bedouin that. He not bald completely?
I think I know the man. Isn't he completely bald?

أيوه . لكن مسكين الرّاجل دلوقت أطرش وأعرج كمان .
SAM. — áywa. lākin maskīn ir-rāgil dilwáqti áṭraš w-áɛrag [kamān.
Yes. But poor the-man now deaf and-lame too,
Yes. The poor man is now deaf and lame too.

23. 1. Adjectives of color and bodily defect. Adjectives indicating the basic colors and physical (bodily) characteristics, usually defects, have, like most other adjectives, three forms: masculine, feminine, and plural. These forms are quite different from those of other adjectives. However, the masculine forms of adjectives of color and defect are identical in form with the comparative form of the three-consonant adjectives:

masculine	*feminine*	*plural*	
أحمر áḥmar	حمرا ḥámra	حمر ḥumr,	red
أشقر ášqar	شقرا šáqra	شقر šuqr,	blond
أخضر áxḍar	خضرا xáḍra	خضر xuḍr,	green
أزرق ázraq	زرقا zárqa	زرق zurq,	blue
أصفر áṣfar	صفرا ṣáfra	صفر ṣufr,	yellow
أسمر ásmar	سمرا sámra	سمر sumr,	brown
أبيض ábyaḍ	بيضا bēḍa	بيض bīḍ,	white
أسود íswid	سودا sōda	سود sūd,	black
أطرش áṭraš	طرشا ṭárša	طرش ṭurš,	deaf
أخرس áxras	خرسا xársa	خرس xurs,	dumb
أعمى áεma	عميا εámya	عمى εúmi,	blind

The comparative/superlative form of these adjectives is the same as their masculine singular form, except for إسود íswid, which has the comparative form أسود áswad 'black'.

Some other color words are formed like most of the derived adjectives, that is, by adding the suffix *-i* to the noun:

بنّى	búnn-i,	brown (color coffee)
برتقانى	burtuqān-i,	orange (color orange)

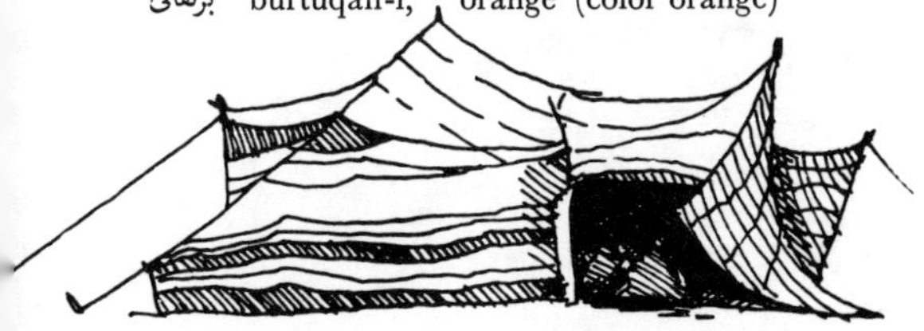

الفرجة على التليفزيون

il-fúrga ʿála it-tilifizyōn

Unit 24. Watching Television

بتعمل ايه يا حلمى ؟

Robert. — bi-tí-ʿmil ēh, ya ḥílmi?
(pt)-you-do what, oh Hilmi?
What are you doing, Hilmi?

أنا باتفرّج على التّليفزيون .

Hilmi. — ána b-a-tfárrag ʿa-t-tilifizyōn.
I (pt)-I-watch on-the-television.
I am watching television.

بيعرضوا إيه النّهارده ؟

Robert. — bi-yi-ʿríḍ-u ēh innahárda?
(pt)-he-show-(pl) what today?
What are they showing today?

بيعرضوا فيلم أمريكانى جميل .

Hilmi. — bi-yi-ʿríḍ-u film amrik-āni gamīl.
(pt)-he-show-(pl) film America-(adj) beautiful.
They are showing a beautiful American film.

يا حلمى ، أنت بتحبّ الأفلام الأمريكانى ؟

Sandra. — ya ḥílmi, ínta bi-t-ḥíbb il-aflām il-amrik-āni?
Oh Hilmi, you (pt)-you-like the-films the-America-(adj)?
Do you like the American films, Hilmi?

أيوه ، أنا بانبسط منهم قوى .

Hilmi. — áywa, ána b-a-mbíṣiṭ mín-hum qáwi.
Yes, I (pt)-I-enjoy from-them very.
Yes, I enjoy them very much.

بتروحوا السّينما برضه ؟

SANDRA. — bi-t-rūḥ-u is-sínima bárḍu?
(pt)-you-go-(pl) the-movie still?
Do you go to the movies any more?

آ . طبعاً . احنا بنروح كتير فى التياترو .

SURAYYA. — āh ṭábعan. íḥna bi-n-rūḥ kitīr f-it-tiyátru.
Oh, naturally. We (pt)-we-go much in-the-theater.
Oh, naturally. We go often to the theater.

فى السّينما بنشوف الأفلام اللّى عايزينها .

HILMI. — f-is-sínima bi-n-šūf il-aflām ílli عayz-ín-ha.
In-the-movie (pt)-we-see the-films which wanting-(pl)-it.
At the movies we see the films we want.

لـكن فى التّليفزيون بيعرضوا أفلام قديمة .

SURAYYA. — lākin f-it-tilifizyōn bi-yi-عríḍ-u aflām qadīm-a.
But in-the-television (pt)-he-show-(pl) films old-(f).
But on television they show old films.

إحنا بنحبّ التّليفزيون عشان بنسمع الأخبار .

HILMI. — íḥna bi-n-ḥíbb it-tilifizyōn عašān bi-ní-smaع il-axbār.
We (pt)-we-love the-television because (pt)-we-listen the-news.
We like television because we can hear the news.

مش بسّ بنسمع ، لـكن بنشوف اللّى بيحصل .

SURAYYA. — miš bass bi-ní-smaع, lākin bi-n-šūf ílli bi-yí-ḥṣal.
Not only ((pt)-we-listen, but (pt)-we-see which (pt)-it-happen.
Not only do we hear, but also we see what happens.

غير كدة ، الأولاد بيحبّوا برامجهم .

SURAYYA. — ġēr kída, il-awlād bi-y-ḥíbb-u baramíg-hum.
Other so, the-boys (pt)-he-like-(pl) programs-their.
Moreover, the children love their programs.

24. 1. Derived double verbs. Double verbs do not have derived verbs of form classes III, VI, and IX. Although the derived double verbs of the other form classes are few in number, they are frequently used. In the following examples, the form class is indicated in parentheses:

complete	*incomplete*	*imperative*
حدّد ḥáddid (II)	يحدّد yi-ḥáddid	حدّد ḥáddid, limit/fix
اتبلّ itbáll (IVb)	يتبلّ yi-tbáll	اتبلّ itbáll, get wet
اتحدّد itḥáddid (V)	يتحدّد yi-tḥáddid	اتحدّد itḥáddid, be fixed
انضرّ inḍárr (VII)	ينضرّ yi-nḍárr	انضرّ inḍárr, get injured
امتدّ imtádd (VIII)	يمتدّ yi-mtádd	امتدّ imtádd, extend
استمرّ istamárr (X)	يستمرّ yi-stamárr	استمرّ istamárr, continue

The three stems of these derived verbs are the same. Their inflection, except for form classes II and V, is the same as for simple double verbs:

	complete		*incomplete*	
3 msg.	اتبلّ itbáll,	got wet	يتبلّ yi-tbáll	gets wet
3 fmsg.	اتبلّت itbáll-it	got wet	تتبلّ ti-tbáll	gets wet
3 pl.	اتبلّوا itbáll-u	got wet	يتبلّوا yi-tbáll-u	get wet
2 msg.	اتبلّيت itballē-t	got wet	تتبلّ ti-tbáll	get wet
2 fmsg.	اتبلّيت itballē-t-i	got wet	تتبلّي ti-tbáll-i	get wet
2 pl.	اتبلّيتوا itballē-t-u	got wet	تتبلّوا ti-tbáll-u	get wet
1 sg.	اتبلّيت itballē-t	got wet	اتبلّ a-tbáll	get wet
1 pl.	اتبلّينا itballē-na	got wet	نتبلّ ni-tbáll	get wet

	imperative		*participle*	
msg.	اتبلّ itbáll	get wet!	متبلّ mitbáll	being wet
fmsg.	اتبلّي itbáll-i	get wet!	متبلّة mitbáll-a	being wet
pl.	اتبلّوا itbáll-u	get wet!	متبلّين mitball-īn	being wet

The inflection of form classes II and V of double verbs is regular and, therefore, similar to the inflection of form class II verbs derived from triconsonantal simple verbs.

24. 2. Derived hollow verbs. Except for derived verbs of form class IVb, which are passive and derived from simple hollow verbs by adding the prefix *it*, other derived hollow verbs are rare:

complete	*incomplete*	*imperative*
	form class IVb	
اتشاف itšāf	يتشاف yi-tšāf	اتشاف itšāf, be seen
اتباع itbāع	يتباع yi-tbāع	اتباع itbāع, be sold
اتشال itšāl	يتشال yi-tšāl	اتشال itšāl, be carried
اتقال itqāl	يتقال yi-tqāl	اتقال itqāl, be said
اتجاب itgāb	يتجاب yi-tgāb	اتجاب itgāb, be brought

other derived verb forms

طوّل ṭáwwil (II)	يطوّل yi-ṭáwwil	طوّل ṭáwwil,	lengthen
جاوب gāwib (III)	يجاوب yi-gāwib	جاوب gāwib,	answer
اطّوّل iṭṭáwwil (V)	يطّوّل yi-ṭṭáwwil	اطّوّل iṭṭáwwil,	be lengthened
اتحاول itḥāwil (VI)	يتحاول yi-tḥāwil	اتحاول itḥāwil,	be attempted
اختار ixtār (VIII)	يختار yi-xtār	اختار ixtār,	choose
ابيضّ ibyáḍḍ (IX)	يبيضّ yi-byáḍḍ	ابيضّ ibyáḍḍ,	turn white
استقال istaqāl (X)	يستقيل yi-staqīl	استقيل istaqīl,	resign

The inflection of the derived hollow verbs is regular because the stems do not change during their inflections. All three stems (complete, incomplete, and imperative) are usually the same (which is not true for simple hollow verbs).

	complete		*incomplete*	
3 msg.	اتباع itbāع	was sold	يتباع yi-tbāع	is sold
3 fmsg.	اتباعت itbāع-it	was sold	تتباع ti-tbāع	is sold
3 pl.	اتباعوا itbāع-u	were sold	يتباعوا yi-tbāع-u	are sold
2 msg.	اتباعت itbáع-t	were sold	تتباع ti-tbāع	are sold
2 fmsg.	اتباعتِ itbáع-t-i	were sold	تتباعى ti-tbāع-i	are sold
2 pl.	اتباعتوا itbáع-t-u	were sold	تتباعوا ti-tbāع-u	are sold
1 sg.	اتباعت itbáع-t	was sold	اتباع a-tbāع	am sold
1 pl.	اتباعنا itbáع-na	were sold	نتباع ni-tbāع	are sold

	imperative			participle		
msg.	اتباع	itbāع	be sold!	متباعين	mitbāع	sold
fmsg.	اتباعى	itbāع-i	be sold!	متباعة	mitbāع-a	sold
pl.	اتباعوا	itbāع-u	be sold!	متباع	mitbaع-īn	sold

24. 3. Derived defective verbs. Simple defective verbs have all derived forms except classes VII and IX, which have no defective members.

complete		incomplete	
ورّى	wárra (II)	يورّى	yi-wárri, show
ساوى	sāwa (III)	يساوى	yi-sāwi, arrange
اترمى	itráma (IVb)	يترمى	yi-trími, be thrown
اتغدّى	itġadda (V)	يتغدّى	yi-tġádda, lunch
اتساوى	itsāwa (VI)	يتساوى	yi-tsāwa, be arranged
اشترى	ištára (VIII)	يشتري	yi-štíri, buy
استنّى	istanna (X)	يستنّى	yi-stanna, wait

imperative		participle	
ورّى	wárri, show!	مورّى	miwárri, shown
ساوى	sāwi, arrange!	مساوى	misāwi, arranged
إترمى	itrími, be thrown!	مترمى	mitrími, (being) thrown
اتغدّى	itġádda, lunch!	متغدّى	mitġáddi, eaten
اتساوى	itsāwa, be arranged!	متساوى	mitsāwi, being arranged
اشترى	ištíri, buy!	مشترى	mištíri, bought
استنّى	istánna, wait!	مستنّى	mistánni, waiting

Notice that in form classes II, III, and VIII the final *a* of the base form is replaced by *i* in the incomplete and imperative forms. All participles of these derived verbs end in *i*.

The inflection of these derived verbs is the same as that of the simple defective verbs:

	complete			*incomplete*		
3 msg.	ودّى	wádda	took away	يودّى	yi-wáddi	takes away
3 fmsg.	ودّت	wádd-it	took away	تودّى	ti-wáddi	takes away
3 pl.	ودّوا	wádd-u	took away	يودّوا	yi-wádd-u	take away
2 msg.	ودّيت	waddē-t	took away	تودّى	ti-wáddi	take away
2 fmsg.	ودّيتِ	waddē-t-i	took away	تودّى	ti-wáddi	take away
2 pl.	ودّيتوا	waddē-t-u	took away	تودّوا	ti-wádd-u	take away
1 sg.	ودّيت	waddē-t	took away	أودّى	a-wáddi	take away
1 pl.	ودّينا	waddē-na	took away	نودّى	ni-wáddi	take away

	imperative			*participle*	
2 msg/fmsg.	ودّى	wáddi	take away!	مودّى	miwáddi
2 pl.	ودّوا	wádd-u	take away!	مودّيه	miwaddí-ya
				مودّيين	miwaddi-yīn!

زيارة لأسوان والسدّ العالي

ziyāra li aswān wi sadd il-ɛāli

Unit 25. A Visit to Aswan and the High Dam

يا عبّاس ، تفتكر انت حتكون فاضي الأسبوع الجايّ ؟

SAM. — ya ɛabbās, ti-ftíkir ínta ḥa-t-kūn fāḍi il-usbūɛ ig-gāy?
Oh Abbas, you-think you (ft)-you-be empty the-week the-coming?
Abbas, do you think you will be free this coming week?

أيوه ، بسّ يوم الاتنين حاشتغل طول النّهار .

ABBAS. — áywa, bass yōm il-itnēn ḥ-a-štáġal ṭūl in-nahār.
Yes, only day the-two (ft)-I-work length the-daylight.
Yes, only Monday I will work the whole day.

ليه يا سام ، انت حتعمل ايه ؟

ABBAS. — lēh, ya Sam, ínta ḥa-tí-ɛmil ēh?
Why, oh Sam, you (ft)-you-do what?
Why, Sam, what are you going to do?

كلّنا حنروح أسوان خمسة ايّام .

SAM. — kull-ína ḥa-n-rūḥ aswān xámas-t-iyyām.
All-us (ft)-we-go Aswan five-(cs)-days.
All of us are going to Aswan for five days.

حنسافر يوم التّلات • حتيجى معانا بقى ؟

SAM. — ḥa-n-sāfir yōm it-talāt. ḥa-tī-gi maɛā-na, báqa?
(ft)-we-leave day the-third. (ft)-you-come with-us, then?
We will leave Tuesday. Are you coming with us, then?

طبعاً ، حاجى ؛ أنا عمرى ما رحت هناك .

ABBAS. — ṭábɛan, ḥ-āgi; ána ɛúmr-i ma-rúḥt hināk.
Naturally, (ft)-I come; I age-my (neg)-go-I there.
Naturally, I will come; I have never been there.

حنسافر بالطيّارة والاّ بالعربيّة ؟
ABBAS. — ḥa-n-sāfir b-iṭ-ṭayyāra wálla b-il-ɛarabíyya?
(ft)-we-leave by-the-airplane or by-the-car?
Are we going to go by plane or by car?

لا كده ولا كده ، حنركب القطر .
SANDRA. — la' kída wála kída, ḥa-ní-rkab il-qáṭr.
No so nor so, (ft)-we-ride the-train.
Neither, we will take the train.

أنا متأكّد ، يا عبّاس ، إنّها حتكون رحلة لطيفة .
SAM. — ána mut'ákkid, ya ɛabbās, inn-áha ḥa-t-kūn ríḥla [laṭīf-a.
I sure, oh Abbas, that-it (ft)-it-be trip nice-(f).
I am sure, Abbas, it will be a nice trip.

أكيد ، حنشوف السدّ العالى .
ABBAS. — akīd, ḥa-n-šūf is-sádd il-ɛāli.
Certain, (ft)-we-see the-dam the-high.
Certainly, we will see the High Dam.

واحنا راجعين حنُقف فى الأقصر .
SANDRA. — w-íḥna ragɛ-īn ḥa-nú-q̇af fi-lúqṣur.
And-we returning-(pl) (ft)-we-stop in-Luxor.
And on our way back, we will stop at Luxor.

السدّ العالى ده مشروع عظيم .
SANDRA. — is-sádd il-ɛāli da mašrūɛ ɛaẓīm.
The-dam the-high that project great.
The High Dam is a great project.

هوّ ده مستقبل مصر .
ABBAS. — húwwa da mustáqbal maṣr.
He this future Egypt.
It is the future of Egypt.

25. 1. The role of كان kān 'was/were', **as a hollow verb.** kān is a hollow verb of the vowel class *u*. Its use corresponds to the English verb "to be" in the past and future tenses. The inflection of the three stems of kān is as follows:

	complete			*incomplete*	
3 msg.	كان	kān,	was	يكون	yi-kūn
3 fmsg.	كانت	kān-it,	was	تكون	ti-kūn
3 pl.	كانوا	kān-u,	were	يكونوا	yi-kūn-u
2 msg.	كنت	kun-t,	were	تكون	ti-kūn
2 fmsg.	كنت	kún-t-i,	were	تكونى	tikūn-i
2 pl.	كنتوا	kún-t-u,	were	تكونوا	ti-kūn-u
1 sg.	كنت	kun-t,	was	أكون	a-kūn
1 pl.	كنّا	kún-na,	were	نكون	ni-kūn

imperative

2 msg.	كون	kūn,	be!
2 fmsg.	كونى	kūn-i,	be!
2 pl.	كونوا	kūn-u,	be!

In Arabic, the incomplete stem of kān is not used to convey the meaning of the verb "to be" in the present tense. Only the complete forms of kān may be used to convey the meaning of the past tense of the verb "to be". The incomplete forms are usually used with the future tense prefix *ha-*.

In a few cases the incomplete forms may be used without the future tense prefix to express a wish or the future tense of the verb "to be" or as a verb auxiliary.

عايز أشترى بيت يكون بعيد عن المطار .
ع̣āyiz a-štíri bēt yi-kūn biع̣īd ع̣an il-maṭār.
Wanting I-buy house he-be far from the-airport.
I want to buy a house that is far from the airport.

إن شاء الله تكون مبسوط .
in šā' allāh ti-kūn mabṣūṭ.
If willed God you(m)-be happy.
I hope you will be happy.

هىّ كانت عيّانة امبارح .
híyya kān-it ع̣ayyān-a imbāriḥ.
She was-she sick-(f) yesterday.
She was sick yesterday.

بكرة هىّ حتكون أحسن كتير .
búkra híyya ha-t-kūn áḥsan kitīr.
Tomorrow she (ft)-she-be better much.
Tomorrow she will be much better.

Usually, the imperative stem forms of kān are not used in Egyptian Arabic; instead, the imperative forms خلّي xálli of the verb خلّى xálla 'let/make' and ابقى íbqa of the verb بقى báqa 'be/become/remain' are used:

خلّيك ولد طيّب ، يا حسّن !
xallī-k wálad ṭáyyib, ya ḥássan!
Let-you(m) boy good, oh Hassan!
Be a good boy, Hassan!

25. 2. The role of كان kān 'was/were' **as a verb auxiliary.** kān may be used before a verb or a modal auxiliary in any verbal sentence or verb cluster.

It can also be used in verbless sentences before the predicate or before prepositions fī 'in', ɛand 'at' and maɛa 'with' in verbless sentences:

A. kān + verb.

In this construction, the stem of kān may be complete or incomplete (with or without the tense prefix *ha* but never with *bi*). The stem of the verb following kān may also be complete or incomplete. If kān is complete, a following incomplete verb may be with or without tense prefixes *bi* or *ḥa*.

كنّا فتحنا الباب .
kún-na fatáḥ-na il-bāb.
Were-we opened-we the-door.
We had/would have opened the door.

In this construction, a complete form of kān followed by a complete verb form conveys the meaning of 'had,' or 'would have'.

كانت بتفتح الباب .
kān-it bi-tí-ftaḥ il-bāb.
Was-she (pt)-she-open the-door.
She was opening/used to open the door.

كانت تفتح الباب .
kān-it tí-ftaḥ il-bāb.
Was-she she-open the-door.
She used to open the door.

كانت حتفتح الباب .
kān-it ḥa-tí-ftaḥ il-bāb.
Was-she (ft)-she-open the-door.
She was about/was going to open the door.

In the preceding three constructions, the first (with *bi*) conveys the meaning of "was doing" or "used to do"; whereas, in the second (without *bi*), the meaning can only be "used to do".

In the preceding and following constructions, both kān and the following verb have the same subject.

احنا حنكون بنفتح الشبّاك .
íḥna (ḥa)-n-kūn bi-ní-ftaḥ iš-šibbāk.
We (ft)-we-were (pt)-we-open the-window.
We will be opening the window.

احنا حنكون فتحنا الشبّاك .
íḥna (ḥa)-n-kūn fatáḥ-na iš-šibbāk.
We (ft)-we-were opened-we the-window.
We will have opened the window.

If kān is incomplete, as in the two examples above (the *ḥa* in parentheses means that it is optional), the following verb may be complete or incomplete (with or without the tense prefix *bi*, but not with *ḥa*).

B. kān + modal auxiliary + verb.

كنّا عايزين نسافر .
kún-na ɛayz-īn n-sāfir.
Were-we wanting-(pl) we-leave.
We wanted to leave.

كان قصدهم يروحوا .
kān qaṣd-úhum yi-rūḥ-u.
Was intention-their he-go-(pl).
They intended to go.

In the preceding constructions, kān is inflected to agree with the following modal auxiliary (and verb), as, for instance, is the case with the modal auxiliaries ɛāyiz, nāwi, ɛammāl, and malzūm or kān remains invariable (third person masculine singular) as, for instance, with bidd, nifs, qaṣd, and ɛála.

C. kān + fī-h = there was/were.
ḥa-y-kūn + fī-h = there will be
kān + ḥa-y-kūn + fī-h = there would have been

In these and the following constructions kān/yi-kūn (with ḥa), third person masculine singular, is invariable:

كان فيه ناس كتير فى السّينما .
kān fī-h nās kitīr fi-s-sínima.
Was in-it people many in-the-cinema.
There were many people at the movies.

حيكون فيه حاجة تانية كمان .
ḥa-y-kūn fī-h ḥāga tány-a kamān.
(ft)-he-be in-it thing other also.
There will be something else too.

كان حيكون فيه دوشة أكتر .
kān ḥa-y-kūn fī-h dáwša áktar.
Was (ft)-he-be in-it trouble more.
There would have been more trouble.

D. kān + ɛand + pr/maɛa + pr = had/had had
ḥa-y-kūn + ɛand + pr/maɛa + pr = will have
kān + ḥa-y-kūn ɛand + pr/maɛa + pr = would have had

كان عندى عربيّة جديدة .
kān ɛánd-i ɛarabíyya gidīd-a.
Was at-me car new-(f).
I had/had had a new car.

حيكون عندنا حفلة كبيرة .
ḥa-y-kūn ɛand-ína ḥáfla kibīr-a.
(ft)-he-be at-us party big-(f).
We will have a big party.

كان حيكون عندك صداع .
kān ḥa-y-kūn ع ánd-ak ṣudāع.
Was (ft)-he-be at-you(m) headache.
You would have had a headache.

E. In all of the above constructions, kān is usually negated by the split negative form ma...š, if not preceded by the tense prefix ḥa; otherwise, miš is placed before ḥa:

ما كنّاش فتحنا الباب .
ma-kun-nā-š fatáḥ-na il-bāb.
(Neg)-were-we-(neg) opened-we the-door.
We hadn't/would not have opened the door.

احنا مش حنكون بنفتح الشبّاك .
íḥna miš ḥa-n-kūn bi-ní-ftaḥ iš-šibbāk.
We not (ft)-we-were (pt)-we-open the-window.
We will not be opening the window.

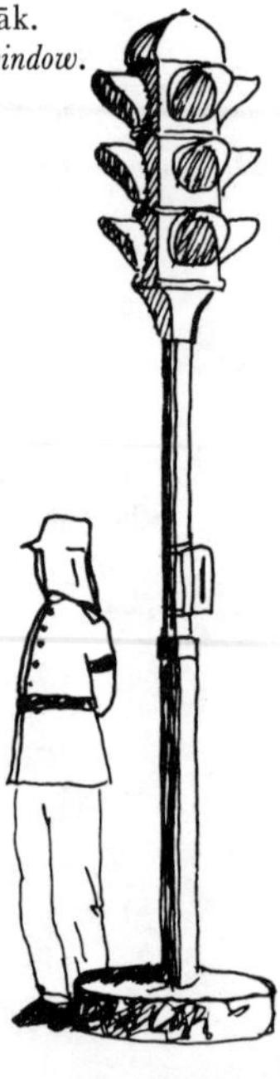

Unit 26. عندي ميعاد

ɛánd-i maɛād

I Have an Appointment

أنا نازل البلد . فيه حدّ جاىّ معاىَ ؟

Ahmad. — ána nāzil il-bálad. fī-h ḥadd gayy maɛā-ya?
I going down the-town. In-it anyone coming with-me?
I am going to town. Anyone coming with me?

استنّ دقيقة ، يا أحمد . أنا خارج كمان .

Sam. — istánna diqīqa, ya áḥmad. ána xārig kamān.
Wait minute, oh Ahmad. I going out also.
Wait a minute, Ahmad. I am going out too.

شهّل شويّه وحياتك ، يا سام ، عشان عندى ميعاد .

Ahmad. — šáhhil šwáyya wi-ḥyā-t-ak, ya Sam, ɛašān ɛánd-i maɛād.
Hurry up little and-life-(cs)-your(m), oh Sam, because at-me appointment.
Hurry up, Sam, please, because I have an appointment.

مش بدرى قوى ؟ كلّ حاجه لسّه مقفوله .

Sam. — miš bádri qáwi? kúll(i) ḥāga líssa maqfūl-a.
Not early very? All thing yet closed-(f).
Isn't it too early? Everything is still closed.

أنت سايق ، يا سام ، والاّ واخد الأتوبيس ؟

Ahmad. — ínta sāyiq, ya Sam, wálla wāxid il-utubīs?
You driving, oh Sam, or taking the-bus?
Are you driving, Sam, or taking the bus?

أنا حاسوق عشان أنا متأخّر كمان .

Sam. — ána ḥ-a-sūq ɛašān ána mit'áxxar kamān.
I (ft)-I-drive because I late also.
I am driving because I am late too.

أقدر آجى معاك ، يا سام ؟
AHMAD. — á-qdar āgi maɛā-k, ya Sam?
I-can come with-you(m), oh Sam?
Can I ride with you, Sam?

أيوه . إنت جاهز ؟ طيّب ياالله بينا .
SAM. — áywa. ínta gāhiz? ṭáyyib, yálla bī-na.
Yes. You ready? Well, come on with-us.
Yes. Are you ready? Let's go then.

صباح الخير . هوّ المدير موجود ؟
AHMAD. — ṣabāḥ il-xēr. húwwa il-mudīr mawgūd?
Morning the-good. He the-director present?
Good morning. Is the director here?

وانا داخل ، هوّ كان خارج ، يا افندم .
SECRETARY. — w-ána dāxil, húwwa kān xārig, y-afándim.
And-I coming in, he was going out, oh-sir.
While I was coming in, he was going out, sir.

أنا عندى ميعاد عشان النّهارده الصّبح .
AHMAD. — ána ɛánd-i maɛād ɛašān innahárda iṣ-ṣúbḥ.
I at-me appointment for today the-morning.
I have an appointment for this morning.

أيوه . هوّ عارف، يا افندم . تتفضّل فنجان قهوة ؟
SECRETARY. — áywa. húwwa ɛārif, y-afándim. ti-tfáḍḍal [fingān qáhwa?
Yes. He knowing, oh-sir. You welcome cup coffee?
Yes. He knows, sir. Would you like a cup of coffee?

لا ، كتّر خيرك ؛ أنا لسّه شارب قهوة .
AHMAD. — la', káttar xēr-ak; ána líssa šārib qáhwa.
No, multiply goodness-your(m); I still drinking coffee.
No, many thanks; I just had coffee.

26. 1. Active and passive participles of simple verbs. Except for hollow verbs, simple verbs usually have two participles: one active and one passive. For triconsonantal and double verbs, the pattern of the active participle is CāCiC.

This pattern is similar to that of the verbs of form class III. The pattern of the passive participle, of the same verbs, is maCCūC. Like adjectives, both these participles have three forms: masculine singular, feminine singular, and plural for both masculine and feminine. The following are some examples:

triconsonantal verb		*active participle*
	msg.	كاتب kātib, clerk/writer
كتب kátab, write	fmsg.	كاتبة kátb-a, clerk/writer
	pl.	كاتبين katb-īn, clerks/writers

passive participle

مكتوب maktūb, written
مكتوبة maktūb-a, written
مكتوبين maktub-īn, written

double verb		*active participle*
	msg.	حابب ḥābib, loving
حبّ ḥabb, love	fmsg.	حبّة ḥább-a, loving
	pl.	حبين ḥabb-īn, loving

passive participle

محبوب maḥbūb, beloved/dear
محبوبة maḥbūb-a beloved/dear
محبوبين maḥbub-īn beloved/dear

The participles of the defective verbs have a different pattern:

defective verb		*active participle*	
	msg.	ماضي māḍi	past/signed
مضى máḍa, sign,	fmsg.	ماضية máḍy-a	past/signed
elapse	pl.	ماضيين maḍy-īn	past/signed

passive participle

ممضي mámḍi,	signed/signer
ممضيّة mamdí-yya	signed/signer
ممضيّين mamḍi-yyīn	signed/signers

The passive voice in Arabic. In English, we say "Ahmad wrote the letter" or "The letter was written by Ahmad". Since the passive construction in Arabic does not name the agent performing the action, the active construction is used when the speaker wants to name the agent. Thus, you may hear:

أحمد كتب الجواب .		الجواب اتكتب .
áḥmad kátab ig-gawāb.	or:	ig-gawāb itkátab.
Ahmad wrote the-letter.		The-letter was written.

The latter construction contains a passive verb and is called in Arabic 'verb constructed with an unknown subject' (مبنى للمجهول mábni li-l-maghūl) because the agent performing the action is not expressed. For the passive in Arabic, the use of the passive participle of the simple verbs is very common.

الجواب مكتوب .
ig-gawāb maktūb.
The-letter written.
The letter is written.

The third person plural of certain active verbs is also used as a passive construction:

قالولى إنّك مش موجود .
qal-ū-l-i ínn-ak miš mawgūd.
Told-(pl)-to-me that-you(m) not present.
I was told that you were not here.

اخبار اليوم

axbār il-yōm

Unit 27. News of the Day

العالم ملخبط الأيّام دى ، يا بيتر .
MOUSA. — il-ع̣ālam miláxbaṭ il-ayyām di, ya Peter.
The-world mixed up the-days this, oh Peter.
The world is mixed up these days, Peter.

هوّ انت شفت جريدة النّهارده الصّبح ؟
MOUSA. — húwwa ínta šuf-t garīd-it innahárda-ṣ-ṣubḥ?
He you saw-you(m) newspaper-(cs) today-the-morning?
Have you seen this morning's paper?

أيوه . لـكن أنا مهتم بالأخبار الرياضيّة بسّ .
PETER. — áywa. lākin ána mihtámm bi-l-axbār ir-riyad-í-yya [bass.
Yes. But I interested with-the-news the-sports-(adj)-(f) only.
Yes. But I am interested in the sports section only.

إزّاى كده ؟ دا إنت ضايع عليك حاجات كتيره .
MOUSA. — izzāy kída? da ínta ḍāyiع ع̣alē-k ḥag-āt kitīr-a.
How so? This you losing on-you(m) thing-(pl) much-(f).
Why? I'm afraid you are missing a great deal.

سيب السّياسة على جمب ، يا موسى . أنت جاىّ والاّ لا ؟
PETER. — sīb is-siyāsa ع̣ála gamb, ya mūsa. ínta gayy wálla [la'?
Leave the-politics on aside, oh Mousa. You coming or not?
Leave politics alone, Mousa. Are you coming?

طيّب . إنت رايح فين ؟ يا ترى للنّادى ؟
MOUSA. — ṭáyyib. ínta rāyiḥ fēn? ya tára li-n-nādi?
Good. You going where? Oh wonder to-the-club?
Fine. Where are you going? To the club?

أيوه ، لـكن حاتغدّى الأوّل .

Peter. — áywa, lākin ḥ-a-tġádda il-áwwil.
Yes, but (ft)-I-have lunch the-first.
Yes, but I am going to have lunch first.

أنا متغدّى خلاص ، الحمد لله ؛

Mousa. — ána mitġáddi xalāṣ, il-ḥámd(u)-li-llāh;
I lunched finished, the-praise-to-God;
I have already had lunch;

لـكن جاىّ معاك . أنا عايز أشوف بيتك .

Mousa. — lākin gayy maع̨ā-k. ána ع̨āyiz a-šūf bēt-ak.
but coming with-you(m). I wanting I-see house-your(m).
but I'm coming with you. I want to see your house.

اتفضّل . بيتى لسّه مدهون بويه جديد .

Peter. — itfáḍḍal. bēt-i líssa madhūn bōya gidīd.
Welcome. House-my still painted paint new.
Please come. My house is newly decorated.

آدى احنا وصلنا . ياالله نشغّل الرّاديو .

Peter. — ād-iḥna wiṣíl-na. yálla ni-šáġġal ir-rádyu.
Here-we arrived-we. Come on we-make work the-radio.
Here we are. Let's turn on the radio.

سامع ؟ الوزارة اجتمعت مرتين الأسبوع ده .

Mousa. — sāmiع̨? il-wizāra igtámaع̨-it marr-it-ēn il-usbūع̨ [da.
Hearing? The-cabinet met-she time-(cs)-(d) the-week this.
Do your hear? The cabinet has met twice this week.

والرئيس الوزارة قابل المعارضة .

Peter. — Wi ra'īs il-wizāra qābil il-muع̨ārḍa.
And head the-cabinet met the-opposition.
And the prime minister has met with the opposition.

27. 1. Active or passive participles of derived and hollow verbs. Derived and hollow verbs have only one participle. The participle of the hollow verbs is formed on the pattern of the active participle of the simple verbs. In this case, the hidden second radical *y* of the hollow verbs appears in the participial form. The participle of the derived verbs is formed by prefixing *mi-* or *m-* to the imperative verb stem.

These participles also have three forms (m, f, and pl):

verb	*participle*
	شايف šāyif
شاف šāf, see	شايفة šáyf-a
	شايفين šayf-īn
	منضّف mináḍḍaf
نضّف náḍḍaf, clean	منضّفة minaḍḍáf-a
	منضّفين minaḍḍaf-īn
	مسافر msāfir
سافر sāfir, leave/ travel	مسافرة msáfr-a
	مسافرين msafr-īn
	مكفّي mikáffi
كفّى káffa (káffi), be sufficient	مكفّيّة mikaffí-yya
	مكفّيين mikaffi-yyīn

The imperative stem is given in parentheses when it differs from the complete stem.

(verb)	*(participle)*
	متأخّر mit'áxxar
اتأخّر it'áxxar, be late	متأخّرة mit'axxár-a
	متأخّرين mit'axxar-īn
	مستحمل mistáḥmil
إستحمل istáḥmil, endure/support	مستحملة mistaḥmíl-a
	مستحملين mistaḥmil-īn

Usually, educated people have *mu-* prefixed to the imperative stem instead of *mi-*. The patterns of the participles of form class IVa and IX are slightly different from the above pattern.

verb	*participle*
	مرسل múrsil
أرسل ársal (irsil), send	مرسلة mursíl-a
	مرسلين mursil-īn
	مصفرّ miṣfírr
إصفرّ iṣfárr, become yellow	مصفرّة miṣfírr-a
	مصفرّين miṣfirr-īn
	مساعد musāɛid
ساعد sāɛid, help	مساعدة musáɛd-a
	مساعدين musaɛd-īn
	مختلف muxtálif
اختلف ixtálaf (ixtílif), differ	مختلفة muxtalíf-a
	مختلفين muxtalif-īn
	مستعمل mustáɛmil
استعمل istáɛmil, use	مستعملة mustaɛmíl-a
	مستعملين mustaɛmil-īn

Derived defective verbs of form class II which end in *a* replace this *a* with *i* in their participial form:

verb	*participle*
	متغدّى mitġáddi
اتغدّى itġádda, have lunch	متغدّيّة mitġaddí-yya
	متغدّيّين mitġaddi-yyīn

زيارة للمتاحف والجوامع

Unit 28. *ziyāra li-l-matāḥif wi-l-gawāmiɛ*
Visiting Museums and Mosques

الزّيارة للمتحف إمبارح كانت لطيفة قوى .

Sam. — iz-ziyāra l-il-máthaf imbāriḥ kān-it laṭīf-a qáwi.
The-visit to-the-museum yesterday was-she nice-(f) very.
The visit to the museum yesterday was very nice.

زرت متحف ايه يا سام ؟

Badri. — zúr-t(i) máthaf ēh, ya Sam?
Visited-you(m) museum what, oh Sam?
What museum did you visit, Sam?

كنّا فى المتحف المصرى .

Sam. — kún-na fi-l-máthaf il-máṣr-i.
Were-we at-the-museum the-Egypt-(adj).
We were at the National Museum of Egypt.

أنا كمان كنت هناك إمبارح ؛ إزّاى ما شفتكش ؟

Badri. — ána kamān kún-t(i) hināk imbāriḥ; izzāy ma- [šuf-t-ák-š?
I also was-I there yesterday; how (neg)-saw-I-you(m)-(neg)?
I also was there yesterday; how come I didn't see you?

أظنّ لمّا انت جيت ، كنّا احنا مشينا .

Sam. — a-ẓúnn lámma ínta gē-t, kún-na íḥna mišī-na.
I-think when you came-you(m), were-we we went-we.
I think that when you came, we were gone.

كان فيه ناس زيادة عن اللّزوم لمّا أنا كنت هناك .

Badri. — kan-fī-h nās ziyāda ɛan il-luzūm lámma ána [kun-t(i) hināk.
Was-in-it people more than the-necessary when I was-I there.
There were too many people when I was there.

واحنا ماشيين ، جودى كانت داخلة .
SAM. — w-íhna mašy-īn, Judy kān-it dáxl-a.
And-we going-(pl), Judy was-she entering-(f).
When we were leaving, Judy was entering.

وبعدين رحتوا جامع عمر ، مش كده ؟
BADRI. — wi baɛdēn rúḥ-t-u gāmiɛ ɛamr, miš-kída?
And then went-you-(pl) mosque Amr, not-so?
Afterwards, you went to the mosque of Amr, didn't you?

أيوه ، أنا شفتك هناك ، كنت بترسم حاجة .
SAM. — áywa, ána šúf-t-ak hināk; kún-t(i) bi-tí-rsim ḥāga.
Yes, I saw-I-you(m) there; were-you(m) (pt)-you-draw thing.
Yes, I saw you there; you were drawing something.

إنت فنّان يا بدرى .
SAM. — ínta fannān, ya bádri?
You artist, oh Badri?
Are you an artist, Badri?

أنا كنت بارسم وكنت باكتب شعر ، يا سام ؛
BADRI. — ána kún-t(i) b-á-rsim wi kún-t(i) b-á-ktib šiɛr, [ya Sam;
I was-I (pt)-I-draw and was-I (pt)-I-write poetry, oh Sam;
I used to draw and write poetry, Sam;

لـكن دلوقتى ما بقيتش أعمله الاّ ساعات .
BADRI. — lākin dilwáqti ma-baq-ít-š a-ɛmíl-uh ílla saɛ-āt.
but now (neg)-became-she-(neg) I-do-it except hour-(pl).
but now I do only occasionally.

وجالى وقت كنت باكل عيش من الرّسم .
BADRI. — Wi gā-l-i waqt kún-t-(i) b-ākul ɛēš min ir-rásm.
And came-to-me time was-I (pt)-eat bread from the-drawing.
Sam, there was a time when I drew for a living.

28. 1. The use and meaning of participles. Participles resemble and behave like both adjectives and verbs. They can also be used as nouns.

A. Like adjectives, active and passive participles have three forms: masculine singular, feminine singular, and plural (see the preceding two sections). They may modify a noun or be a predicate in a verbless sentence. If a participle modifies a noun, it agrees with the noun in definiteness, number, and gender. A participle modifying a definite noun usually takes ílli 'who/that/which', instead of the definite article:

الدكّان اللّى قافل	الباب مفتوح .
id-dukkān ílli qāfil	il-bāb maftūḥ.
the-store which closed	*The-door open.*
the closed store	The door is open.

The participles of derived verbs may be used as active or passive participles, according to the context. Many of the active participles may also be used as passive participles:

الدكّان قافل id-dukkān qāfil, the store is closed.

B. Like verbs, active participles may be followed by an object noun, pronoun or an adverb:

الولد ضارب الكلب .
il-wálad ḍārib ik-kálb.
The-boy (is the one who) beat the-dog.
The boy has beaten the dog.

همّ مسافرين بكرة .
húmma msafr-īn búkra.
They (are the ones who) leaving tomorrow.
They are leaving tomorrow.

أنا عارفك كويّس .
ána ɛárf-ak kwáyyis.
I (am the one who) know-you(m) well.
I know you well.

Passive participles indicate a state or condition, and active participles the doer of the action. Active participles of the verbs of locomotion usually indicate the doer of the action in such situations which correspond to English expressions ending in *-ing* (present participle).

احنا رايحين نتفسّح .
íḥna rayḥ-īn ni-tfássaḥ.
We going-(pl) we-take a walk.
We are going to take a walk.

Active participles of some other verbs (like šāyif, fākir, ع ārif, fāhim, sākin) usually indicate the doer of the action at the present time, which corresponds to the English present tense:

أنا فاهم الحكايه .
ana fāhim il-ḥikāya.
I (am the one who) understand the-story.
I understand the story.

Active participles of verbs other than those mentioned above indicate the doer or the one who has done the action, which corresponds to the English expression *having done* (present perfect):

هوّ عامل واجبه .
húwwa ع āmil wágb-uh.
He (is the one who) has done duty-his.
He has done his duty.

أنا شارب قزازتين بيرة .
ána šārib qizaz-t-ēn bīra.
I (am the one who) have drunk bottle-(cs)-(d) beer.
I have drunk two bottles of beer.

Active participles may replace verbs in verbal sentences.

أنا ناسى أكتب الجواب .
ána nāsi á-ktib il-gawāb.
I (am the one who) have forgotten I-write the letter.
I forgot/have forgotten to write the letter.

C. Some participles are used as nouns and may, therefore, have broken plurals.

singular		*plural*
كاتب kātib,	clerk/writer	كتبة kátaba
ظابط ẓābiṭ,	officer	ظبّاط ẓubbāt

28. 2. Verbal adjectives. Most of the participles are used as adjectives; however, there are participles of some particular verbs which have a characteristic pattern different from that of other participles and which are used as pure and simple adjectives. Usually, the pattern of the verbal adjectives is CVCān:

verb		*verbal adjective*	
زعل zíɛil,	become angry	زعلان zaɛlān,	angry
ملا mála,	fill	مليان malyān,	filled
غار ġār,	be jealous	غيران ġayrān,	jealous
عطش ɛíṭiš,	be thirsty	عطشان ɛaṭšān,	thirsty

Unit 29. على مهلك

ɛála máhl-ak

Take It Easy

يا توماس ، رحت فين إمبارح ؟

ALI. — ya Thomas, rúḥ-t fēn imbāriḥ?
Oh Thomas, went-you(m) where yesterday?
Thomas, where did you go yesterday?

إمبارح إحنا زرنا الهرم .

THOMAS. — imbāriḥ íḥna zúr-na-l-háram.
Yesterday we visited-we-the-Pyramid.
Yesterday we visited the Pyramids.

أنا باشتغل هناك فى مينا هاوس، لـكن ما شفتكمش . [ukúm-š.

ALI. — ána b-a-štáġal hināk fi mīna háws, lākin ma-šuf-t-
I (pt)-I-work there in Mena House, but (neg)-saw-I-you(pl)-
I work there at Mena House, but I did not see you. *(neg).*

إحنا رحنا بدرى قوى عشان الحرّ .

BARBARA. — íḥna rúḥ-na bádri qáwi ɛašān il-ḥárr.
We went-we early very because the-heat.
We went very early because of the heat.

وأنا بابتدى أشتغل بعد الضهر .

ALI. — w-ána b-a-btídi a-štáġal baɛd iḍ-ḍúhr.
And-I (pt)-I-begin I-work after the-noon.
And I start to work in the afternoon.

إحنا حنروح تانى بكرة ، يا على .

BARBARA. — íḥna ḥa-n-rūḥ tāni búkra, ya ɛáli.
We (ft)-we-go again tomorrow, oh Ali.
We are going again tomorrow, Ali.

الحقيقة إحنا كنّا ناويين نروح النّهارده .

Thomas. — il-ḥaqīqa íḥna kún-na nawy-īn ni-rūḥ innahárda.
The-fact we were-we intending-(pl) we-go today.
Actually, we had planned to go today.

لَكن زىّ العادة ، صحينا وخرى .

Thomas. — lākin zayy il-ɛāda, ṣiḥī-na wáxri.
But as the-custom, woke up-we late.
But as usual, we got up late.

بكرة حنطلع هناك كلّنا بدرى .

Ali. — búkra ḥa-ní-ṭlaɛ hināk kull-ína bádri.
Tomorrow (ft)-we-get out there all-us early.
Tomorrow all of us will go out there early.

تعالى نتّفق من دلوقتِ ، يا على ؛

Barbara. — taɛāla ni-ttífiq min dilwáqti, ya ɛáli;
Come here we-agree from now, oh Ali;
Let's agree right now, Ali;

إنت مش حتسوق بسرعة .

Barbara. — ínta miš ḥa-t-sūq bi-súrɛa.
you not (ft)-you(m)-drive with-speed.
you are not going to drive fast.

أنا نادر لمّا أزيد عن السّرعة المسموح بها .

Ali. — ána nādir lámma a-zīd ɛan is-súrɛa il-masmūḥ bī-ha.
I rare when I-increase on the-speed the-permitted with-it.
I rarely exceed the speed limit.

أنا لازم أمشى حالاً . أنا وراىَ ميعاد .

Thomas. — ána lāzim á-mši ḥālan; ána warā-ya maɛād.
I must I-go immediately; I behind-me appointment.
I must leave immediately; I have an appointment.

على مهلك . خد بالك من العربيّة دى ، يا اخى .

Ali. — ɛála máhl-ak. xud bāl-ak min il-ɛarabíyya di, y-āx-i.
On slowness-your(m). Take care-your(m) from the-car that, oh-
Take it easy. Watch that car, pal. *[brother-my.*

29. 1. Verb clusters. A verb cluster, which in Egyptian Arabic is also a verbal sentence, consists of two or three verbs in sequence. It may also consist of the active participle of the first verb plus one or two other verbs in sequence. There are, therefore, two types of verb clusters.

A. Verb/active participle + verb:

يعرف يعوم .	هوّ عارف يعوم .
Yí-ɛaraf yi-ɛūm.	huwwa ɛārif yi-ɛūm.
He-know he-swim.	*He (is the one who) knows he-swim.*
He knows how to swim.	He knows how to swim.

B. Verb/active participle + verb + verb:

هوّ نسى يخرج يشترى عيش .
huwwa nísi yú-xrug yi-štíri ɛēš.
He forgot he-go out he-buy bread.
He forgot to go out and buy bread.

هوّ ناسى يخرج يشترى عيش .
huwwa nāsi yú-xrug yi-štíri ɛēš.
He (is the one who) has forgotten he-go out he-buy bread.
He forgot to go out and buy bread.

Verbs in each of the two constructions above have the same subject. In the first construction (A), only verbs of the four pairs in group I and verbs in group II below or their respective participles can occur in the first position.

GROUP I

راح rāḥ, go	جه gih, come
خرج xárag, go out	دخل dáxal, come in/enter
طلع ṭíliɛ, go up	نزل nízil, come down/descend
قعد qáɛad, sit down	وقف wíqif, stand up

GROUP II

قدر qídir, be able	فضل fíḍil, continue/remain
عرف ɛírif, know	فضّل fáḍḍal, prefer
حاول ḥāwil, try/practice	ابتدا ibtáda, begin/start
حبّ ḥabb, like/love	طلب ṭálab, ask/demand
نسى nísi, forget	خللى xálla, let/make

The restriction on the occurrence of verbs in the position just discussed and in the first and second position of the second construction (B) is similar to the restriction of certain English verbs followed by verbals as in "I want to start to collect stamps" or "He tried to sit and listen calmly."

The first verb may be either complete or incomplete (with or without tense prefixes):

عرفت أكتب .	بأعرف أكتب .
ɛiríf-t a-ktib.	b-á-ɛraf á-ktib.
knew-I I-write.	*(pt)-I-know I-write.*
I knew how to write.	I know how to write.

The second verb may be any verb in complete or incomplete form, depending on the first verb: if the first verb is incomplete, it can be followed only by an incomplete verb form; and if it is complete, it may be followed by either an incomplete or a complete verb form. A verb in group II, however, can be followed only by an incomplete form:

أقدر أروح .	ابتدى يمطر .
á-qdar a-rūḥ.	ibtáda yú-mṭur.
I-be able I-go.	*began he/it-rain.*
I can go.	It began to rain.
جينا كلنا .	حايحاول يغنّى .
gē-na kál-na.	ha-y-ḥāwil yi-ġánni.
came-we ate-we.	*(ft)-he-try he-sing.*
We came and ate.	He will try to sing.

In the second construction, the first verb can only be one of the verbs in group II, complete or incomplete (with or without tense prefixes). The second verbs can only be one of the verbs of the four pairs in group I. The third verb may be any verb. However, the second and the third verbs can only be incomplete (without tense prefixes):

هوّ طلب يخرج يروح فسّينما .
huwwa tálab yú-xrug yi-rūḥ fi-s-sínima.
He asked he-go out he-go in-the-movies.
He asked to go out to go to the movies.

بيحبّ يقعد يسمع الرّاديو .
bi-y-ḥíbb yú-qɛud yí-smaɛ ir-rádyu.
(pt)-he-like he-sit he-listen the-radio.
He likes to sit and listen to the radio.

29. 2. Adverbs and adverbials (words used as adverbs) of Egyptian Arabic are approximately used as their counterparts in English.

A. Adverbs or words used as adverbs are not inflected.

B. Adverbs may occur as predicates in verbless sentences or as clauses in verbal sentences:

الدّفتر هنا .
id-dáftar hína.
The-notebook here.
The notebook is here.

حاجى بعد ما اخلص من الشّغل .
ḥ-āgi báɛd(i) m-á-xlaṣ min iš-šúġl.
(ft)-I come after-I-finish from the-work.
I will come when I am through with my work.

C. Adverbials (nouns and prepositions used as adverbs) may often occur with bound pronouns:

الطرابيزة تحتها قطّة .
iṭ-ṭarabēza taḥt-áha qúṭṭa.
The-table under-her/it cat.
There is a cat under the table.

هوّ سافر سنتها .
húwwa sāfir saná-t-ha.
He left year-(cs)-her/it.
He left the same year.

D. Usually, adverbs are placed after the verb (or its object, if there is one) they modify.

Frequently used adverbs/adverbials of time, place, and manner:

Adverbs of time

إنّهرضى	innahárḍa, today	دلوقت	dilwáqti, now
إمبارح	imbāriḥ, yesterday	بكرة	búkra, tomorrow
حالاً	ḥālan, immediately	على طول	ɛala-ṭūl, immediately
بعدين	baɛdēn, later on	بعد ما	báɛd(i) ma, after

دائمن	dáyman, always	ابداً	ábadan, ever/never
بدري	bádri, early	وخري	wáxri, late

أوّل ما áwwal ma, as soon as
اوّل إمبارح áwwil imbāriḥ, the day before yesterday
بعد الضّهر baɛd-iḍ-ḍúhr, in the afternoon
بعد بكرة báɛd(i) búkra, after tomorrow
كلّ يوم kull(i)-yōm, every day
باليل bi-l-lēl, in the evening
بمنسبه bi-munásba, on the occasion
وقتها waqt-áha, then/ at that time
سعتها saɛ-ít-ha, at that time
سنتها saná-t-ha, that year
كلّ ما kúll-(i)-ma, every time

Usually adverbs of time stand at the end of a sentence; for emphasis they may be placed at the beginning of a sentence.

لازم نتفرج على البلد بكرة .
lāzim ni-tfárrag ɛa-l-bálad búkra.
Must we-go sightseeing on-the-town tomorrow.
We must go sightseeing around town tomorrow.

Adverbs of place

هنا	hína, here	ف	fi, in
هناك	hinākٍ, there	جمب	gamb, near/beside
فوق	fōq, up	على اليمين	ɛa-l-yimīn, to the right
تحت	taḥt, down	على الشّمال	ɛa-š-šimāl, to the left
ورة	wára, behind/after	قدّام	quddām, in front
على	ɛála/ɛa, on	جوّا	gúwwa, inside
عند	ɛand, at	برّا	bárra, outside
		بين	bēn, between

Usually, adverbs of place stand after the verb (or its object if there is any) they modify:

حانروح هناك على طول .
ha-n-rūḥ hināk ɛala-ṭūl.
(ft)-we-go there on-length.
We will go there immediately.

Adverbs of manner

قوام	qawām, fast/quickly	بسهله	bi-shúla, easily
كويّس	kwáyyis, well	بظّبط	bi-ẓ-ẓábṭ, exactly
سوة	sáwa, together	على غفلة	ɛála ġáfla, suddenly
مع بعض	máɛa báɛaḍ, together	طبعاً	tábɛan, naturally/of cours
بشويش	bi-šwēš, slowly	عادتاً	ɛādatan, usually
بسرعة	bi-súrɛa, quickly	شخصياً	šaxṣíyyan, personally
بصّدفة	bi-ṣ-ṣúdfa, accidentally	لوحد	li-wáḥd + pr. suff., alone
على مهل	ɛála máhl-ak, carefully	بنفس	bi-náfs + pr. suff., by one

أنا شلت الصندوق بنفسي .
ána šil-t is-sandūq bi-náfs-i.
I carried-I the-case by-self-my.
I carried the case by myself.

Adverbs of manner are used after the verb (or its object, if there is one) they modify. However, if all three types of adverbs occur in a sentence the adverb of place follows the verb; then comes the adverb of manner and finally the adverb of time:

انا قبلت الرّاجل هناك بصّدفة الصّبح .
ána qabíl-t ir-rāgil hināk bi-ṣ-ṣúdfa iṣ-ṣúbḥ.
I met-I the-man there by-the-chance the-morning.
I met the man there by chance this morning.

حلم الطالب

ḥilm iṭ-ṭālib

Unit 30. The Student's Dream

انت باين مبسوط النّهارده ، يا كريم . خير ان شاء الله .

NICK. — ínta bāyin mabṣūṭ innahárda, ya karīm. xēr in [šā' allāh?

You appearing happy today, oh Karim. Well being if willing God?

Karim, you seem happy today. What is the good news?

يادوبي خلّصت الكلّيّة ، يا نك .

KARIM. — yadōb-i xalláṣ-t ik-kullíyya, ya Nick.

Just-me finished-I the-college, oh Nick.

I have just graduated from college, Nick.

إنت عاوز تعمل ايه دلوقتي ؟ تروح الجامعة ؟

NICK. — ínta ɛāwiz tí-ɛmil ēh dilwáqti? ti-rūḥ ig-gámɛa?

You wanting you-do what now? You-go the-university?

What do you want to do now? Go to the university?

أيوه ، أنا قصدى أدرس القانون إذا قدرت .

KARIM. — áywa, ána qáṣd-i á-dris il-q̇anūn íza qidír-t.

Yes, I intention-my I-study the-law if could-I.

Yes, I intend to study law if I can.

ويمكن أروح أمريكا أعمل دراسات عُليا .

KARIM. — wi yímkin a-rūḥ amrīka á-ɛmil diras-āt ɛúlya.

And may I-go America I-do study-(pl) high(pl).

And I may go to America to do graduate studies.

عمرك رُحت أمريكا قبل كده ؟

NICK. — ɛúmr-ak ruḥ-t amrīka qabl kída?

Age-your(m) went-you America before so?

Have you ever been in the United States before?

يا ريت كنت رحت أمريكا ، يا نك .
KARIM. — yarēt kun-t ruḥ-t amrīka, ya Nick.
Wish were-I went-I America, oh Nick.
I wish I had been in the States, Nick.

إنت عارف ، يا كريم ، عليك تقدّم طلب لمنحة .
NICK. — ínta ɛārif, ya karīm, ɛalē-k ti-qáddim ṭálab li-mínḥa.
You knowing, oh Karim, on-you you-present application for-grant.
You know, Karim, you ought to apply for a fellowship.

وفين عايز انت تروح فى أمريكا ؟
NICK. — wi fēn ɛāyiz ínta ti-rūḥ f-amrīka?
And where wanting you you-go in-America?
And where do you want to go in the States?

أنا نفسى أروح الغرب الأوسط ، خصوصاً إنديانا .
KARIM. — ána nífs-i a-rūḥ il-ġárb il-áwsaṭ, xuṣūṣan indyāna.
I self-my I-go the-west the-middle, especially Indiana.
I would like to go to the Midwest, especially Indiana.

انت عمّال تقول كده ؛ إش معنى انديانا ؟
NICK. — ínta ɛammāl ti-qūl kída; išmíɛna indyāna?
You all the time you-say so; why Indiana?
You say this all the time; why Indiana?

من اللّى باسمعه ، انديانا لازم تكون ولاية عظيمة ؛
KARIM. — min ílli b-a-smáɛ-uh indyāna lāzim ti-kūn wilāya [ɛaẓīm-a;
From which (pt)-I-hear-it Indiana must she-be state great-((f));
From what I hear, Indiana must be a great state;

وعشان انا ناوى أكمّل دراسات علم اللغات .
KARIM. — wi ɛašān ana nāwi a-kámmil diras-āt ɛilm il-luġ-āt.
and because I intend I-complete study-(pl) science the-language-(pl).
and furthermore because I intend to complete my studies [in linguistics.

30. 1. Modal auxiliaries and their use. In Egyptian Arabic, a few verbs and some other parts of speech may be used as modal auxiliaries to express various shades of meaning of obligation, wish, intention, determination, and length of time for having done something. The modal auxiliaries in Egyptian Arabic are used approximately in the same way as the English modals, such as "can, may, will, shall, must, ought to," are used. They always precede the main verb. Some modal auxiliaries are used with a bound pronoun (pr.), which agrees in person, number, and gender with the subject of the following verb. A few modal auxiliaries have adjectival forms (masculine, feminine, and plural) which agree in number and gender with the subject of the following verb. The stem of the latter may be complete or incomplete. Such incomplete stems are without tense prefixes unless otherwise indicated. The following are some of the most common modal auxiliaries:

A. بقى báqa 'become' + l(i) + pr + verb/participle

This construction conveys the meaning of having been doing something for a certain length of time. The following verb stem is incomplete with or without tense prefixes.

بقالهم بياكلوا طول الصّبح .
baqá-l-hum bi-y-ákl-u ṭūl iṣ-ṣúbḥ.
It became-to-them (pt)-he-eat-(pl) length the-morning.
They have been eating all morning.

بقالى مستنّيك ساعتين .
baqā-l-i mistannī-k saع-t-ēn.
It became-to-me waiting-you(m) hour-(cs)-(d).
I have been waiting for you two hours.

B. قام qām 'stand (up)' + verb

This construction conveys the meaning of starting or undertaking to do something. The following verb stem may be complete or incomplete without tense prefixes.

قام اشتغل فى التصميم الجديد .
qām ištáġal fi-t-taṣmīm ig-gidīd.
Stood worked in-the-project the-new.
He started to work on the new project.

The following three modal auxiliaries (C, D, and E) and others, with participial pattern, have three forms (masculine, feminine, and plural), unless otherwise stated.

C. عايز ʕāyiz 'wanting' + pr + verb

This construction expresses willingness to do something specified by the verb. ʕāyiz may or may not have the bound pronoun, and the verb stem is incomplete.

عايزين نسافر بكره .	عايزينا نسافر دلوقتى .
ʕayz-īn n-sāfir búkra.	ʕayz-ín-na n-sāfir dilwáqti.
Wanting-(pl) we-leave tomorrow.	*Wanting-(pl)-us we-leave now.*
We want to leave tomorrow.	They want us to leave now.

D. ناوى nāwi 'intending' + verb

This construction expresses intention of doing something specified by the verb, the stem of which is incomplete.

ناوية ترجع المدرسة .
náwy-a tí-rgaʕ il-madrása.
Intending-(f) she-return the-school.
She intends to return to school.

E. عمال ʕammāl 'continually' + verb

This construction expresses the idea of doing something continually. The stem of the verb is incomplete, with or without the prefix *bi*.

لاقيته عمّال بيذاكر .
laqē-t-uh ʕammāl bi-y-zākir.
Found-I-him continually (pt)-he-study.
I found him studying all the time.

الولد عمّال يعيّط .
il-wálad ʕammāl yi-ʕáyyaṭ.
The-boy continually he-cry.
The boy cries all the time.

F. قعد qáʕad 'stay/sit' / قاعد qāʕid + verb.

This construction expresses the idea of doing something for a certain amount of time. The verb stem is incomplete.

قاعدين يتكلّموا ساعة ونص .
qaʕd-īn yi-tkallím-u sāʕa wi nuṣṣ.
Sitting-(pl) he-speak-(pl) hour and half.
They kept talking for an hour and a half.

G. راح rāḥ, go / رايح rāyiḥ + verb

The modal auxiliary in this construction gives a future meaning to the following verb, the stem of which is incomplete. This construction is rare.

هوّ رايح يكلّمك بكره .
húwwa rāyiḥ yi-kallím-ak búkra.
He going he-speak to-you(m) tomorrow.
He will talk to you tomorrow.

H. على ɛála, on + pr + verb = ought to
نفس nifs, self + pr + verb = long to/wish
قصد qaṣd, intention + pr + verb = intend to
بدّ bidd, desire + pr + verb = would like to
غرض ġáraḍ, purpose + pr + verb = be determined to

The verb stem in these constructions is incomplete.

عليك تروح يشوفك الحكيم .
ɛalē-k t-rūḥ yi-šūf-ak il-ḥakīm.
On-you(m) you-go he-see-you(m) the-doctor.
You ought to go and see the doctor.

نفسنا تيجوا عندنا .
nifs-ína t-īg-u ɛand-ína.
Self-our you-come-(pl) at-us.
We want to have you at our place.

قصدكم تبيعوا البيت ده ؟
qaṣd-úkum ti-bīɛ-u il-bēt da?
Intention-your(pl) you-sell-(pl) the-house this?
Do you intend to sell this house?

لا . أنا بدّى أصلّحه قُريّب .
la'. ána bídd-i a-ṣalláḥ-uh qurāyyib.
No. I desire-me I-repair-it soon.
No. I would like to repair it soon.

يعنى غرضك ما تبيعوش أبدًا ؟
yáɛni ġáraḍ-ak ma-t-biɛ-ū-š ábadan?
That is purpose-your(m) (neg)-you-sell-it-(neg) never?
That is to say, you are determined never to sell it?

I. عُمر ʕumr, life + pr + ma + verb = never
عُمر ʕumr, life + pr + verb = ever

The first construction conveys the meaning of never having done, or be doing something specified by the verb. The second construction conveys the meaning of ever having done, or be doing something. In both constructions the verb stem may be either complete or incomplete, with or without tense prefixes.

عمرك كنت فى مصر ؟
ʕúmr-ak kún-t(i) fi-máṣr?
Life-your(m) were-you(m) in-Egypt?
Have you ever been in Egypt?

لا . عمرى ما زرت مصر .
la'. ʕúmr-i ma-zúr-t maṣr.
No. Life-my (neg)-visited-I Egypt.
No. I have never visited Egypt.

J. لازم lāzim + verb/participle = must
يلزم yílzam + pr + verb/noun = need
ملزوم malzūm + verb = be obliged to

1. In the first construction, lāzim does not change; it may be followed by a verb or a participle. The verb stem may be complete or incomplete, with or without tense prefixes, with different meanings as a result.

لازم كل / واكل .
lāzim kal/wākil.
Must ate/eating.
He must have eaten.

لازم ياكل .
lāzim y-ākul.
Must he-eat.
He must eat.

لازم بياكل .
lāzim bi-y-ākul.
Must (pt)-he-eat.
He must be eating.

لازم حياكل .
lāzim ḥa-y-ākul.
Must (ft)-he-eat.
Probably he will eat.

2. In the second construction, yílzam is also invariable, though it can take a bound pronoun. It may be followed by a verb (incomplete stem) or a noun.

يلزمك تستحمّ.
yilzám-ak ti-staḥámma.
It need-you(m) you-bathe.
You need to take a bath.

يلزمك حاجة ؟
yilzám-ak ḥāga?
It need-you(m) thing?
Do you need anything?

3. In the third construction, malzūm 'obliged', like an adjective, has three forms, and the verb stem following it is incomplete.

هوّ ملزوم يحضر المقابلة.
húwwa malzūm yí-ḥḍar il-muqábla.
He is obliged he-be present the-meeting.
He is obliged to attend the meeting.

K. يمكن yímkin + pr + verb/participle = perhaps/may
ممكن múmkin + verb = could/can/possible

1. yimkin 'perhaps' is invariable; if used with a bound pronoun, a difference in meaning results. It may be followed by a verb or a participle. The verb stem may be complete or incomplete; if used with tense prefixes, a difference in meaning results.

يمكن راح / رايح بدري.
yímkin rāḥ/rāyiḥ bádri.
Perhaps went/going early.
Perhaps he went/is going early.

يمكن يروح بدري.
yímkin yi-rūḥ bádri.
Perhaps he-go early.
Perhaps he will go early.

يمكنه يروح بدري.
yimkín-uh yi-rūḥ bádri.
May-him he-go early.
He may (can) go early.

يمكن حيروح بدري.
yímkin ḥa-y-rūḥ bádri.
May (ft)-he-go early.
Perhaps he will go early.

2. Usually, múmkin is used in negative and interrogative constructions. The verb stem is incomplete. múmkin can also be used in verbless sentences.

مش ممكن يروح بدري.
muš múmkin yi-rūḥ bádri.
Not possible he-go early.
He cannot go early.

ممكن تدّيني الشوكة دي ؟
múmkin ti-ddī-ni-š-šōka di?
Possible you-give-me-the-fork that?
Could you give me that fork?

ممكن ده؟
múmkin da?
Possible this/that?
Is that possible?

لا ، ده مش ممكن.
la', da muš múmkin.
No, this/that not possible.
No, that is impossible.

L. جايز gāyiz + *l(i)* + pr + verb = can/be allowed to
يجوز yigūz + *l(i)* + pr + verb = can/be allowed to

These two modal auxiliaries are invariable and are both used in the same way. The verb stem following them is incomplete.

جايزلكم تدخلوا دلوقتي.
gayiz-l-úkum ti-dxúl-u dilwáqti.
Permissible-to-you(pl) you-enter-(pl) now.
You can go in now.

يجوزلها تسافر بكره.
yiguz-l-áha t-sāfir búkra.
Permissible-to-her she-leave tomorrow.
She is permitted to leave tomorrow.

M. يا دوب yadōb + pr + complete verb stem
زمان zamān + pr + complete verb stem
يا ريت yarēt + pr + complete verb stem
يا ريت yarēt + incomplete verb stem

yadōb, in the first construction, conveys the meaning of just having performed some action, and zamān indicates that some action must have been performed by now or that some action will be performed very soon.

يا دوبها خلّصت الشغل.
yadúb-ha xállaṣ-it iš-šúġl.
Just-her finished-she the-work.
She has just finished the work.

زمانه جايّ.
zamān-uh gayy.
Long time-his coming.
He must have come by now/he is on his way.

yarēt may be used with or without a bound pronoun with a following complete verb stem. It may be followed by an incomplete verb stem without a bound pronoun. In the first case, it expresses a wish that some action might have taken place in the past; in the second case, a wish that some action may be performed in the future.

يا ريتهم جُم امبارح .
yarít-hum gum imbāriḥ.
I wish-them came(pl) yesterday.
I wish they had come yesterday.

يا ريت ييجوا بكره .
yarēt y-īg-u búkra.
I wish he-come-(pl) tomorrow.
I wish they would come tomorrow.

رايحين السينما

rayḥīn is-sínima

Unit 31. Going to the Movies

بتقول ايه ، يا شكرى ، نروح السّينما اللّيلة دى ؟
CARL. — bi-t-qūl ēh, ya šúkri, ni-rūḥ is-sínima il-lēla di?
(pt)-you-say what, oh Shoukri, we-go the-movies the-night this?
What do you say, Shoukri, shall we go to the movies tonight?

إنت شاطر قوى ؛ أنا نفسى كنت لسّه بافكّر فيها .
SHOUKRI. — ínta šāṭir qáwi; ána náfs-i kun-t líssa b-a-fákkar [fī-ha.
You smart very; I self-my was-I still (pt)-I-think in-it.
How smart you are; I was just thinking that myself.

يا جمال ، أنت جاىّ معانا ؟
SHOUKRI. — ya gamāl, ínta gayy maɛā-na?
Oh Gamal, you coming with-us?
Are you coming with us, Gamal?

أيوه ، لاكن لازم نسأل لورا وفيفى كمان .
GAMAL. — áywa, làkin, lāzim ní-s'al Laura wi Fīfi kamān.
Yes, but must we-ask Laura and Fifi also.
Yes, but we should ask Laura and Fifi too.

همّ قالوا لى إنّهم رايحين المسرح .
CARL. — húmma qalū-l-i inn-úhum rayḥ-īn il-másraḥ.
They told-to-me that-them going-(pl) the-theater.
They told me that they were going to the theater.

على فكرة ، فيه فيلم ايه فى السينما مترو اللّيلة دى ؟
CARL. — ɛála fíkra, fī-h film ēh fi-s-sínima mítru il-lēla di?
On thought, in-it film what in-the-movies Metro the-night this?
By the way, what film is showing at the Metro tonight?

المجلّة دى فيها لستة كاملة عن الأفلام .

Shoukri. — il-magálla di fī-ha lísta káml-a عan il-aflām.
The-magazine this in-it list complete-(f) on the-films.
This magazine has a complete list of films.

آه ! دول أفلام قدام ، ومش كويّسين أبداً .

Gamal. — āh! dōl aflām qudām, wi miš kwayyis-īn ábadan.
Oh! These films old, and not good-(pl) never.
Oh! These are old films, and they are not good at all.

دول الممثّلتين اللى أحبّ أشوفهم .

Carl. — dōl il-mumassil-t-ēn ílli a-ḥíbb a-šúf-hum.
These the-actor-(f)-(d) which I-love I-see-them.
These are the two actresses I would like to see.

هوّ الممثّل المضحك اللى بيلعب معاهم مين ؟ [maعā-hum mīn?

Shoukri. — húwwa il-mumássil il-múḍḥik ílli bi-yí-lعab
He the-artist the-comedian that (pt)-he-play with-them who?
Who is the comedian that is playing with them?

اسمه شكوكو ؛ هوّ ممثّل مشهور .

Gamal. — ísm-uh šukūku; húwwa mumássil mašhūr.
Name-his Shoukoukou; he actor famous.
His name is Shoukoukou; he is a famous actor.

هىّ سينما ريفولى بعيدة من هنا ؟

Carl. — híyya is-sínima rívoli biعīd-a min hína?
She the-movie house Rivoli far-(f) from here?
Is the Rivoli theater far from here?

أهو وصلنا ! دى قريّبة منّا ، على ناصية الشارع . [iš-šāriع.

Shoukri. — ahú wiṣíl-na! di qurayyíb-a mín-na, عála náṣy-it
Here arrived-we! This near-(f) from-us, on corner-(cs) the-street.
Here we are! It is close to us, just around the corner.

31. 1. The use of free personal pronouns. As we have seen in unit 6, free personal pronouns are:

هوّ húwwa, he	انتَ ínta, you (m)	أنا ána, I
هىّ híyya, she	انتِ ínti, you (f)	إحنا íḥna, we
همّ húmma, they	انتوا íntu, you (pl)	

Free personal pronouns are mainly used:

A. As the subject of a verbless sentence:

هوّ راجل طيّب .
húwwa rāgil ṭáyyib.
He man good.
He is a good man.

B. For emphasis in a verbal sentence:

همّ حيسافروا بكره .
húmma ḥa-yi-sáfr-u búkra.
They (ft)-he-leave-(pl) tomorrow.
They will leave tomorrow.

C. To signal the person in a verbal sentence when the bound subject pronouns are the same:

بتلعب تنس .
bi-tí-lɛab tínis.
(pt)-she/you(m)-play tennis.
She/you is/are playing tennis.

هىّ بتلعب تنس .
híyya bi-tí-lɛab tínis.
She (pt)-she-play tennis.
She is playing tennis.

خلّصت الدّرس .
xalláṣ-t id-dárs.
Finished-you(m)/I the-lesson.
You/I finished the lesson.

أنا خلّصت الدّرس .
ána xalláṣ-t id-dárs.
I finished-I the-lesson.
I finished the lesson.

D. For emphasis, as the object pronoun in a verbal sentence:

همّ شافوه هوّ .
húmma šaf-ū-h húwwa.
They saw-(pl)-him he.
They saw him.

E. As a question word:

هوّ أنا اللّى ما باشتغلش ؟
húwwa ána ílli ma-b-a-štaġál-š?
He I who (neg)-(pt)-I-work-(neg)?
Am I the one who is not working?

31. 2. The demonstratives. The more frequent and simple demonstratives are:

ده	da	this/that (m)
دى	di	this/that (f)
دول	dōl	these/those

Usually, these demonstratives occur after a definite noun. Like adjectives, they agree with the noun: dōl agrees in number only; da and di agree in gender and number.

الولد ده	il-wálad da	this/that boy
البنت دى	il-bínt di	this/that girl
الحاجات دول	il-ḥag-āt dōl	these/those things

Demonstratives may be used as subjects in verbless sentences and like English demonstratives in verbal sentences:

ده كتاب .	ده بيشتغل تمام .	أنا كسرت ده .
da kitāb.	da bi-štáġal tamām.	ána kasár-t da.
This book.	*This/that(pt)-work perfect.*	*I broke-I this/that.*
This is a book.	This/that works/is working well.	I broke that.

Less frequently used demonstratives are:

دُكهه	dúkha or díkha	that (m)
دِكهه	díkha	that (f)
دُكهم	dúkhum	those

These demonstratives are usually used in comparative constructions:

الدّفتر ده أحسن من دُكهه .
id-dáftar da áḥsan min dúkha.
The-notebook this better from that.
This notebook is better than that one.

For expressions like "here it is" or "here they are", the following demonstratives are used:

أهو	ahú,	here he/it is
أهى	ahí,	here she/it is
أهم	ahúm,	here they are

Usually, these demonstratives occur before or after a noun.

أهو أحمد ! هوّ لسّه جاى.
ahú áḥmad! húwwa líssa gayy.
Here is Ahmad! He yet came.
Here is Ahmad! He just came.

Another demonstrative آدى ādi conveys the meaning of the last three demonstratives and is placed before a noun:

آدى السّت ādi is-sítt, here is the lady

A demonstrative is negated by placing مش miš before it:

مش ده ولا دُكهه.
miš da wála dúkha.
Not this nor that.
Neither this nor that one.

صور تذكار

ṣúwar tizkār

Unit 32. Snapshots for Remembrance

يا صبرى، تعرف محلّ بيبيع أفلام؟
NELSON. — ya ṣábri, tí-ɛraf maḥáll bi-y-bīɛ aflām?
Oh Sabri, you-know store (pt)-he-sell films?
Sabri, do you know a store that sells film?

الرّاجل اللّى فات من هنا عنده محلّ كبير.
SABRI. — ir-rāgil ílli fāt min hína ɛánd-uh maḥáll kibīr.
The-man who passed from here at-him store big.
The man who passed by has a big store.

يا صبرى، شفت الصّور اللّى جبناهالك؟
JANE. — ya ṣábri, šuf-t iṣ-ṣúwar ílli gib-na-hā-l-ak?
Oh Sabri, saw-you the-pictures which brought-we-her-for-you?
Did you see the pictures we brought for you, Sabri?

فيهم صور خدتها معانا فى أمريكا.
JANE. — fī-hum ṣúwar xad-t-áha maɛā-na f-amrīka.
In-them pictures took-you-her with-us in-America.
There are pictures you took with us in the States.

ياالله نقعد فى القهوة اللّى على النّيل.
NELSON. — yálla nú-qɛud fi-l-qáhwa ílli ɛála-n-nīl.
Come on we-sit in-the-cafe which on-the-Nile.
Let's sit at the cafe on the Nile.

ليه مانروحش الهرم دلوقتى؟
SABRI. — lēh ma-n-rúḥ-š il-háram dilwáqti?
Why (neg)-we-go-(neg) the Pyramid now?
Why don't we go to the Pyramids now?

فيه ولد موجود هناك بياخد صور كويّسة .

SABRI. — fī-h wálad mawgūd hinā̄k bi-y-āxud ṣúwar kway-[yís-a.
In-it boy present there (pt)-he-take pictures good.
There is a boy there who takes good pictures.

البنت اللّى كانت معاىَ قالت كده برضه .

JANE. — il-bínt ílli kān-it maʕā-ya qāl-it kída bárḍu.
The-girl who was-she with-me said-she so also.
The girl who was with me said the same thing.

جاهزين ؟ ارفعوا روؤسكم ، ما تتحرّكوش ، ابتسموا ، خلاص .

BOY. — gahz-īn? irfáʕ-u ru'ús-kum, ma-ti-tḥarrak-ū-š, [ibtísm-u, xalāṣ.
Ready-(pl)? Lift-you(pl) head-your(pl), (neg)-you-move-you(pl)-(neg), smile-you(pl), finished.
Ready? Lift your heads, stand still, smile, finished.

يا صبرى ، حيحصل ايه فى الصّور اللّى خدهالنا دى ؟

NELSON. — ya ṣábri, ḥa-yí-ḥṣal ēh fi-ṣ-ṣúwar ílli xad-há-l-na [di?
Oh Sabri, (ft)-it-happen what in-the-pictures which took-it-to-us this?
Sabri, what will happen to the pictures he took of us?

الصّور اللّى حتطلع حابعتها اللّوكاندة .

BOY. — iṣ-ṣúwar ílli ḥa-tí-tlaʕ ḥ-a-bʕát-ha il-lukánda.
The-pictures which (ft)-she-turn out (ft)-I-send-it the-hotel.
I will send the pictures which turn out well to the hotel.

متشكّرين يا ابنى . انت عايز منّى كام ؟

NELSON. — mutašakkir-īn, ya íbn-i. ínta ʕāyiz mínn-i kām?
Thankful-(pl), oh son-my. You wanting from-me how much?
Thank you, son. How much do we owe you?

ولا حاجة ، يا أستاذ . إنت دفعت اللّى عليك ، خلاص .

BOY. — wála ḥāga, ya ustāz. ínta dafáʕ-t ílli ʕalē-k, xalās.
Nor thing, oh professor. You paid-you which on-you; finished.
Nothing, sir. You paid what you owe me; it's taken care of.

32. 1. The use of the relative pronoun إللّى ílli. This pronoun corresponds exactly to English relative pronouns "who(m)/which/that" and to the English expressions "the one(s) who/which/that".

Unlike English relative pronouns, which are sometimes optional (for example: "the letter which I wrote yesterday" and "the letter I wrote yesterday" are equally correct), the Arabic ílli is either used or not used according to simple rules. ílli, in Arabic, functions exactly like the Arabic definite article ال il.

A. Like the definite article, ílli does not have gender or number inflections:

B. Like an adjective, a prepositional phrase or a whole verbal sentence may modify a noun. In such cases, if the noun is definite, the prepositional phrase or verbal sentence is preceded by ílli: in these cases, it conveys the meaning of 'one' or 'the one (s) who'; 'he/she/they who'; 'whoever/whichever/whatever':

الكتاب اللّى على الطّرابيزة بتاعى .
ik-kitāb ílli ع ala-ṭ-ṭarabēza bitā ع-i.
The-book which on-the-table belonging to-me.
The book which is on the table is mine.

C. If the noun is indefinite, ílli is omitted:

أنا عارف راجل عنده عشرين ولد .
ána ع ārif rāgil ع ánd-uh ع išrīn wálad.
I knowing man at-him twenty boy.
I know a man who has twenty children.

D. ílli may stand at the beginning of a sentence, alone or after a free pronoun, an interrogative, or an imperative; in these cases, it conveys the meaning of 'one' or 'the one(s) who'; 'he/she/they who'; 'whoever/whichever/whatever':

اللّى عايز ينجح لازم يذاكر .
ílli ع āyiz yí-ngaḥ lāzim yi-zākir.
Who wanting he-succeed must he-study.
The one who wants to succeed must study.

قول اللّى انت عايز تقوله .
qūl ílli ínta ع āyiz ti-qūl-uh.
Say that you wanting you-say-it.
Say whatever you want to say.

E. Usually, ílli is used instead of the definite article before a participle preceded by a definite noun:

الولد اللّى لابس نضّاره أخويا .
il-wálad ílli lābis naḍḍāra axū-ya.
The-boy who wearing spectacles brother-my.
The boy who is wearing spectacles is my brother.

F. Frequently, the retrocive pronoun (in brackets) accompanies ílli in a sentence:

البنت اللّى انت قاعد جانبها أختى.
il-bínt ílli ínta qāɛid gamb-[áha] úxt-i.
The-girl that you sitting beside-[her] sister-my.
The girl that you are sitting beside is my sister.

على كورنيش النيل

ɛála kurnīš in-nīl

Unit 33. On the Promenade by the Nile

يا أحمد ، فين فلوكتك الصّغيّرة ؟

PETER. — ya áḥmad, fēn fulúk-t-ak iṣ-ṣuġayyár-a?
O Ahmad, where sailboat-(cs)-your(m) the-small-(f)?
Ahmad, where is your small sailboat?

الصّغيّرة دى اللّى جانب الكبرى بتاعتى .

AHMAD. — iṣ-ṣuġayyár-a di ílli gamb ik-kúbri bitáɛ-t-i.
The-small-(f) this which beside the-bridge belonging to-(cs)-me.
The small one close to the bridge is mine.

والمركب الكبيرة دى بتاعة مين ؟

MARY. — w-il-márkib ik-kibīr-a di bitāɛ-it mīn?
And-the-ship the-big-(f) that belonging to-(cs) whom?
And to whom does that big ship belong?

دى بتاعة شركة السّياحة .

AHMAD. — di bitāɛ-it šírk-it is-siyāḥa.
That belonging to-(cs) company-(cs) the-tourism.
That one belongs to the Tourist Office.

ياالله ، ناخد الحاجات بتاعتكم فى المركب .

HASSAN. — yálla, n-āxud il-ḥag-āt bitaɛ-ít-kum f-il-márkib.
Come on, we-take the-thing-(pl) belonging to-(cs)-you(pl) in-the-[ship.
Let's take your things to the boat.

الحاجات بتاعتنا فى العربيّة بتاعتك .

PETER. — il-ḥag-āt bitaɛ-ít-na f-il-ɛarabíyya bitáɛ-t-ak.
The-thing-(pl) belonging to-(cs)-us in-the-car belonging to-(cs)-[you(m).
Our things are in your car.

هوّ الكتاب ده بتاعك ، يا بيتر ؟

AHMAD. — húwwa ik-kitāb da bitāع-ak, ya Peter?
He the-book this belonging to-you(m), oh Peter?
Is this your book, Peter?

ايوه ، ده بتاعى ، لَكن التّانى بتاعها .

PETER. — áywa, da bitāع-i, lākin it-tāni bitáع-ha.
Yes, this belonging to-me, but the-other belonging to-her.
Yes, this is mine, but the other one is hers.

متشكّر ، يا أحمد . قل لى ، السّراية دى بتاعة مين ؟

PETER. — mutšákkir, ya áḥmad. qúl-l-i, is-sarāya di bitāع-it [mīn?
Thankful, oh Ahmad. Tell-to-me, the-palace that belonging to-(cs)-whom?
Thank you, Ahmad. Tell me, to whom does that palace [belong?

دى بتاعة الحكومة ، لَكن ما فيش حدّ جوّه .

AHMAD. — di bitáع-t il-ḥukūma, lākin ma-fī-š ḥadd gúwwa.
That belonging to-(cs) the government, but (neg)-in-(neg) anyone [inside.
That belongs to the government, but it is unoccupied.

إنت ، يا بتاع السّجاير ، ادّينى علبة كليوباتره .

HASSAN. — ínta, ya bitāع is-sagāyir, iddī-ni عílb-it kilubátra.
You, oh belonging to the-cigarettes, give-me box-(cs) Cleopatra.
Hey, cigarette seller, give me a pack of Cleopatra.

يا ولد ، عندك سجاير بتاعة برّه ؟

MARY. — ya wálad, عánd-ak sagāyir bitāع-it barra?
Oh boy, at-you cigarettes belonging to-(cs) outside?
Boy, do you have any foreign cigarettes?

أيوه ، عندى سجاير مصرى وسجاير أمريكانى .

SELLER. — áywa, عánd-i sagāyir máṣr-i wi sagāyir amrik-āni.
Yes, at-me cigarettes Egypt-(adj) and cigarettes America-(adj).
Yes, I have both local and American cigarettes.

33. 1. The use of the word بتاع bitāʿ 'belonging to'. Another way to indicate possession is through the use of bitāʿ.

A. In a sentence, bitāʿ always follows the noun indicating the thing possessed and precedes the possessor. The noun preceding bitāʿ usually has the definite article:

الفستان بتاع السّتّ جديد .
il-fustān bitāʿ is-sítt gidīd.
The-dress belonging to the-lady new.
The lady's dress is new.

B. Like an adjective, bitāʿ agrees in gender and number with the preceding noun (the thing possessed) and has, therefore, three forms: masculine singular, feminine singular, and plural (for both masculine and feminine):

بتاع bitāʿ (m)   بتاعة bitāʿ-a (f)   بتوع bitūʿ (pl)

However, this word always occurs in construct state; therefore, the feminine form always occurs (in pronunciation only) as bitāʿ-t or bitāʿ-it (before a word beginning with a consonant):

العربيّة بتاعة الظبّاط
il-ʿarabíyya bitāʿ-t iẓ-ẓubbāt
the-car belonging to-(cs) the-officers
the officers' car

العربيّة بتاعتهم
il-ʿarabíyya bitaʿ-ít-hum
the-car belonging to-(cs)-them
their car

C. Like a noun, bitāʿ is used with bound possessive pronouns for such English expressions as "mine, yours, his, hers, its, ours, theirs":

البيت بتاعى
il-bēt bitāʿ-i
the-house belonging to-me
my house

الشنطة بتاعتى
iš-šánta bitáʿ-t-i
the-purse belonging to-(cs)-me
my purse

المدرسة بتاعتكم
il-madrása bitaʿ-ít-kum
the-school belonging to-(cs)-you(pl)
your school

D. Sometimes bitāع is used with nouns to indicate various kinds of relationships:

بتاع نسوان
bitāع niswān
belonging to women
ladies' man

بتاع السّمك
bitāع is-sámak
belonging to the-fish
the fish seller

جزم بتوع ستّات
gízam bitūع sitt-āt
shoes belonging to lady-(pl)
ladies' shoes

E. Except for some parts of the body, bitāع is usually used to indicate possession of dual nouns:

الولدين بتوع المدرّس
il-walad-ēn bitūع il-mudárris
the-boy-(d) belonging to the-teacher
the two boys of the teacher

F. bitāع is used with a preceding noun (the thing possessed) qualified by an adjective:

الباب الكبير بتاع البيت
il-bāb ik-kibīr bitāع il-bēt
the-door the-big belonging to the-house
the big door of the house

G. bitāع is used with the question word مين mīn in such questions as those corresponding to the English 'whose is' or 'whose are'?

بتاع مين القلم ده ؟
bitāع-mīn il-qálam da?
Belonging to-whom the-pencil this?
Whose pencil is this?

بتاعة مين الأوضة دى ؟
bitāع-it mīn il-ōḍa di?
Belonging to-(cs) whom the-room this?
Whose room is this?

H. With members of the family, bitāʿ is used only to indicate possession of the wife and plural forms:

السّتّ بتاعة المدير حلوة .
is-sítt bitáʿ-t il-mudīr ḥílw-a.
The-lady belonging to-(cs) the-director pretty-(f).
The director's wife is pretty.

الولاد بتوعنا كبار .
il-awlād bitúʿ-na kubār.
The-boys belonging to-us big(pl).
Our boys are big.

حديث مع وكيل السياحة

ḥadīs máɛa wakīl is-siyāḥa

Unit 34. Talking with the Travel Agent

أهلاً ، يا أستاذ ، اتفضّل . أىّ خدمة ؟

Travel Agent. — áhlan, ya ustāz, itfáḍḍal. áyy(i) xídma?
Hello, oh professor, please. Any service?
Hello, sir, please come in. What can I do for you?

أهلاً بيك ، يا سيدى . إحنا مسافرين رحلة ،

Phil. — áhlan bī-k, ya sīdi. íḥna msafr-īn ríḥla,
Hello with-you(m), oh mister. We traveling-(pl) trip,
Hello, sir. We are going to take a trip,

ومحتاجين لشويّة معلومات .

Phil. — wi miḥtag-īn li-šwáyy-it maɛlum-āt.
and needy-(pl) for-little-(cs) information-(pl).
and we need some information.

ناويين تروحوا فين ، يا افندم ؟

Travel Agent. — nawy-īn t-rūḥ-u fēn, y-afándim?
Intending-(pl) you-go-(pl) where, oh sir?
Where do you intend to go, sir?

ناويين نسافر الشّام قريّب .

Phil. — nawy-īn ni-sāfir iš-šām quráyyib.
Intending-(pl) we-go the-Syria soon.
We intend to go to Syria soon.

وعايزين نسافر بالبحر .

Dorothy. — wi ɛayz-īn ni-sāfir bi-l-báḥr.
And wanting-(pl) we-travel by-the-sea.
And we want to go by sea.

إن شاء الله ، عايزين تسافروا الشّام إمتى ؟

Travel Agent. — in-ša'-allāh, ɛayz-īn ti-sáfr-u iš-šām [ímta?
If-willed-God, wanting-(pl) you-travel-(pl) the-Syria when?
When do you wish to leave for Syria?

أفتكر الأسبوع إللى جاىّ يبقى كويّس .

Dorothy. — a-ftíkir il-usbūɛ ílli gayy, yí-bqa kwáyyis.
I-think the-week which coming, it-become good.
I think next week will be fine.

لكم حدّ معرفة فى الشّام ؟

Travel Agent. — l-úkum ḥadd maɛrífa fi-š-šām?
To-you(pl) anyone acquaintance in-the-Syria?
Do you know anyone in Syria?

أيوه . لنا أصحاب عايشين هناك من تلات سنين .

Phil. — áywa. lī-na aṣḥāb ɛayš-īn hināk min tálat sin-īn.
Yes. To-us friends living-(pl) there from three year-(pl).
Yes. We have friends who have lived there for three years.

التذاكر حايكلّفوا كام من فضلك ؟

Phil. — it-tazākir ḥa-yi-kallíf-u kām min-fáḍl-ak?
The-tickets (ft)-it-cost-(pl) how much from-bounty-your(m)?
How much will the tickets cost, please?

ستّين جنيه رايح جاىّ للنّفر . معاكم عفش ؟

Travel Agent. — sittīn ginēh rāyiḥ gáyy li-n-náfar. maɛā- [kum ɛafš?
Sixty pounds going coming to-the-person. With-you(pl) luggage?
Sixty Egyptian pounds per person round trip. Do you have [any luggage?

لا . شنطتين صغيّرتين بسّ ، بناخدهم معانا .

Phil. — la'. šanṭ-it-ēn ṣuġayyar-īn bass, bi-n-axúd-hum [maɛā-na.
No. Bag-(cs)-(d) small-(pl) only, (pt)-we-take-them with-us.
No. Only two small suitcases which we will carry with us.

34. 1. Interrogative constructions. There are two devices for the formation of interrogative constructions: intonation and question words.

A. Intonation. Raising the voice on the last syllable in a declarative sentence changes it from affirmative to interrogative:

الباب مفتوح .	الباب مفتوح ؟
il-bāb maftūḥ.	il-bāb maftūḥ?
The-door open.	*The-door open?*
The door is open.	Is the door open?

B. Question words. Most question words are used with prepositions and may be placed either at the end or at the beginning of a phrase or sentence; in both cases, the question word has a rising intonation. The most frequently used question words are the following:

ايه ؟	ēh? what?	بايه ؟ bi-ēh? with what?
ليه ؟	lēh? why?	عشان ايه ؟ ɛašan-ēh? why?
قدّ ايه ؟	qaddi-ēh?	what size? how long?
فين ؟	fēn?	where?
من فين ؟	min-fēn?	where from?
من اين ؟	min-ēn?	where from?
على فين ؟	ɛala-fēn?	where to?
مين ؟	mīn? who?	لمين ؟ li-mīn? for/to whom?
إمتى ؟	ímta?	when?
من إمتى ؟	min ímta?	since when?
كام ؟	kām?	how much/how many?
بكام ؟	bi-kām?	how much?
ازّاى ؟	iz-zāy? how?	كيف ؟ kēf? how?
أنهو ؟	ánhu?	which one (m)?
أنهى ؟	ánhi?	which one (f)?
أنهم ؟	ánhum?	which one (pl)?
أىّ ؟	ayy?	which/any?

ايه الحكاية ؟	ليه / عشان ايه بتضحك ؟
ēh il-ḥikāya?	lēh/ɛašan-ēh bi-tí-ḍḥak?
What the-story?	*Why (pt)-you(m)-laugh?*
What is the matter?	Why are you laughing?

حضرتك من اين ، يا أستاذ ؟
ḥaḍrít-ak min-ēn, ya ustāz?
Sir-you(m) from-where, oh professor?
Where are you from, sir?

أحمد فين ؟
áḥmad fēn?
Ahmad where?
Where is Ahmad?

من امتى إنت هنا ؟
min ímta ínta hína?
From when you(m) here?
How long have you been here?

بكام التّفّاح ؟
bi-kām it-tiffāḥ?
For-how much the-apples?
How much do the apples cost?

كام يوم حانستنّى ؟
kām yōm ḥa-ni-stánna?
How many day (ft)-we-wait?
How many days will we wait?

انهو من دول عايزه إنت ؟
anhú min dōl ع áyz-uh ínta?
Which one from these wanting-it you?
Which one of these do you want?

إنت رايح ايّ مدرسة ؟
ínta rāyiḥ ayy madrása?
You(m) going which school?
Which school are you attending?

C. The free personal pronouns هوّ húwwa 'he', هيّ híyya 'she', and همّ húmma 'they' are often used as a question word before the subject of a sentence. هوّ húwwa is also used as a question word before first and second person subject pronouns, regardless of their gender and number:

هوّ المدير موجود ؟
húwwa il-mudīr mawgūd?
He the-director present?
Is the director here?

هوّ إحنا إللّى قابلناك أوّل امبارح ؟
húwwa íḥna ílli qabil-nā-ki áwwil imbāriḥ?
He we who met-we-you(f) first yesterday?
Are we the ones who met you the day before yesterday?

D. Question tags, such as the English 'correct?, right?, o.k.?, please?', and rhetorical questions are very common in

Egyptian Arabic. The following question tags are used to emphasize questions.

The question tags in the sentences below are in brackets.

قلت له صحيح ؟
qul-t-íl-uh [ṣaḥīḥ]?
Told-you(m)-to-him really?
Did you really tell him?

إنت أمريكانى مش كده ؟
ínta amrik-āni [miš kídá]?
You(m) America-(adj) not so?
You are American, aren't you?

هوّ ماشى والاّ لسّه ؟
húwwa māši [wálla líssa]?
He going or yet?
Has he gone yet or not?

The following words also are used as question tags:

والنّبى wi-n-nábi by-the-Prophet
أبداً ábadan never
عمرك ɛúmr-ak your life

والنّبى حاتيجى والاّ لا ؟
wi-n-nábi ḥa-t-īgi wálla la'?
And-the-Prophet (ft)-you-come or no?
Look here, are you coming or not?

34. 2. Coordinating conjunctions are:

و wi, and
والاّ wálla, or, or rather
أو aw, or
يا ... يا ya...ya, either...or
يا ... أو ya...aw, either...or
لا ... ولا la...wála, neither...nor
مش ... ولا miš...wála, neither...nor
ما ... ولا ma...wála, neither...nor

التّلميذ والمدرّس
it-tilmīz w-il-mudárris
the-student and-the-teacher
the student and the teacher

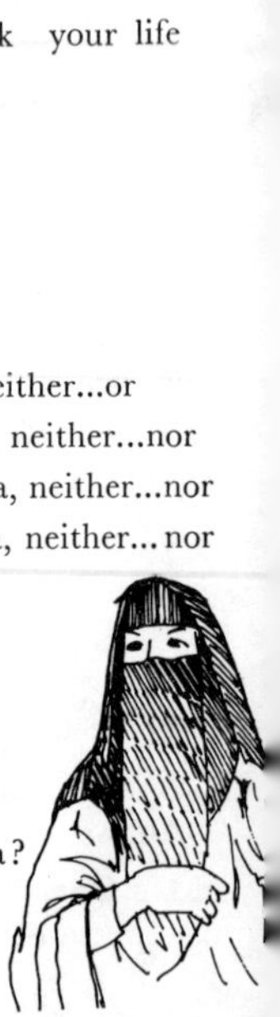

هىّ تلميذة والاّ / أو مدرّسة ؟
híyya tilmīz-a wálla/aw mudarrís-a?
She student-(f) or teacher-(f)?
Is she a student or a teacher?

هىّ يا تلميذة يا مدرّسة .
híyya ya tilmīz-a ya mudarrís-a.
She either student-(f) or teacher-(f).
She is either a student or a teacher.

هوّ لا / مش تلميذ ولا مدرّس .
húwwa la/miš tilmīz wála mudárris.
He no/not student nor teacher.
He is neither a student nor a teacher.

ما بيلعبش ولا يذاكرش .
ma-b-yi-lɛáb-š wála y-zakír-š.
(neg)-(pt)-he-play-(neg) nor he-study-(neg).
He is neither playing nor studying.

هوّ مشّ حاياكل ولا حاينام .
húwwa miš ḥa-y-ākul wála ḥa-y-nām.
He not (ft)-he-eat nor (ft)-he-sleep.
He will neither eat nor sleep.

wálla is usually used in interrogative and less frequently used in declarative sentences.

ya....ya/aw is used as its English counterpart is used.

la....wála is used both with verbal and verbless sentences.

miš....wála is used with verbs preceded by the future tense prefix ḥa- or with verbless sentences.

ma.... wála is used only with verbal sentences; however, verbs are followed by the negative suffix -š. wálla may be followed by an incomplete verb with or without the tense prefixes.

34. 3. Subordinating conjunctions. Subordinating conjunctions connect clauses. Most subordinating conjunctions are formed from prepositions or some other words and the use of the particle *ma*.

Usually, a preposition is followed by an object (noun or pronoun); whereas, a subordinating conjunction is usually followed by a verbal sentence. ما *ma* is usually placed before the verb; however, it can come before the subject also. An incomplete verb following a subordinating conjunction does not have a tense prefix.

There are two types of subordinating conjunctions: of time and of purpose. The most common subordinating conjunctions of time are:

لمّا	lámma, when/until
عندما	ɛánd(i) ma, when/while
يوم ما	yōm ma, the day when
من يوم ما	min yōm ma, since
ساعة ما	sāɛ-it ma, at the time that
من ساعة ما	min sāɛ-it ma, since
أوّل ما	áwwil ma, as soon as
قبلما / قبل ... ما	qábl(i) ma, before
بعد ما	báɛd(i) ma, after
وقت ما	wáqt(i) ma, at the time that
من وقت ما	min wáqt(i) ma, since
كلّما / كلّ ... ما	kúll(i) ma, every time
لغاية ما	li-ġāyit ma, until/up to
لحدّ ما	li-ḥádd ma, until
و	wi, while

لمّا وصل كان تعبان خالص .
lámma wíṣil kān taɛbān xāliṣ.
When he arrived he was tired completely.
When he arrived, he was dead tired.

قال لى الحكاية واحنا فى الاجتماع .
qál-l-i-l-ḥikāya w-íḥna fi-l-igtimāɛ.
He said-to-me-the-story and-we in-the-meeting.
He told me the story while we were at the meeting.

Usually the subordinating conjunctions of time can also occur at the beginning of a sentence. Note that لمّا lámma and عند ما ɛánd(i)ma also mean "until" and "while", respectively.

Following is a list of the most common subordinating conjunctions of purpose:

إنّ inn, that	بدل ما bádal ma, instead
مهما máhma, whatever	مع إنّ maع ínn, although
عشان عašān, because/ in order to/for	كأنّ ka-ínn, as if
	لَكن lākin, but
ما دام madām, because	أمّا ámma, but/as for
لإنّ li-ínn, because	إذا íza, if
لأحسن l-áḥsan, lest	لو law, if
من غيرما min ġēr ma, without	إن in, if

(For the use of the last three conjunctions [if] see conditional sentences).

المدرّس أعلن إنّ يوم الخميس أجازة .
il-mudárris áعlan ínn(i) yōm il-xamīs agāza.
The-teacher notified that day the-fifth holiday.
The teacher said that Thursday is a holiday.

طلع فوق بدل ما ينزل تحت .
ṭíliع fōq bádal ma yí-nzil taḥt.
Went up instead he-come down under.
We went up instead of coming down.

إنّ inn and some other subordinating conjunctions of purpose do not occur at the beginning of a sentence. Most conjunctions of purpose may be followed by either verbal or verbless sentences. The pronouns following إنّ inn are always bound. This conjunction follows certain verbs (or their active participles) like:

افتكر iftákar or ظنّ ẓann, think	شاف šāf, see
عرف عírif, know	قال qāl, say
سمع símiع, hear	خاف xāf, be afraid

Note that و wi is used as a coordinating or subordinating conjunction. This conjunction and لاحسن l-áḥsan may be followed by a noun or a free pronoun, but not by a bound pronoun.

Unit 35. عند الحكيم
ɛand il-ḥakīm
Visiting the Doctor

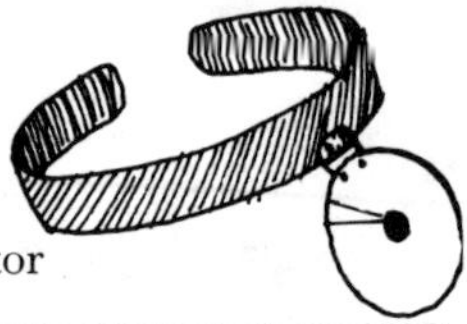

صباح الخير ، يا هانم . الدّكتور هنا ؟
PATIENT. — ṣabāḥ il-xēr, ya hānim, id-duktūr hína?
Morning the-good, oh lady. The-doctor here?
Good morning, young lady. Is the doctor here?

لا ، الدّكتور مش موجود ؛ ولَكن زمانه جايّ .
NURSE. — la', id-duktūr miš mawgūd; wi lākin zamān-uh [gayy.
No, the-doctor not present; and but time-his coming.
No, the doctor is not here; but he will be coming soon.

اتفضّل . فيه إيه ؟ إنت تعبان ؟
DOCTOR. — itfáḍḍal. fī-h ēh? ínta taɛbān?
Please. In-it what? You(m) tired?
Come in, please. What is it? Don't you feel well?

أنا ما عنديش ألم ، لَكن حاسس بضعف ، يا دكتور .
PATIENT. — ána ma-ɛand-ī-š álam, lākin ḥāsis bi-ḍáɛf, ya [duktūr.
I (neg)-to-me-(neg) pain, but feeling with-weakness, oh doctor.
I don't have any pain, doctor, but I feel very weak.

فكّ قميصك ، من فضلك ، يا أستاذ .
NURSE. — fukk qamīṣ-ak min-fáḍl-ak, ya ustāz.
Unbutton shirt-your(m), from-bounty-your(m), oh professor.
Please unbutton your shirt, sir.

باين عليك ما بتاكلش كويّس ، يا سيدى .
DOCTOR. — bāyin ɛalē-k ma-b-t-akúl-š kwáyyis, ya sīdi.
Appearing on-you(m) (neg)-(pt)-you(m)-eat-(neg) well, oh sir.
It seems you don't eat well, sir.

أنا ما اعرفش ليه ، لكن ما عنديش قوّة خالص .

PATIENT. — ána m-a-ȝráf-š lēh, lākin ma-ȝand-ī-š qúwwa [xāliṣ.
I (neg)-I-know-(neg) why, but (neg)-at-me-(neg) strength com- [*pletely.*
I don't know why, but I don't have any energy at all.

إنت ما بتاخدش الفيتامينات إللّى وصفتها لك ؟

DOCTOR. — ínta ma-b-t-axúd-š il-fitamin-āt ílli waṣaf-t- [ihā-l-ak?
You (neg)-(pt)-you-take-(neg) the-vitamin-(pl) which prescribed- [*I-it-to-you?*
Aren't you taking the vitamins I prescribed for you?

لا ، عشان ما لقيتهاش فى الأجزاخانة .

PATIENT. — la', ȝašān ma-laqi-t-hā-š fi-l-agzaxāna.
No, because (neg)-found-I-her-(neg) in-the-pharmacy.
No, because there weren't any at the pharmacy.

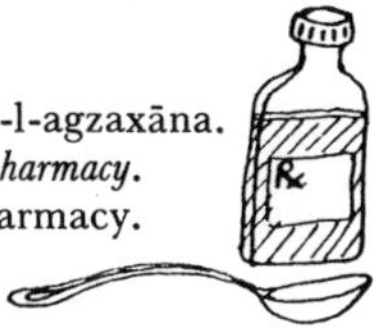

ما عندكش صداع الصّبح ؟

DOCTOR. — ma-ȝand-ák-š ṣudāȝ iṣ-ṣúbḥ?
(Neg)-at-you(m)-(neg) headache the-morning?
Don't you have headaches in the morning?

لا ، ما عنديش ؛ بسّ باحسّ بدوخة بسيطة .

PATIENT. — la', ma-ȝand-ī-š; bass b-a-ḥíss bi-dūxa baṣīṭ-a.
No, (neg)-at-me-(neg); only (pt)-I-feel with-dizziness little-(f).
No, I don't; I just feel a little dizzy.

ده مش تمام . حادّى لك شويّة حبوب عشان تخفّ .

DOCTOR. — da miš tamām. ḥ-a-ddí-l-ak šwáyy-it ḥubūb [ȝašān ti-xíff.
That not right. (ft)-I-give-to-you(m) little-(cs) pills because [*you(m)-recover.*
That's not good. I will give you some pills so you will get [better.

آه ! وحاجة تانية كمان : ما تشتغلش كتير .

DOCTOR. — ah! wi ḥāga tány-a kamān: ma-t-ištaġál-š kitīr.
Oh! And thing other-(f) also: (neg)-you-work-(neg) too much.
Then, another thing: don't work too hard.

35. 1. Negative constructions. There are two types of negative constructions: one using the word مش miš or muš, and the other using the split form ما...ش ma...š.

A. The word miš is invariable and is placed before the word, phrase, or sentence to be negated. Usually, miš is used:

1. With nouns, pronouns, adjectives, participles, adverbs and prepositions in verbless sentences or in isolation.

مش الكتاب ده	لا ، مش هوّ .
miš ik-kitāb da	la', miš húwwa.
not the-book this/that	*No, not him.*
not this book	No, it is not him.

2. With the future tense by placing miš before the future tense prefix ḥa-.

مش حاكتب الجواب .
miš ḥ-á-ktib il-gawāb.
Not (ft)-I-write the-letter.
I will not write the letter.

مش حانجيب الكتب معانا .
miš ḥa-n-gīb ik-kútub maɛā-na.
Not (ft)-we-bring the-books with-us.
We will not bring the books with us.

3. With modal auxiliaries (for the form, meaning and use of the modal auxiliaries like ɛāyiz, 'wanting' and lāzim, 'necessary, must' refer to unit 30) followed by the incomplete verb form.

مش عايزين يرجعوا تانى .
miš ɛayz-īn yi-rgáɛ-u tāni.
Not wanting-(pl) he-return-(pl) other.
They do not want to return again.

مش لازم ناخدهم كلّهم .
miš lāzim n-axúd-hum kull-úhum.
Not necessary we-take-them all-them.
Is is not necessary that we take all of them.

4. With verbal interrogative sentences by placing miš directly before the verb.

مش بعت لك الفلوس ؟
miš baɛát-l-ak il-filūs?
Not he sent-to-you(m) the-money?
Didn't he send you the money?

B. The split form ما...ش ma...š (ma- is a prefix, and -š is a suffix) is usually used to negate verb forms in verbal sentences and prepositions (prepositions ɛand, máɛa, li and fi can also be used in verbless sentences to render a meaning equivalent to English verbs "to have" [the first three prepositions] and "to be" [the last one]) used in verbless sentences and infrequently used with free personal pronouns when the latter are used instead of the above preposition in the negative form. The formula is:

ma + verb/preposition/personal pronoun + š.

In pronunciation (not in Arabic spelling), the negative split form ma...š takes slightly different forms, depending on the item being negated:

1. The prefix ma- is placed before the item being negated. The vowel *a* drops (in pronunciation) before a verb beginning with the same vowel. Before a verb beginning with the vowel *i*, the *i* drops before adding ma-.

أقدر أروح .	ما أقدرش أروح .
á-qdar a-rūḥ.	m-a-qdár-š a-rūḥ.
I-can I-go.	*(neg)-I-can-(neg) I-go.*
I can go.	I can't go.
اشتريت جرنال .	ما اشتريتش جرنال .
ištarē-t gurnāl.	ma-štarí-t-š gurnāl.
Bought-I/you(m) newspaper.	*(neg)-bought-I/you(m)-(neg) newspaper.*
I/you bought a newspaper.	I/you didn't buy a newspaper.

2. The suffix -š is placed after the item being negated.

In pronunciation, however, this suffix takes different forms, according to the ending of the item being negated.

a. If the verb form or preposition used as a verb has the object suffix pronoun -ik (second person feminine singular), the negative suffix is -īš. The vowel of -ik drops, unless three consecutive consonants would result.

باشوفك .	ما باشوفيكش .
b-a-šūf-ik.	ma-b-a-šuf-k-īš.
(pt)-I-see-you(f).	*(neg)-(pt)-I-see-you(f)-(neg).*
I see you.	I don't see you.

b. If the verb form or preposition used in verbless sentences has the object suffix pronoun -h (third person masculine singular, which is never pronounced in this position) preceded by a short vowel, the negative suffix is -š; however, the -h is never pronounced in this position either, and the short vowel is lengthened before adding the negative suffix.

إنت كتبته .	إنت ما كتبتوهش .
ínta katáb-t-uh.	ínta ma-katab-t-ūh-š.
You(m) wrote-you(m)-it.	*You(m) (neg)-wrote-you(m)-it-(neg).*
You wrote it.	You didn't write it.

c. If the verb form or preposition used as a verb has the object suffix pronoun -h (third person masculine singular) preceded by a long vowel, the negative suffix is -ūš; in this case, the -h is pronounced, and the long vowel is shortened when the negative suffix is added.

كتبت .	كتبتيه .
katáb-ti.	katab-tī-h.
Wrote-you(f).	*Wrote-you(f)-it.*
You wrote.	You wrote it.

ما كتبتيهوش .
ma-katab-ti-h-ūš.
(neg)-wrote-you(f)-it-(neg).
You didn't write it.

d. If the verb form or preposition used in verbless sentences ends in one consonant, the negative suffix is -š; if the verb or preposition contains a long vowel, it is shortened when the negative suffix is added.

ضربت .	ما ضربتش .
ḍárab-it.	ma ḍarab-ít-š.
Hit-she.	*(neg) hit-she-(neg).*
She hit.	She didn't hit.
هوّ سافر .	هوّ ما سافرش .
húwwa sāfir.	húwwa ma-safír-š.
He traveled.	*He (neg)-traveled-(neg).*
He left.	He didn't leave.

e. If a verb form or preposition used as a verb ends in two consonants, the negative suffix is -iš.

كتبت .	ما كتبتش .
katáb-t.	ma katáb-t-iš.
Wrote-I/you(m).	*(neg) wrote-I/you(m)-(neg).*
I/you wrote.	I/you didn't write.

f. If a verb form or a preposition used as a verb ends in a short vowel (in pronunciation), the negative suffix is -š; however, the short vowel is lengthened when adding the negative suffix.

بيلعبوا .	ما بيلعبوش .
bi-yi-lɛáb-u.	ma-b-yi-lɛab-ū-š.
(pt)-he-play-(pl).	*(neg)-(pt)-he-play-(pl)-(neg).*
They play/are playing.	They don't play/aren't playing.
أنا شفتها .	أنا ما شفتهاش .
ána šuf-t-áha.	ána ma-šuf-t-ahā-š.
I saw-I-her.	*I (neg)-saw-I-her-(neg).*
I saw her.	I didn't see her.

g. The following are negative forms of the prepositions عند ɛand, مع máɛa, لِ li and فِ fi when they are used as verbs. Usually, the negative prefix ma- is optional before the preposition maɛa, and the *h* in the following example before the negative suffix -š is not pronounced:

ما فيهش حاجة .
ma-fī-h-š ḥāga.
(neg)-in-it-(neg) thing.
There isn't anything.

	ما عندوهش	ما لوهش	معهش
3 m.	ma-ɛand-ūh-š	ma-l-ūh-š	maɛá-h-š (he does not have)
	ما عندهاش	ما لهاش	معهاش
3 f.	ma-ɛand-ahā-š	ma-l-hā-š	maɛa-hā-š (she does not have)
	ما عندهمش	ما لهمش	معهمش
3 pl.	ma-ɛand-uhúm-š	ma-l-húm-š	maɛa-húm-š (they do not have)
	ما عندكش	ما لكش	معكش
2 m.	ma-ɛand-ák-š	ma-l-ák-š	maɛá-k-š (you(m) do not have)
	ما عندكيش	ما لكيش	معكيش
2 f.	ma-ɛand-ik-īš	ma-l-k-īš	maɛa-kī-š (you (f.) do not have)
	ما عندكمش	ما لكمش	معكمش
2 pl.	ma-ɛand-ukúm-š	ma-l-kúm-š	maɛa-kúm-š (you (pl.) do not have)
	ما عنديش	ما ليش	معيش
1 sg.	ma-ɛand-ī-š	ma-l-ī-š	maɛ-ī-š (I do not have)
	ما عندناش	ما لناش	معناش
1 pl.	ma-ɛand-inā-š	ma-l-nā-š	maɛa-nā-š (we do not have)

A few forms each have another commonly used form:

ما عندوهش .   ما عندهوش .
ma-ɛand-ūh-š or ma-ɛand-uh-ūš he does not have

h. The negative forms of the free personal pronouns are the following:

(هوّ) ما هوش / ما هوّاش
(húwwa) ma-hū-š or ma-huwwā-š he does not have

(هىّ) ما هيّاش
(híyya) ma-hiyyā-š she does not have

(همّ) ما همّاش
(húmma) ma-hummā-š they do not have

(إنتَ) ما انتاش
(ínta) ma-ntā-š you (m.) do not have

(إنتِ) ما انتيش
(ínti) ma-n-tī-š you (f.) do not have

(إنتو) ما انتوش
(íntu) ma-ntū-š you (pl.) do not have

(أنا) ما انيش
(ána) ma-nī-š I do not have

(احنا) ما احناش
(íḥna) ma-ḥnā-š we do not have

The above negative forms are the only forms in which free personal pronouns are used in verbless sentences like the prepositions discussed in the preceding paragraph.

ما نيش فاكر خالص.
ma-nī-š fākir xāliṣ.
(neg)-I-(neg) thought completely.
I have no idea at all.

C. The negation of imperatives is the same as the negation of the incomplete verb forms of the second person masculine, feminine, and plural.

افتح !	ما تفتحش !
íftaḥ!	ma-ti-ftáḥ-š!
Open (m)!	*(neg)-you-open-(neg)!*
	Don't open (m)!

35. 2. Exclamations. Most of the following Arabic exclamations have their appropriate English counterparts. However, the Arabic interjection يا ya 'oh'!, which is always used before names or titles of persons in direct address, has no counterpart in English:

يا محمّد !	يا ريّس !	يا أستاذ !
ya muḥámmad!	ya ráyyis!	ya ustāz!
Oh Muhammad!	*Oh Chief!*	*Oh professor!*
Muhammad!	Waiter!	Sir!

This interjection is also used before some exclamatory expressions:

يا ساتر ، يا ربّ !	يا سلام !	يا خسارة !
ya sātir, ya rább!	ya salām!	ya xṣāra!
Oh protector, oh Lord!	*Oh peace!*	*Oh loss!*
God forbid!	How wonderful!	What a pity!
يا خبر أبيض !	يا شيطان !	يا بختك !
ya xábar ábyaḍ!	ya šiṭān!	ya báxt-ak!
Oh news white!	*Oh devil!*	*Oh luck-your!*
How awful!	You rascal!	How lucky you are!

The following exclamations express the speaker's astonishment, fear, or dislike.

الله !	سبحان الله !	والله !	لا يا شيخ !
állah!	subḥān allāh!	wállah!	la' ya šēx!
God!	*Praise God!*	*And God!*	*No oh master!*
What!	Good Lord!	Really!	You don't say!
أعوذُ بالله !		إشمعنى كده !	شي غريب !
aɛūzu billāh!		išmíɛna kída!	šē ġarīb!
Asking the protection of God!		*What meaning so!*	*Thing strange!*
Oh Lord!		Why do you do/ [say that!	Strange!

The following exclamations have the connotation of approval:

عظيم !	عال ، عال !	ممتاز !	يا ريت !
ɛaẓīm!	ɛāl, ɛāl!	mumtāz!	ya rēt!
Mighty!	*Fine, fine!*		*Oh wish!*
Great!	Excellent!	Outstanding!	I wish it were!

35. 3. Oaths. Here we give some of the oaths used by the Arabs of Egypt. Since oaths reflect culture patterns, we offer them for the student's information rather than for his use. Oaths are usually used as exclamations, for emphasis, for ascertaining the truth of statements made by others, or for pleading. The kinds of oaths used depend on the background and the status (for example, married or single) of the speaker.

Most of these oaths may be preceded by la' in negative statements or followed by a question mark in interrogative sentences.

والله !
w-allāh-i!
By-God-my!
By heavens!

والله العظيم !
w-allāh-i-l-ɛaẓīm!
By-God-my-the-Great!
Good Lord!/By the great Lord!

وربّنا !
wi-rabb-ína!
By-God-our!
By heavens!

والنّبى !
wi-n-náb-i!
By-the-Prophet-my!
By heavens!

بذمّتى !
bi-zimm-ít-i!
By-conscience-(cs)-my!
By my conscience!

بشرفى !
bi-šáraf-i!
By-honor-my!
By my honor!

إن شاء الله !
in-šā' allāh!
If-willed God!
God willing!

وحياة ابنى / أبويَ !
wi-ḥyāt íbn-i/abū-ya!
By-life son-my/father-my!
By the life of my son/my father!

وحياة ربّنا !
wi-ḥyāt rabb-ína!
By-life God-our!
Please!

وحياتك !
wi-ḥyāt-ak!
By-life-your(m)!
Please!

Unit 36. الساعة كام؟ *is-sāɛa kām?* What Time Is It?

أنا متأخّر ؛ يا على السّاعة كام معاك ؟
SAM. — ána mit'áxxar; ya ɛáli-s-sāɛa kām maɛā-k?
I late; oh Ali-the-hour how much with-you(m)?
I am late; what time is it, Ali?

ما اعرفش ، يا سام ؛ معاييش ساعة .
ALI. — m-a-ɛráf-š, ya Sam; maɛ-ī-š sāɛa.
(Neg)-I-know-(neg), oh Sam; with-me-(neg) watch.
I don't know, Sam; I don't have a watch.

أنا عندى ساعة ، لـكن عند السّاعاتى بيصلّحها .
ALI. — ána ɛánd-i sāɛa, lākin ɛand is-saɛāti bi-y-ṣalláḥ-ha.
I at-me watch, but at the-watchmaker (pt)-he-repair-it.
I have a watch, but it's at the watchmaker for repair.

تقريباً ضهر دلوقتِ . السّاعة اتناشر إلاّ عشرة . [ɛášara.
AHMAD. — taqrīban ḍúhr(i) dilwáqti. is-sāɛa iṭnāšar ílla
Approximately noon now. The-hour twelve minus ten.
It's about noon now. It is ten to twelve.

إنت باين عليك مستعجل ، يا سام .
AHMAD. — ínta bāyin ɛalē-k mistáɛgil, ya Sam.
You appearing on-you(m) in a hurry, oh Sam.
You seem to be in a hurry, Sam.

أيوه . أنا لازم أروح أجيب الأولاد من المدرسة السّاعة اتناشر ونصّ .
SAM. — áywa. ána lāzim a-rūḥ a-gīb il-awlād min il-madrása
[is-sāɛa itnāšar wi nuṣṣ.
Yes. I must I-go I-bring the-children from the-school the-hour twelve
[and half.
Yes. I have to bring the children from school at twelve-thirty.

الأولاد؟ كام ولد عندك ، يا سام؟
ALI. — il-awlād? kām wálad ɛánd-ak, ya Sam?
The-children? How many child at-you(m), oh Sam?
Children? How many children do you have, Sam?

لى ّ تلات أولاد وبنتين كلّهم فى المدرسة .
SAM.—lí-yya talát-t awlād wi bint-ēn kull-úhum fi-l-madrása.
To-me three-(cs) children and girl-(d) all-them in-the-school.
I have three boys and two girls in school.

هوّ انت بتاخدهم معاك كلّ يوم الصّبح كمان؟ [iṣ-ṣúbḥ kamān?
AHMAD. — húwwa ínta bi-t-axúd-hum maɛā-k kúll(i) yōm
He you (pt)-you-take-them with-you(m) all day the-morning also?
Do they come with you every morning also?

أيوه . إحنا بنصحى كلّ يوم السّاعة ستّة وتلت .
SAM. — áywa. íḥna bi-ní-ṣḥa kúll(i) yōm is-sāɛa sítta wi tilt.
Yes. We (pt)-we-wake up all day the-hour six and one third.
Yes. We get up at six-twenty every day.

ليه بدرى كده؟ دى المدارس فصولها بتبتدى السّاعة تمانية .
ALI. — lēh bádri kída? di-l-madāris fuṣúl-ha bi-ti-btídi [is-sāɛa tamánya.
Why early so? That the-schools classes-her (pt)-she-begin the-hour [*eight.*
Why so early? The schools start at eight.

ومع كده ، إنت عندك عربيّة ، مش كده؟
AHMAD. — wi máɛa kída, ínta ɛánd-ak ɛarabíyya, miš kída?
And with so, you at-you(m) car, not so?
And then, you have a car, don't you?

أيوه ، أنا عندى عربيّة ، لٰكن مش معاى النّهارده .
SAM. — áywa, ána ɛánd-i ɛarabíyya, lākin miš maɛā-ya [innahárda.
Yes, I at-me car, but not with-me today.
Yes, I have a car, but I don't have it with me today.

36. 1. Verbless sentences with prepositions عند ɛand 'at', مع máɛa 'with', and لِ li 'to, for'. A verb corresponding to the English verb "have" is lacking in Arabic. In order to convey the meaning of this verb, the above prepositions are used with bound pronouns. Prepositions in this type of sentence may be preceded by a free subject pronoun and are negated by the split negative form ما...ش ma...š:

لىّ أصحاب كتير فى مصر .	معاك فلوس ، يا لطفى ؟
lí-yya aṣḥāb kitīr fi-máṣr.	maɛā-k filūs, ya lúṭfi?
To-me friends many in-Egypt.	*With-you(m) money, oh Lutfi?*
I have many friends in Egypt.	Do you have any money, Lutfi?

عندك عربيّة ، يا حسّن ؟	لا ، ما عنديش عربيّة .
ɛánd-ak ɛarabíyya, ya ḥássan?	la', ma-ɛand-ī-š ɛarabíyya.
At-you(m) car, oh Hassan?	*No, (neg)-at-me-(neg) car.*
Do you have a car, Hassan?	No, I don't have a car.

There is a difference in meaning between the use of ɛand and máɛa for the translation of the English verb "have". ɛand conveys the meaning "have" in the general sense, that is, to possess or own something; whereas máɛa denotes the meaning "have" in the strict sense of carrying something with or on oneself.

عندهم عربيّة .	معاهم عربيّة .
ɛand-úhum ɛarabíyya.	maɛā-hum ɛarabíyya.
At-them car.	*With-them car.*
They have (or own) a car.	They have (with them) a car.

عنده ɛánd-uh	معاه maɛā-h	له lī-h	he has
عندها ɛand-áha	معاها maɛā-ha!	لها lī-ha	she has
عندهم ɛand-úhum	معاهم maɛā-hum	لهم lī-hum	they have
عندك ɛánd-ak	معاك maɛā-k	لك lī-k	you (m) have
عند ك ɛánd-ik	معاك maɛā-ki	لك lī-ki	you (f) have
عندكم ɛand-úkum	معاكم maɛā-kum	لكم lī-kum	you (pl) have
عندى ɛánd-i	معاى maɛā-ya	لىّ lí-yya	I have
عندنا ɛand-ína	معانا maɛā-na	لنا lī-na	we have

For expressions corresponding to "had" or "did have", كان kān 'was', is placed before ɛand, máɛa, or li.

كان عندى عربيّة جديدة .
kan-ɛánd-i ɛarabíyya gidīd-a.
Was-to-me car new-(f).
I had a new car.

In a negative construction of this type, only kān is negated by the negative split form ma...š:

ما كانش عندى فلوس أبداً .
ma-kán-š ɛánd-i filūs ábadan.
(Neg)-was-(neg) at-me money never.
I didn't have any money at all.

36. 2. The verbless sentence with فيه fī-h 'there is/are'. This type of sentence is very common in Egyptian Arabic; it consists of a prepositional phrase: fi plus the third person masculine singular pronoun -h (fi + h), usually followed by an indefinite noun or noun phrase. This sentence is negated by the split negative form ما...ش ma...š:

فيه حفلة .	ما فيش حفلة .
fī-h ḥáfla.	ma-fīh-š ḥáfla.
In-it party.	*(Neg)-in-it-(neg) party.*
There is a party.	There is no party.

For the formation of the construction "there was/were", the verb auxiliary كان kān 'was' is placed before the verbless sentence fī-h:

كان فيه حفلة امبارح .	كان فيه ناس كتير فى الأوضة .
kan-fī-h ḥáfla imbāriḥ.	kan-fī-h nās kitīr fi-l-ōḍa.
Was-in-it party yesterday.	*Was-in-it people many in-the-room.*
There was a party yesterday.	There were many people in the [room.

In this type of construction, only كان kān can be negated by the split form:

ما كانش فيه عيش كفاية .
ma-kán-š fī-h ɛēš kifāya.
(Neg)-was-(neg) in-it bread enough.
There was not enough bread.

هدايا من أمريكا

hadāya min amrīka

Unit 37. Gifts from America

أهلاً ، أهلاً ، يا سام . انت وصلت إمتى ؟

ALI. — áhlan, áhlan, ya Sam. ínta wiṣíl-t ímta?
Welcome, welcome, oh Sam. You arrived-you(m) when?
Good to see you, Sam. When did you arrive?

أنا هنا من أسبوعين تقريباً ، يا على .

SAM. — ána hína min isbuع-ēn taqrīban, ya ع áli.
I here from week-(d) approximately, oh Ali.
I have been here about two weeks, Ali.

كان لازم تخبرنا عن وقت وصولك .

ALI. — kān lāzim ti-xbír-na ع an waqt wuṣūl-ak.
Was necessary you-notify-us on time arrival-your(m).
You should have notified us of your arrival.

ازّاى بقى ؟ دانا بعتّ لك جواب من حوالى شهر .

SAM. — izzāy báqa? da ána baع at-t-íl-ak gawāb min ḥawāli [šahr.
How then? This I sent-I-to-you(m) letter from about month.
How's that? I sent you a letter about a month ago.

بالحق ، والدى طلب منّى أكتب لك جواب بالنّيابة عنه .

SAM. — bi-l-ḥáqq, wáld-i ṭálab mínn-i a-ktíb-l-ak gawāb [bi-n-niyāba ع ánn-uh.
In-the-truth, father-my asked from-me I-write-to-you(m) letter by-[the-behalf on-his.
Actually, my father asked me to write to you for him.

أنا عارف ، لـكن للاسف أنا ما ردّيتش عليه لسّه .

ALI. — ána ع ārif, lākin l-il-ásaf ána ma-raddí-t-š ع alē-h líssa.
I knowing, but to-the-sorrow I (neg)-answered-I-(neg) on-it yet.
I know, but unfortunately I haven't answered his letter yet.

طيّب ، ياالله بينا على البيت . أنا عندى شويّة حاجات للاولاد .
SAM. — ṭáyyib, yálla bī-na ʿala-l-bēt. ána ʿánd-i šwáyy-it [ḥag-āt li-l-awlād.
Well, come on with-us on-the-home. I at-me little-(cs) thing-(pl) [to-the-children.
O.K., let's go home. I have something for the children.

آدى سام يا ناس ؛ بقاله هنا من أسبوعين .
ALI. — ādi Sam, ya nās; baqā-l-uh hína min isbuʿ-ēn.
Here is Sam, oh people; has been-to-him here from week-(d).
Here is Sam, folks; he has been here for two weeks.

العيله بتبعت لكم أحسن التّمنيّات .
SAM. — il-ʿēla bi-ti-bʿat-l-úkum áḥsan it-timanniyy-āt.
The-family (pt)-she-send-to-you(pl) best the-wish-(pl).
My family send you their best wishes.

العلبة دى فيها هدايا لكلّ واحد منكم .
SAM. — il-ʿílba di fī-ha hadāya li-kúll(i) wāḥid mín-kum.
The-box this in-it presents for-all one from-you.
In this box there are gifts for each one of you.

ليه بسّ كده ، يا سام ؟ والله ألف شكر .
FATMA. — lēh bass kída, ya Sam? w-allāh-i alf šukr.
Why only so, oh Sam? By-God-my thousand thanks.
Why all this, Sam? Many thanks.

ما تفتحيهاش ، يا ليلى ؛ خلّى سام يفتحهالك .
ALI. — ma-ti-ftaḥ-i-hā-š, ya láyla; xálli Sam yi-ftaḥ-hā-l-ik.
(Neg)-you-open-(f)-it-(neg), oh Leila; let Sam he-open-it-for-[you(f).
Don't open it, Leila; let Sam open it for you.

طيّب . آدى كرافتّة لك ، يا على ؛ بابا اشتراهالك .
SAM. — ṭáyyib. ādi karafátta li-k, ya ʿáli; bāba ištara-hā-l-ak.
Well. Here is tie for-you(m), oh Ali; father bought-it-for-you(m).
Fine. This tie is for you, Ali; father bought it for you.

37. 1. li **as a preposition.** Like most prepositions, *li* takes (in pronunciation) different forms depending on its position in the sentence. Its meaning too varies with the context: it may be translated into English as "to", "for", "in", "on behalf of", or "toward". *li* can be used as follows:

A. As a preposition before a word, its form does not change:

لمين الكتاب ده ؟	الكتاب ده لصاحبي .
li mīn ik-kitāb da?	ik-kitāb da li ṣáḥb-i.
For who the-book this?	*The-book this for friend-my.*
For whom is this book?	This book is for my friend.

B. As a preposition with bound pronouns, its form is:

له	l-uh	to, for him	لك	l-íki	to, for you (f)
لها	l-íha	to, for her	لكم	l-úkum	to, for you (pl)
لهم	l-úhum	to, for them	لي	l-íyya	to, for me
لك	l-ik	to, for you (m)	لنا	l-ína	to, for us

الكتاب ده لي ؟	لا ، الكتاب ده لها .
ik-kitāb da l-íyya?	la', ik-kitāb da l-íha.
The-book this for-me?	*No, the-book this for-her.*
Is this book for me?	No, this book is for her.

37. 2. li **introducing indirect objects.** With verbs which take two objects (direct and indirect) *li* is used in verbal sentences to introduce indirect objects.

Like direct objects, indirect objects may be free (nouns) or bound (pronouns). If both objects are nouns, either one may immediately follow the verb. However, if the indirect object follows the direct object, it takes the preposition *li* as a prefix and if the indirect object precedes the direct object, it may or may not take the preposition *li*, according to the type of verb:

ورّى الجواب لصاحبه .	ورّى صاحبه الجواب .
wárra ig-gawāb liṣáḥb-uh.	wárra ṣáḥb-uh ig-gawāb.
He showed the-letter to friend-his.	*He showed friend-his the-letter.*
He showed the letter to his friend.	He showed his friend the [letter.

كتب جواب لصاحبه .	كتب لصاحبه جواب .
kátab gawāb li-ṣáḥb-uh.	kátab li-ṣāḥb-uh gawāb.
He wrote letter to-friend-his.	*He wrote to-friend-his letter.*
He wrote a letter to his friend.	He wrote his friend a letter.

If one of the objects (direct or indirect) is a bound pronoun, it is attached to the verb and the free object follows. In this case also, the indirect object may or may not take the preposition *li*, according to the type of verb:

جاب لى هديّة .	إدّاها وردة .
gáb-l-i hadíyya.	iddā-ha wárd-a.
He brought-to-me present.	*He gave-her flowers-(one).*
He brought me a present.	He gave her a flower.

If both objects (direct and indirect) are pronouns, the direct precedes the indirect, which takes the preposition *li:*

إدّاهالها .
idda-há-l-ha.
He gave-her/it-to-her.
He gave it to her.

If both objects are pronouns and the direct object is third person masculine singular, its form is *hū* or *hu* (before a cluster or two consonants):

كتبه .	كتبهوله .	كتبهولنا .
kátab-uh.	katab-hū-l-uh.	katab-hú-l-na.
He wrote-him/it.	*He wrote-it-to-him.*	*He wrote-it-to-us.*
He wrote it.	He wrote it to him.	He wrote it to us.

When *li* + indirect object pronoun is attached to a verb form (with or without a direct object pronoun), it assumes different forms, according to the ending of the verb form: one consonant, two consonants, a short vowel, or a long vowel.

In the following listing, V = short vowel, $\bar{V}$ = long vowel and C = consonant. The forms of *li* + indirect object after a verb form ending in:

a short vowel:

V → $\bar{V}$	+ l-uh	to, for him
V	+ l-ha	to, for her
V	+ l-hum	to, for them
V → $\bar{V}$	+ l-ak	to, for you (m)
V → $\bar{V}$	+ l-ik	to, for you (f)
V	+ l-kum	to, for you (pl)
V → $\bar{V}$	+ l-i	to, for me
V	+ l-na	to, for us

Note that in the case of a verb form ending in a short vowel, this vowel is lengthened before adding l-uh, l-ak, l-ik, or l-i:

جابوا	gāb-u	they brought
جابوله	gab-ū-l-uh	they brought for him
جابوها	gab-ú-l-ha	they brought for her
جابوهم	gab-ú-l-hum	they brought for them
جابولك	gab-ū-l-ak	they brought for you (m)
جابولك	gab-ū-l-ik	they brought for you (f)
جابولكم	gab-ú-l-kum	they brought for you (pl)
جابولى	gab-ū-l-i	they brought for me
جابولنا	gab-ú-l-na	they brought for us

a long vowel:

$\bar{V}$ → V + hū + l-uh	him/it to, for him
$\bar{V}$ → V + hú + l-ha	him/it to, for her
$\bar{V}$ → V + hú + l-hum	him/it to, for them
$\bar{V}$ → V + hū + l-ak	him/it to, for you (m)
$\bar{V}$ → V + hū + l-ik	him/it to, for you (f)
$\bar{V}$ → V + hú + l-kum	him/it to, for you (pl)
$\bar{V}$ → V + hū + l-i	him/it to, for me
$\bar{V}$ → V + hú + l-na	him/it to, for us

Notice that the long vowel (caused by the addition of the third masculine singular suffix pronoun *-h*, him/it, to a verb form ending in a short vowel) becomes short and the object pronoun *-h* is replaced by *-hū* or *-hu* (before a two consonant cluster) before *li* + pronoun. Unlike the suffix *-h*, which is not pronounced in final position, the *h* of *hū* or *hu* is pronounced in this position:

قالوا	qāl-u	they said/told
قالوه	qal-ū-h	they told it/him
قالوهوله	qal-u-hū-l-uh	they told it to him
قالوهولنا	qal-u-hú-l-ha	they told it to her
قالوهولهم	qal-u-hú-l-hum	they told it to them
قالوهولك	qal-u-hū-l-ak	they told it to you (m)
قالوهولك	qal-u-hū-l-ik	they told it to you (f)
قالوهولكم	qal-u-hú-l-kum	they told it to you (pl)
قالوهولى	qal-u-hū-l-i	they told it to me
قالوهولنا	qal-u-hú-l-na	they told it to us
كتبتِ	katáb-t-i	you (f) wrote
كتبتيه	katab-t-ī-h	you (f) wrote it
كتبتيهوله	katab-t-i-hū-l-uh	you (f) wrote it to him
كتبتيهولها	katab-t-i-hú-l-ha	you (f) wrote it to her
كتبتيهولهم	katab-t-i-hú-l-hum	you (f) wrote it to them
كتبتيهولى	katab-t-i-hū-l-i	you (f) wrote it to me
كتبتيهولنا	katab-t-i-hú-l-na	you (f) wrote it to us

one consonant:

C + l-uh	to/for him	C + l-ik	to/for you (f)
C + l-áha	to/for her	C + l-úku(m)	to/for you(pl)
C + l-úhum	to/for them	C + l-i	to/for me
C + l-ak	to/for you(m)	C + l-ína	to/for us

قال	qāl	he said/told
قال له	qál-l-uh	he told him
قال لها	qal-l-áha	he told her
قال لهم	qal-l-úhum	he told them
قال لك	qál-l-ak	he told you (m)

قال لِك	qál-l-ik	he told you (f)
قال لَكُم	qal-l-úkum	he told you (pl)
قال لى	qál-l-i	he told me
قال لنا	qal-l-ína	he told us

two consonants:

CC + íl-uh	to/for him
CC + íl-ha	to/for her
CC + íl-hum	to/for them
CC + íl-ak	to/for you (m)
CC + íl-ik	to/for you (f)
CC + íl-kum	to/for you (pl)
CC + íl-i	to/for me
CC + íl-na	to/for us

قلت له	qul-t-íl-uh	I/you (m) told him
قلت لها	qul-t-íl-ha	I/you (m) told her
قلت لهم	qul-t-íl-hum	I/you (m) told them
قلت لك	qul-t-íl-ak	I told you (m)
قلت لِك	qul-t-íl-ik	I told you (f)
قلت لَكُم	qul-t-íl-kum	I told you (pl)
قلت لى	qul-t-íl-i	you (m) told me
قلت لنا	qul-t-íl-na	you (m) told us

Unit 38. تغيير الفلوس
tağyīr il-filūs
Changing Money

يا موسى ، ممكن أغيّر شويّة دولارات فين ؟
PETER. — ya mūsa, múmkin a-ġáyyar šwáyy-it dular-āt fēn?
Oh Moussa, possible I-change little-(cs) dollar-(pl) where?
Mousa, where can I change some American dollars?

ممكن تغيّرهم فى اللّوكاندة أو فى البنك .
MOUSA. — múmkin ti-ġayyár-hum f-il-lukánda aw f-il-bánk.
Possible you-change-them in-the-hotel or in-the-bank.
You can change them at a hotel or a bank.

يا ستّ هانم ، ممكن تصرفى لى الشّيك ده ؟
PETER. — ya sítt(i) hānim, múmkin ti-ṣrifī-l-i iš-šēk da?
Oh woman lady, possible you-cash-to-me the-check this?
Madam, would you cash this check for me?

حاضر ، يا افندم . ده شيك بخمسمية دولار .
TELLER. — ḥāḍir, y-afándim. da šēk bi-xúms(u) mīt dollār.
Ready, oh gentleman. This check of-five hundred dollar.
Certainly, sir. This is a five hundred dollar check.

ممكن تورّينى أىّ شهادة شخصيّة .
TELLER. — múmkin t-warrī-ni ayy šihāda šaxṣ-í-yya.
Possible you-show-me any certificate person-(adj)-(f)?
Would you show me some identification?

أهو ! من فضلك إدينى خمسة جنيه فكّة .
PETER. — ahú! min fáḍl-ik iddī-ni xámsa ginēh fákka.
Here is! From-bounty-your(f) give-me five pound change.
Here! Please give me five pounds in change.

ليه بتصرف مبلغ كبير كده ، يا بيتر ؟
MOUSA. — lēh bi-tí-ṣrif máblaġ kibīr kída, ya Peter?
Why (pt)-you-cash amount big so, oh Peter?
Why do you cash such a large amount, Peter?

ما تنساش ، يا موسى ، عندنا أربع ولاد وخمس بنات .
LAURA. — ma-ti-nsā-š, ya mūsa, ع‍and-ína arbáع wilād wi [xámas banāt.
(Neg)-you-forget-(neg), oh Mousa, at-us four boys and five girls.
Remember, Mousa, we have four boys and five girls.

يا بيتر ، ضرورى لازم نشترى شويّة صحون .
LAURA. — ya Peter, ḍarūri lāzim ni-štíri šwáyy-it ṣuḥūn.
Oh Peter, essential must we-buy little-(cs) plates.
Peter, we have to buy some dishes.

فى العشرة أيام الأخيرة كسرنا تسع فناجين .
LAURA. —f-il-ع‍ášar-t-iyyām il-axīr-a kasár-na tísaع fanagīn.
In-the-ten-(cs)-days the-last-(f) broke-we nine cups.
In the last ten days, we have broken nine cups.

حلو ده ! وتمان صحون وسبع كبّايات .
PETER. — ḥilw da! wi táman ṣuḥūn wi sábaع kubbayy-āt.
Sweet this! And eight dishes and seven glass-(pl).
That is nice! And eight plates and seven glasses.

طبعاً ، فيه حداشر نفر فى العيلة .
LAURA. — tábع‍an, fī-h ḥidāšar náfar f-il-ع‍ēla.
Naturally, in-it eleven person in-the-family.
Naturally, there are eleven people in the family.

وكده يبقى اتنين وعشرين ايد .
MOUSA. — wi kída yí-bqa itnēn wi-ع‍išrīn īd.
And so it-become two and-twenty hand.
And that makes twenty-two hands.

38. 1. Cardinal numbers. Numbers 0 through 10 are:

0	٠	صفر	ṣifr, zero.
1	١	واحد	wāḥid (m)
1	١	واحدة	wáḥd-a (f)

2	٢	اتنين itnēn		
3	٣	تلاتة talāta	تلاتة talát-t	تلات talāt
4	٤	أربعة arbáɛa	أربعة arbáɛ-t	أربع árbaɛ
5	٥	خمسة xámsa	خمسة xamás-t	خمس xámas
6	٦	ستّة sítta	ستّ sitt	ستّ sitt
7	٧	سبعة sábɛa	سبعة sabáɛ-t	سبع sábaɛ
8	٨	تمانية tamánya	تمانة tamán-t	تمان táman
9	٩	تسعة tísɛa	تسعة tisáɛ-t	تسع tísaɛ
10	١٠	عشرة ɛášara	عشرة ɛašár-t	عشر ɛášar

A. Number 1 has two forms: masculine and feminine. It may follow or precede a noun, and in either case it agrees with the noun in gender. If it precedes the noun, the number 1 may function as an indefinite article or mean "a certain"; and if it follows the noun, the only meaning it can have is "one":

> واحد صاحبك ماشى مع واحدة بنت .
> wāḥid sáḥb-ak māši máɛa wáḥd-a bint.
> *One friend-your(m) going with one-(f) girl.*
> A friend of yours is going with a (certain) girl.

> صاحبك ماشى مع بنت واحدة .
> sáḥb-ak māši máɛa bint wáḥd-a.
> *Friend-your(m) going with girl one-(f).*
> Your friend is going with one girl (only).

B. Number 2 is invariable. It is seldom used because most nouns take the dual suffix. Usually, it is used as a counting number in isolation, with nouns which do not take the dual suffix, and with a few nouns of measure (weight and money). The nouns of measure use the singular form after 2; all the other nouns are used in their plural form:

اتنين كيلو	اتنين فلاحين
itnēn kīlu	itnēn fallaḥ-īn
two kilo	*two farmer-(pl)*
two kilos	two farmers

C. Each of the numbers 3 through 10 has three different forms: one ending in *-a* (first column above), one ending in *-t* (second column), and one ending in a consonant (third column). This difference in the endings of the forms is not a matter of gender (masculine *vs.* feminine), but rather a phonological (pronunciation) problem. Except for a few cases (mentioned below), numbers 3 through 10 are always used before plural nouns.

1. Forms in the first column are used when counting in isolation (1, 2, 3, 4, 5, etc.); after the singular nouns e.g. ساعة sāʿa 'hour', to indicate the time, and نمرة nímra 'number', to indicate the quantity; before the tens (20, 30, 40, etc.) connected by و wi, 'and':

خمسة وعشرين	السّاعة تلاتة .	البيت نمرة أربعة
xámsa wi ʿišrīn	is-sāʿa talāta.	il-bēt nímra arbáʿa
five and twenty	*The-hour three.*	*the-house number four*
twenty-five	It is three o'clock.	the house number four

أربعة تعريفة	تمانية صاغ	عشرة متر
arbáʿa taʿrīfa	tamánya ṣāġ	ʿášara mitr
four half-piasters	*eight piasters*	*ten meter*
(about 5 cents)	(about 19 cents)	ten meters

2. Forms in the second column are used before plural nouns beginning with a vowel; before عشرة ʿášara 'ten' for the formation of numbers 13 through 19; and before the number آلاف alāf 'thousands'. Historically, the suffix *-t* has developed (in pronunciation) as the construct state suffix which replaces *a*, the feminine ending:

سبعة آلاف	تسعة اشهر	تلاتة ارباع
sabáʿ-t alāf	tisáʿ-t úšhur	talát-t irbāʿ
seven-(cs) thousands	*nine-(cs) months*	*three-(cs) quarters*
7,000	nine months	three-quarters

3. Forms in the third column are used before plural nouns beginning with a consonant:

تلات مرّات	أربع ساعات	خمس كتب
talat-marr-āt	árbaɛ saɛ-āt	xámas kútub
three-time-(pl)	*four hour-(pl)*	*five books*
three times	four hours	five books

D. Numbers 11 through 19 are:

11	١١	حداشر	ḥiḍāšar	16	١٦	ستّاشر	siṭṭāšar
12	١٢	اتناشر	iṭnāšar	17	١٧	سبعتاشر	sabaɛṭāšar
13	١٣	تلتّاشر	talaṭṭāɛšar	18	١٨	تمنتاشر	tamanṭāšar
14	١٤	أربعتاشر	arbaɛṭāšar	19	١٩	تسعتاشر	tisaɛṭāšar
15	١٥	خمستاشر	xamasṭāšar				

Notice the difference in Arabic spelling and pronunciation of the original number 10: the consonant ع is replaced by the long vowel ا *ā*, and the consonants are made emphatic (in pronunciation only).

Numbers above 10 are always used before singular nouns, and the adjective following a noun occurs in its plural form:

خمستاشر ولد نبها
xamastāšar wálad nubáha
fifteen boy intelligent(pl)
fifteen intelligent boys

E. The tens from 20 through 90 are:

20	٢٠	عشرين	ɛišrīn	60	٦٠	ستّين	sittīn
30	٣٠	تلاتين	talatīn	70	٧٠	سبعين	sabɛīn
40	٤٠	أربعين	arbiɛīn	80	٨٠	تمانين	tamanīn
50	٥٠	خمسين	xamsīn	90	٩٠	تسعين	tisɛīn

The numbers between the tens are formed by placing the units 1 through 9 (for 3 through 9, the forms which end in *a*) before the tens; however, between the units and the tens, the conjunction و wi 'and' is inserted:

21	٢١	واحد وعشرين	wāḥid wi ɛašrīn
32	٣٢	اتنين وتلاتين	itnēn wi talatīn
43	٤٣	تلاتة وأربعين	talāta wi arbiɛīn
54	٥٤	أربعة وخمسين	arbáɛa wi xamsīn
65	٦٥	خمسة وستين	xámsa wi sittīn
76	٧٦	ستّة وسبعين	sítta wi sabɛīn
87	٨٧	سبعة وتمانين	sábɛa wi tamanīn
98	٩٨	تمانية وتسعين	tamánya wi tisɛīn
99	٩٩	تسعة وتسعين	tísɛa wi tisɛīn

F. The hundreds are:

100	١٠٠	ميّة	míyya	مية	mīt
200	٢٠٠	ميتين	mitēn		
300	٣٠٠	تلتميّة	tultumíyya	تلتمية	tultumīt
400	٤٠٠	ربعميّة	rubɛumíyya	ربعمية	rubɛumīt
500	٥٠٠	خمسميّة	xumsumíyya	خمسمية	xumsumīt
600	٦٠٠	ستّميّة	suttumíyya	ستّمية	suttumīt
700	٧٠٠	سبعميّة	subɛumíyya	سبعمية	subɛumīt
800	٨٠٠	تمنميّة	tumnumíyya	تمنمية	tumnumīt
900	٩٠٠	تسعميّة	tusɛumíyya	تسعمية	tusɛumīt

The forms on the left (míyya) are used in counting in isolation (not followed by a noun) or in compounds with units and tens:

120	١٢٠	ميّة وعشرين	míyya wi ɛišrīn
131	١٣١	ميّة واحد وتلاتين	míyya wāḥid wi talatīn
506	٥٠٦	خمسميّة وستّة	xumsumíyya wi sítta

The forms on the right, which end in *-t* (in pronunciation only), are in construct state:

خمسميّة سنة	مية عربيّة
xumsumīt sána	mīt ɛarabíyya.
five hundred year	*hundred car*
500 years	100 cars

G. Numbers, 1,000 . . . to 10,000 . . . are:

1,000	ألف	alf	6,000	ستّ آلاف	sitt-alāf
2,000	ألفين	alf-ēn	7,000	سبعة آلاف	sabaع-t-alāf
3,000	تلاتة آلاف	talat-t-alāf	8,000	تمانة آلاف	taman-t-alāf
4,000	أربعة آلاف	arbaع-t-alāf	9,000	تسعة آلاف	tisaع-t-alāf
5,000	خمسة آلاف	xamas-t-alāf	10,000	عشرة آلاف	عašar-t-alāf

Above 10,000, the number ألف alf is added to the tens and hundreds:

11,000	حداشر ألف	ḥidāšar alf
21,000	واحد وعشرين ألف	wāḥid wi عišrīn alf

H. The millions are formed by either the units (ending in-*a*), tens, or hundreds (ending in -*t*) plus the number مليون milyōn 'one million' which is usually invariable:

2,000,000	اتنين مليون	itnēn milyōn
5,000,000	خمسة مليون	xámsa milyōn
100,000,000	مية ميلون	mit-milyōn

38. 2. The definite article with numbers. Numbers usually precede the noun and, if the construction is definite, only the numeral has the definite article. However, if the numeral follows the noun, the noun, with numbers from 3 on, is plural and the number has the counting form. Moreover, both the noun and the numeral must have the definite article:

خمس كتب
xámas kútub
five books

الخمس كتب دول بتوعي .
il-xámas kútub dōl bitūع-i.
The-five books these belong to-me.
These five books are mine.

الكتب الخمسة دول بتوعي .
ik-kútub il-xámsa dōl bitūع-i.
The-books the-five these belong to-me.
These five books belong to me.

أيام الاسبوع

ayyām il-usbūع

Unit 39. The Days of the Week

النّهارده أوّل يناير ، يعني ، راس السّنة .

JERRY. — innahárda áwwil yanāyir, yáعni, rās is-sána.
Today first January, that is, head the-year.
Today is the first of January, that is, New Year's Day.

إحنا عندنا السّنة الهجريّة مختلفة عن السّنة الميلادية .

SALAH. — íḥna عand-ína is-sána il-higr-í-yya muxtálif-a عan [is-sána il-milad-í-yya.
We at-us the-year the-Higra-(adj)-(f) different-(f) than the-year [the-birth-(adj)-(f).
Our Moslem calendar is different from the Christian calendar.

لكن رسمياً إحنا بنمشي على السّنة الغربيّة .

SALAH. — lākin rasmíyyan íḥna bi-ní-mši عála is-sána il- [ġarb-í-yya.
But officially we (pt)-we-go on the-year the-west-(adj)-(f).
However, officially we follow the western calendar.

ياالله نعدّ أيّام الأسبوع بالعربي .

JERRY. — yálla ni-عídd ayyām il-usbūع b-il-عárab-i.
Come on we-count days the-week in-the-Arab-(adj).
Let's name the days of the week in Arabic.

أوّل يوم هوّ الاتنين ؛ والتّاني التّلات ؛ والتّالت الأربع .

JERRY. — áwwil yōm húwwa il-itnēn; w-it-tāni it-talāt; [w-it-tālit il-árbaع.
First day he the-two; and-the-second the-three; and-the-third [the four.
The first day is Monday; the second, Tuesday; and the [third, Wednesday.

والرّابع الخميس ، والخامس الجمعة .

SALAH. — w-ir-rābiع il-xamīs, w-il-xāmis ig-gúmعa.
And-the-fourth the-fifth, and-the-fifth the-Friday.
And the fourth is Thursday, and the fifth is Friday.

يا صلاح ، انا نسيت سادس وسابع يوم .

JERRY. — ya ṣalāḥ, ána nisī-t sādis wi sābiع yōm.
Oh Salah, I forgot-I sixth and seventh day.
Salah, I have forgotten the sixth and the seventh days.

اليوم السادس والسابع همّ السّبت والحدّ .

SALAH. — il-yōm is-sādis w-is-sābiع húmma is-sábt w-il-[ḥádd.
The day the-sixth and-the-seventh they the-seven and-the-one.
The sixth and the seventh are Saturday and Sunday.

خد بالك من اختلاف الأعداد .

SALAH. — xud bāl-ak min ixtilāf il-aعdād.
Take care-your(m) from difference the-numbers.
Notice the different forms of the numbers.

أيوه ، بيختلفوا حسب الجنس والمكان .

JERRY. — áywa, bi-y-ixtílif-u ḥásab il-gíns w-il-makān.
Yes, (pt)-he-differs-(pl) account the-gender and-the-place.
Yes, they differ according to gender and position.

انت بتقول تالت بنت . لَكن ، البنت التّالتة .

SALAH. — ínta bi-t-qūl, tālit bint; lākin, il-bínt it-tált-a.
You (pt)-you-say, third girl; but, the-girl the-third-(f).
You say, the third girl; but, the girl the third.

أو ، تالت ولد والوالد التّالت .

SALAH. — aw, tālit wálad w-il-wálad it-tālit.
Or, third boy and-the-boy the-third.
Or, the third boy and the boy the third.

أنا متأكّد انت فهمت الفرق بينهم .

SALAH. — ána mut'ákkid ínta fihím-t il-fárq bín-hum.
I assured you understood-you(m) the-difference between-them.
I am sure you understand the difference between these [examples.

39. 1. Ordinal numbers. The ordinal numbers first through tenth are:

masculine		*feminine*		
أوّل	áwwil	اولى	ūla	first
تانى	tāni	تانية	tánya	second
تالت	tālit	تالتة	tált-a	third
رابع	rābiع	رابعة	rábع-a	fourth
خامس	xāmis	خامسة	xáms-a	fifth
ساتت	sātit	ساتّة	sátt-a	sixth
سابع	sābiع	سابعة	sábع-a	seventh
تامن	tāmin	تامنة	támn-a	eighth
تاسع	tāsiع	تاسعة	tásع-a	ninth
عاشر	ع āšir	عاشرة	عášr-a	tenth

A. أوّل áwwil 'first' has an adjectival pattern like آخر āxir 'last' with three forms; masculine, feminine, and plural (notice also تانى tāni 'second/other/next/again').

أوّلانى	awwalāni, awlāni,	first (m)
أوّلانيّة	awwalaní-yya, awlaní-yya,	first (f)
أوّلانيّين	awwalani-yyīn, awlani-yyīn,	first (pl)
أخرانى	axrāni,	last (m)
أخرانيّة	axraní-yya,	last (f)
أخرانيّين	axrani-yyīn,	last (pl)
تانى	tāni,	second or other (m)
تانية	tāny-a,	second or other (f)
تانيين	tany-īn,	second or other (pl)

Another form for "other" is:

آخر āxar (m) أخرى úxr-a (f)

B. The above ordinal numbers may be used after or before a noun. If they are used *after a noun*, they behave like adjectives, that is, they agree in gender, number, and definiteness with the preceding noun. If they are used *before the* *noun*, they do not change, that is, only the masculine form is used without the definite article:

ولد تالت	wálad tālit, third boy
بنت تالتة	bint-tált-a, third girl
الولد الخامس	il-wálad il-xāmis, the fifth boy
البنت الخامسة	il-bínt il-xáms-a, the fifth girl
أوّل ولد	áwwil wálad, the first boy
أوّل بنت	áwwil bint, the first girl

C. For ordinal numbers from the eleventh on, the regular cardinal numbers are used after the noun. These ordinal numbers are invariable and agree with the preceding noun in definiteness only.

اليوم الاتناشر il-yōm il-itnāšar, the twelfth day

39. 2. Fractions and percentages.

A. Fractions of numbers 1 though 10 are nouns with broken plurals. They may also take the dual suffix -ēn:

Singular	*Dual*	*Plural*	
نص nuṣṣ	نصّين nuṣṣ-ēn	أنصاص anṣāṣ	1/2
تلت tilt	تلتين tilt-ēn	اتلات itlāt	1/3
ربع rubع	ربعين rubع-ēn	ارباع irbāع	1/4
خمس xums	خمسين xums-ēn	اخماس ixmās	1/5
سدس suds	سدسين suds-ēn	اسداس isdās	1/6
سبع subع	سبعين subع-ēn	اسباع isbāع	1/7
تمن tumn	تمنين tumn-ēn	اتمان itmān	1/8
تسع tusع	تسعين tusع-ēn	اتساع itsāع	1/9
عشر عušr	عشرين عušr-ēn	اعشار aعšār	1/10

تلاتة ارباع التفّاح مش كويّس .
talát-t-irbāع it-tiffāḥ miš kwáyyis.
Three-(cs)-fourths the-apples not good.
Three-fourths of the apples are not good.

تلتين الفصل غايبين .
tilt-ēn il-fáṣl ġayb-īn.
Third-(d) the-class absent-(pl).
Two-thirds of the class are absent.

B. For fractions of numbers above 10, the pattern is: unit number + ع‍ála + number above 10 (the unit noun 3-10 ends in *a*).

خمسة على اتناشر
xámsa ع‍ála itnāšar
five over twelve (5/12)
five twelfths

C. The percentages are formed by the numeral + fi + míyya (the unit noun 3-10 ends in *a*).

عشرة فى الميّة
ع‍ášara fi-l-míyya
ten in-the-hundred (10 %)
ten percent

باشتري عربية جديدة

Unit 40. *b-a-štíri ɛarabíyya gidīd-a*
I Am Buying a New Car

اسمع يا على ، انا تعبت من الشفروليه دى .
CARL. — ísmaɛ, ya ɛáli, ána tiɛíb-t min iš-šivrulē di.
Listen, oh Ali, I got tired-I from the-Chevrolet this.
Listen, Ali, I am tired of this Chevrolet.

يعنى عايز تشترى عربيّة جديدة ؟
ALI. — yáɛni ɛāyiz ti-štíri ɛarabíyya gidīd-a?
That is wanting you-buy car new-(f)?
You mean you want to buy a new car?

أيوه . لو رحت المانيا حاجيب مرسيدس بنز .
CARL. — áywa. law ruḥ-t almánya ḥ-a-gīb mirsīdis binz.
Yes. If went-I Germany (ft)-I-bring Mercedes Benz.
Yes. If I go to Germany, I will get a Mercedes Benz.

اذا رحت هناك ، يا كارل ، تقدر تشتريها أرخص .
ALI. — íza ruḥ-t hināk, ya Carl, tí-qdar ti-štirī-ha árxaṣ.
If went-you there, oh Carl, you-be able you-buy-it cheaper.
If you went there, Carl, you would be able to buy it cheaper.

لـَكن ، لو لاقيت مشترى ، أنا عايز أبيع دى قبله .
CARL. — lākin, law laqē-t muštári, ana ɛāyiz a-bīɛ di qábla.
But, if found-I buyer, I wanting I-sell this before.
However, I want to sell this first, if I can find a buyer.

لو بعتها هنا ، تجيب لك فلوس كويّسة .
ALI. — law biɛ-t-áha hína, ti-gíb-l-ak filūs kwayyís-a.
If sold-you-it here, it-bring-to-you(m) money good-(f).
If you sold it here, you would get a good price.

يا خسارة ! إذا كنت بعتها السّنة اللّى فاتت ،
CARL. — ya-xṣāra! íza kun-t biع-t-áha is-sána ílli fāt-it,
Oh-damage! If was-I sold-I-it the-year which passed-(she),
What a pity! If I had sold it last year,

كنت قبضت تمن معقول .
CARL. — kun-t qabáḍ-t táman maعqūl.
was-I received-I price reasonable.
I would have received a reasonable price.

أنا قلت لك تبيعهالى ؛ فاكر ؟
ALI. — ána qul-t-íl-ak ti-biع-hā-l-i; fākir?
I told-I-to-you you-sell-it-to-me ;remembering?
I told you to sell it to me; do you remember?

ولو كنت أديتهالى ،
ALI. — wi law kun-t iddi-t-hā-l-i,
And if were-you gave-you-it-to-me,
And if you had given it to me,

كنت حادفع لك ألف جنيه .
ALI. — kun-t ḥ-a-dfáع-l-ak alf ginēh.
was-I (ft)-I-pay-to-you thousand pound.
I would have paid you a thousand pounds.

يا على ، لو تدفع لى خمسميّة جنيه ،
CARL. — ya عáli, law ti-dfáع-l-i xúms(u) mīt ginēh,
Oh Ali, if you-pay-to-me five hundred pound,
Ali, if you pay me five hundred pounds,

أدّى لك العربيّة على طول .
CARL. — a-ddī-l-ak il-عarabíyya عala-ṭūl.
I-give-to-you(m) the-car on-length.
I will give you the car right now.

40. 1. Conditional sentences. The Arabic words إذا íza, إن in, and لو law are each equivalent to the English "if." They differ from each other in both usage and frequency. íza is the most frequently used. íza and in are always used before a complete verb form; whereas, law is usually used before an incomplete verb form. For some speakers, these particles are interchangeable. The most common conditional constructions are listed below. Each construction consists of two parts: the part with "if" (part I), followed by the response part (part II):

A. *part I* *part II*

íza + kān + verb/participle/adjective — ḥa + verb.

In this construction, kān may be invariable or inflected for person, number, or gender to agree with the subject of the following verb. The following verb is incomplete and usually without tense prefixes. kān is inflected if followed by a participle or adjective which agrees in number and gender with the subject of kān. The second part may contain either the future tense prefix ḥa, always followed by an incomplete verb form, or a verb in the imperative form. Usually this construction and the following (B) and (C) concern the present or the future and indicate probability of occurrence:

إذا كان نشدّه حنكسره .
íza kān/kún-na n-šídd-uh—ḥa-ni-ksár-uh.
If was/were-we we-pull-him/it—(ft)-we-break-him/it.
If we pull it, we will break it.

إذا كانوا فاتحين اشترى علبة سجاير .
íza kān-u fatḥ-īn— ištíri ع ílb-it sigāyir.
If was-(pl) open-(pl)—buy box-(cs) cigarettes.
If they are open, buy a package of cigarettes.

إذا كنت عيّان روح يكشف عليك الدّكتور .
íza kún-t(i) ع ayyān—rūḥ yí-kšif ع alē-k id-duktūr.
If were-you(m) sick—go he-examine on-you(m) the-doctor.
If you are sick, go to the doctor and have a check-up.

B. *part I* *part II*

íza + verb (complete) — verb (complete)/ḥa + verb (incomplete).

إذا شدّيناه كسرناه / حنكسره .
íza šaddi-nā-h—kasar-nā-h/ḥa-ni-ksár-uh.
If pulled-we-him—broke-we-him/(ft)-we-break-him.
If we pull it, we will break it.

This and the first example in A are two different constructions which convey the same meaning in Arabic. Moreover, both constructions may be translated into English as:

"If we pulled it, we would break it".

C. *part I* *part II*

law + verb (incomplete) — ḥa + verb.

In this construction, only law is used followed by an incomplete verb form. This construction conveys the meaning of a future action or condition:

لو تيجى بكرة حاقولك الحكاية .

law t-īgi búkra ḥ-a-qūl-ak il-ḥikāya.

If you-come tomorrow (ft)-I-tell-you(m) the story.

If you come tomorrow, I'll tell you the story.

D. *part I* *part II*

íza + kān + verb — kān + verb/kān + ḥa + verb.

In this construction, kān is inflected for person, number, or gender to agree with the subject of the following verb. The verb immediately following kān, in both parts, is complete. This construction concerns past action or a condition which was not realized; therefore, it indicates an impossibility of occurrence.

إذا كنّا شدّيناه كنّا كسرناه .

íza kún-na šaddi-nā-h—kún-na kasar-nā-h.

If were-we pulled-we-him/it—were-we broke-we-him/it.

If we had pulled it, we would have broken it.

إذا كنّا شدّيناه كنّا حنكسره .

íza kún-na šaddi-nā-h—kún-na ḥa-ni-ksár-uh.

If were-we pulled-we-him/it—were-we (ft)-we-break-him/it.

If we had pulled it, we were going to break it.

E. *part I* *part II*

íza/law + kān ʿand + pr — kān + verb/verb.

In this construction, kān in part I is invariable and in part II is inflected for person, number, or gender to agree with the following verb, the stem of which is complete. Part II may consist of an imperative verb form. According to context, íza may convey either an English past/past perfect or present/future tense meaning:

إذا كان عندك قلم سلّفهولى .
íza kan-ع ánd-ak qálam—sallif-hū-l-i.
If was-at-you(m) pencil—lend-it-to-me.
If you have a pencil, lend it to me.

إذا / لو كان عندى قلم كنت سلّفتهولك ٠
íza/law kan-ع ánd-i qálam—kun-t sallif-t(i)-hū-l-ak.
If was-at-me pencil—was-I lend-I-it-to-you(m).
If I had/had had a pencil, I would lend/would have lent [it to you.

F. In a negative conditional sentence, either kān or the following verb may be negated by the split negative form ma...š:

اذا ما كانش نشدّه íza ma-kán-š ni-šídd-uh } if we don't pull it
اذا كان ما نشدّوش íza kān ma-n-šidd-ū-š }

In these examples, a long vowel in kān becomes short because of the following two consecutive consonants, and a last short vowel in šidd-uh becomes long because of the addition of a suffix beginning with a consonant. The *h* (third person masculine singular) in final position is not pronounced. If another suffix is added, *h* is elided even in writing.

Notes